Metacognitive Approaches to Developing Oracy

The acquisition of speech and language represent significant achievements for all children. These aspects of child development have received substantial attention in the research literature and a considerable body of theoretical knowledge exists to chart progress from infancy to maturity. Cross-cultural studies have identified the common purposes served by the acquisition of oral language by children, and the essential similarity in the sequence through which speech develops irrespective of geography and culture.

What is less clear is precisely 'how' children learn to say what they mean and 'how' teachers and parents can support and enhance the development of meaningful speech in their children. Until now, children's speech has been underused as a means of promoting learning in the formal school setting. New requirements within the National Curriculum are trying to address this gap, but there remains a lack of clarity as to what this means for practice, and how it relates to the broad base of curricular objectives.

This book brings together a body of work, from different countries; it offers an improved understanding of how strategies for developing speaking and listening may impact metacognitive awareness, and raise standards of literacy and dialogic thinking for all children.

This book was previously published as a special issue of *Early Child Development and Care*.

Roy Evans is Professor of Education and Research Coordinator in the School of Sport and Education, Brunel University.

Deborah Jones is a Reader in Education at Brunel University. She currently teaches on undergraduate, postgraduate & doctoral programmes, where her focus is on the development of literacy skills in young children.

Metacognitive Approaches to Developing Oracy

Developing Speaking and Listening with Young Children

Edited by

Roy Evans and Deborah Jones

Routledge
Taylor & Francis Group

LONDON AND NEW YORK

First published 2008 by Routledge
2 Park Square, Milton Park, Abingdon, Oxon, OX14 4RN

Simultaneously published in the USA and Canada
by Routledge
270 Madison Avenue, New York, NY 10016

Routledge is an imprint of Taylor & Francis, an informa business

© 2007, 2008 Taylor & Francis, Routledge

Typeset in Plantin by Genesis Typesetting Ltd, Rochester, Kent
Printed and bound in Great Britain by MPG Books Ltd, Bodmin, Cornwall

British Library Cataloguing in Publication Data
A catalogue record for this book is available from the British Library

ISBN 10: 0-415-44766-6 (hbk)
ISBN 13: 978-0-415-44766-9 (hbk)

CONTENTS

Perspectives on oracy—towards a theory of practice

Roy Evans and Deborah Jones

Throughout recorded history scholars have made evident their deep concern to explore the relationships between thought and language in its various forms. From the logic-based metaphysics of Parmenides, the dialectic of Zeno and Socrates, through Descarte's *cogito*, to the empiricism of Locke and Kant's *Critique of practical reason*, philosophers have attempted to deal with supremely important but troubling issues connected with the nature of knowing, the relationship between thought and language and the role of experience in the construction of meaningful thought.

Locke's rejection of innate ideas was quite revolutionary for his time and from some perspectives he may be accorded a special place in the rise of empiricism and the rejection of a priori knowledge. Whatever ideas we have, Locke argued (*Essay concerning human understanding*), derive from sensation and perception. Thinking requires ideas, which come from experience. Locke's contemporary importance lay in his clear assertion that knowledge about the world was purely verbal. From this perspective a major challenge for all peoples is to abstract meaning from experience through language. From a twenty-first-century position, Locke's philosophical stance is part of 'educated commonsense' as Russell (1991) puts it, except we are still left with the baffling psycho-neurological question as to how the mind builds conception from perception of sensations. Piaget's early work on cognition emphasized the role of sensation and experience, as the organism developed increasingly sophisticated mental structures through adaptation and accommodation, driven by a phylogenetically inherited capacity for developmental change. Such pedagogy as has been derived from Piagetian research, however has often taken the point on the provision of an environment rich in experience, and missed the point by conflating children's activity with psychological action. Vygotsky's criticism of Piagetian cognitive modelling turned on a neglect of the social cultural contexts within which learning occurred and the role of dialogical engagement in the construction of meaning.

Vygotsky (1978, 1981) recognized that language encodes the transmissible culture and that meanings are made within the shared social and cultural context. For both these major figures in twentieth-century psychology, children came to understand the world through their mental representations of it. Following the early sensori-motor stage language acquired an increasingly potent role in constructing cognitive schema. Theories built on constructivist or interactionist principles, however, have different implications for pedagogic practice from those built around principles of social constructivism and social interactionism. While Piaget's notion of the nature of representational competence and its development through constructive mismatch in the learning environment appears superficially similar to Vygotsky's ZPD, their respective pedagogical epistemologies differ and the texture of dialogic experiences serve different purposes.

The study of language acquisition by young children and their subsequent emergence as competent language users has been pursued to an extraordinary degree in the past century, partly as a key aspect of the study of human growth and development in the expanding social sciences and relatedly as a consequence of the perceived need for high-quality mass education to service the economic aspirations of post-industrial, post-scientific and post-modern societies. Globalization puts emphasis on the knowledge economy, which, in turn, necessarily implicates language acquisition and the internationalization of key languages.

The current significance accorded language in all its forms finds expression through the emphasis placed on cross-curricular language experiences within schools and preschools internationally, and may be further recognized through the impetus given to home and community literacy practices and the significant growth in language schools for foreign students and migrant labour groups.

The power of language to both imprison and liberate the lives of young learners is a paradox that has been increasingly recognized within the formal systems of education, as socio-linguists have revealed through exploration of the contextual features of learning environments in local neighbourhoods, at home and at school. While psychologists and language theorists have explored the psycho-linguistic mechanisms underpinning the ways in which children learn to say what they mean (e.g. Chomsky, 1957, 1959; Bruner, 1975; Donaldson, 1978; Cromer, 1981; Francis, 1986), others have focused on the dialogic character of supportive learning environments through which children acquire language competence across its variety of functions. Increasingly since the mid-twentieth century, and following Bernstein's illuminating work on the sociology of language, studies of children's language have focused on the social and power relations associated with particular forms of language and linguistic codes. From ancient metaphysics it has been recognized that knowledge (with the possible exception of mathematics) is essentially language, and from the Middle Ages in England governing elites overtly espoused the power–knowledge principle. Foucault's (1971) evocation of this principle was not new. The link between language and power, social or otherwise, is inescapable. Nevertheless, this relationship and its implications for pedagogy across the educational spectrum has yet to provide the motive force needed to give practical effect to the pursuit of inclusiveness and the eradication of social inequalities.

This Special Issue of *Early Child Development and Care* features language, and, in particular, spoken language. For some this will be taken to mean *oracy* and for others *oral language* development. However, all have come to recognize that the oral competencies children need to develop to become fully participative citizens in a highly mobile global context cannot be left to chance. The implications for schooling relate substantially to the reform of pedagogical practices that in the past have valued the acquiescence of children to quiet working practices. Developing oral language and the precursive skills of listening, carry the requirement that innovative pedagogical practices are encouraged which stimulate dialogic learning and emphasize metacognitive approaches to oracy. The 14 papers that comprise this Special Issue have been selected to include contemporary research-based perspectives on language acquisition, language learning in different cultural settings and aspects of second language learning. The text is divided into two main sections, the first emphasizing essentially theoretical concerns and the second focusing on pedagogical developments and classroom innovation. There is a real sense in which these sections overlap but the division is based on 'emphasis' within the respective papers. Papers from the UK reference the National Curriculum key stage 1 when referring to the school-based education of children between 5 and 6 years. Elsewhere the education of this age group is either referred to directly or though national conventions such as kindergarten through early grades of public schooling.

In keeping with the basic purpose here, the early papers are devoted to theoretical concerns and issues around language learning, the development of communicative competence and the critical relationship between dialogue, narrative and metacognitive development. Important dimensions are covered through explorations of mother tongue learning and mind-related exchanges between mothers and their infants. In the final section a significant emphasis is placed on the importance of home and school oral pedagogies for enhancing the language learning of infants between birth and 7 or 8 years of age.

1. Theoretical perspectives on oracy, cognition and intellectual development

Robert Fisher's paper on dialogic teaching and developing thinking raises critical issues which are subsequently taken up and further developed here. He explores the important relationship between dialogue, cognitive and metacognitive development in young children. The characteristics of dialogue are identified and a case is presented for involving young children in talking to think through philosophical discussion. The paper provides a theoretical context for kinds of metacognitive development that it defines as 'me-cognition'. It draws on classroom research, including the Philosophy in Primary Schools research project, to describe how the theory and practice of dialogue can be used to develop cognition and 'me-cognition' in young children. It concludes that dialogic enquiry is a primary thinking skill from which other skills follow, that 'Philosophy for Children' approaches provide effective methods for dialogic teaching that can support and develop children's capacities for cognition and metacognition. Fisher's main argument is that talk is intrinsic to literacy and to our ability to form relationships with others. It is the foundation of both verbal and emotional intelligence. Dialogue is important because it is the primary means for developing intelligence in the human species. It is through the capacity to verbalize that consciousness and understanding develop.

Alice Honig explores language development from the perspective of a clinician and academic steeped in the theory and practice of infant and child development. Drawing on her lifetime of research with young children and their families, she provides a highly accessible review of children's acquisition of language, its significance for human creativity and personal empowerment and the oft-held myth that one does not have to teach children oral language. Honing deals with vocabulary development, pragmatics of language, semantics and cognitive mapping. The importance of storytelling and narrative interrogation for language and cognitive development is explored with the aid of examples taken from clinical practice.

Martin Cortazzi and Lixian Jin provide a particular focus on narrative learning, learning English as an additional language and metacognitive development. Their paper elaborates some aspects of narrative learning—defined as learning to tell stories and learning from, about and through narratives—in the context of primary-age pupils who use English as an additional language (EAL). The paper introduces some principles to support their language development in classroom interaction. They argue that linguistically orientated research on metacognitive strategy development is not necessarily readily applied to EAL learners. After presenting a background on narrative, narrative development and social aspects of telling stories, they introduce an approach to narrative development which encourages a cycle of telling and retelling of stories providing EAL learners with layered opportunities for developing the metacognitive features of planning, remembering, understanding and reflecting on storytelling. This is enabled through the use of written 'keywords', which are used in conjunction with 'story maps' (outlining the narrative structure and content), together with classroom photos. While the focus of the paper is on EAL learners, the visual approach described here can be used with narrative (or factual information) for many other young children and has been used by speech and language therapists to develop specific aspects of language for speech and language impaired children.

Helen Robinshaw's paper addresses the issues around speaking and listening from the perspective of an early years teacher who is also a research psychologist and trained teachers of the deaf. She emphasizes the dependence of developments in speech, writing and reading upon child's acquisition of age-appropriate hearing and listening skills. She notes particularly that the auditory-neurological foundations for listening are still being developed during the early years period, a time when children are more likely to experience middle ear infections and experience reduced hearing sensitivity. A reduction of just a few decibels in hearing levels is enough to impact upon the child's ability to detect and discriminate the sounds of speech. Reduction of hearing sensitivity impacts on the child's acquisition of receptive and expressive language skills. Robinshaw also deals with environmental factors that put children at risk for poor listening and subsequent oral skills in the classroom. She points out that normally hearing children may also be disadvantaged by a poor listening environment. Three factors that influence the quality of the classroom environment for listening are distance, noise and reverberation; therefore, teachers also need to have a good grasp of these factors. Whether hearing or hearing impaired, the critical period for developing auditory–neural connections across each level of the cortex is the first three years of life, and the process is not thought to be complete until the child reaches about 15 years of age. So even the most attentive and normally hearing children in our classrooms do not have fully developed auditory processing or listening skills.

Niklas Pramling and Ingrid Pramling Samuelsson's paper on the prosaics of figurative language in early years settings draws attention to the importance of metaphor in everyday speech. Following other researchers, they note that in making observations on experiences for which we as yet lack a language, we tend to use the language we have, in terms of which we will try to come to grips with the new and unfamiliar. Children try to make sense of the world in ways that are meaningful to them. One strategy people use in such situations is to use metaphors as vehicles of thinking and communication. By means of a few brief examples, the authors point to instances of such talk in the setting of preschool. They also discuss opportunities for learning that such talk could offer children and what the implications for the development of children's thinking and communication might be. Using principles rooted in socio-cultural theory, these authors note that:

> communicative patterns to which the child is exposed will become the mould of its subsequent individual development. Appropriating such tools is not just a cognitive act, it is also a communicative one, that is a social act, in the sense that it requires the child to be sensitive to what s/he needs to make clear in her/his speech in order to be understood by someone else.

This returns to the importance of dialogue and the meta-cognitive as well as oral significance of dialogic teaching. Pramling and Pramling Samuelsson conclude their discussion of the importance of studying the prosaics of metaphor by noting that other 'analyses worth pursuing in this context would include the *in situ* development of this figurative ability and its implications for children's development and learning, and the learning opportunities provided young children in preschool practices'.

With Gee Macrory's paper a return is made to the challenges of language construction for children growing up with more than one language. The case of a French–English bilingual child is used to generate evidence on the processes used to support development in each language. Macrory visits the available theory on *how* language is acquired from the perspective that such understanding is necessary for appropriate contexts to be defined to foster this successfully. It is argued that such understandings are particularly necessary in the case of children growing up bilingually or multilingually. Moreover, an understanding of the theoretical perspectives underpinning and informing training courses and books is vital for professionals working in early years settings. Only in this way can they bring to their role an informed understanding of the development of children in their care and a critical view of any advice offered. Macrory points up the theoretical debates in generative grammar and the more recent contributions of cognitive linguists in providing non-nativist accounts of language acquisition. By reference to previous work in this field, it is argued that such accounts lead ultimately to the view that: 'linguistic constructions are essentially cognitive schemas that are of the same type that exist in other domains of cognition, and derive from recurrent events with respect to which the people of a culture have recurrent communicative roles.' From a somewhat different perspective Macrory aligns with a view similar to that presented by Pramling and Pramling Samuelsson in their paper— i.e. that children make sense of their linguistic environment in their own terms. Put another way, linguistic constructions are 'generalizations children make on the basis of their own categorization skills working on the language they hear'. This reinforces the significance of the language environment to children's lexical and grammatical development.

Daniel Weigel, Jennifer Lowman and Sally Martin provide a particular focus on linguistic environmental influences in two settings, the home and child care. Their concern is to assess the impact on children's speaking and listening skills of each setting prior to formal school entry. It is proposed that a developmental assets approach, one that focuses on strengths of these settings, can aid an understanding of the development of young children's language skills and in the enrichment of those skills. In bringing together the research of others as well as their own work, the authors provide evidence of the contributions of the developmental assets in the home and child care settings alone, as well as combined, to preschool children's language development. Furthermore, these contributions seem to have long-term impacts. They conclude by discussing the contributions a developmental assets approach can offer to the study of the language development of young children. In this work also the position is taken that, as children age, factors external to them become increasingly influential as determiners of receptive and expressive linguistic competence. Their paper makes the assumption that two key external sources of variation in children's listening (receptive language) and speaking (expressive language), as well as communicative competence with others, are the home and the child care environment. The authors review literature on factors affecting children's language development in home and child care environments, present a selection of results from their own work and subsequently examine the implications of the research for ensuring the optimal language development of children.

The paper by S. Degotardi and J. Torr reports on a longitudinal investigation of mothers' mind-related talk to their 12- to 24-month-old infants. This presents a further research-based perspective on aspects of the issues explored by Weigel *et al.* in their work. The present authors call upon previous research to support the position that children's exposure to mind-related talk has been shown to foster young children's metacognitive understanding and to orient them to the patterns of literate language long before they commence formal literacy instruction at school. They note that recent theory-of-mind research emphasizes the importance of children's understanding of, and talk about, the mind for their emerging literacy development.

Metacognitive understanding during children's first years of school is related to their reading ability and their comprehension of narrative content, themes and character motivation. Children's use of metacognitive talk has also been found to predict their comprehension of written narrative at age 8, and their change in reading ability between the ages of 4 and 5 years. Such findings bolster claims that the ability to think and talk about the mind constitutes a vital tool for narrative understanding and the intentional and selective employment of cognitive processes, such as attention and memory, implicated in the process of literacy learning. In this paper, they report on a longitudinal study of the mind-related talk of 22 mothers when their infants were aged 12, 18 and 24 months. Results reveal broad and stable individual differences in mothers' propensity to use encouragement-of-autonomy, mental-state and modula-tion-of-certainty talk to their infants during a free play session. Mothers' talk about beliefs increased with infant age, and higher-educated mothers used significantly more mental-state and modulation-of-certainty talk than lower-educated mothers. These findings are discussed in terms of current understandings of the discourse contexts supporting children's developing understanding of the mind, and implica-tions are derived for early childhood pedagogy in settings for children in the first two years of life.

Olivia Saracho and B. Spodek continue the focus on environmental factors affect-ing children's oral development. Their paper reflects the concerns related to the cultural context in which language is learned and developed, as well as to the relation-ship of language development to cognition. The authors note how, in different countries, this general concern has been made manifest in different ways. Referring to the UK, they note that educators have focused their concerns on the development of communicative expression in relation to intellectual abilities. This has led to the integration of speaking and listening skills, which is referred to as *oracy*, within the National Curriculum. The concept of oracy involves both the discourse activities and a variety of speech events. The importance of talk and narrative in the children's self-expression is included in the concept of oracy, and it is important in promoting children's learning and intellectual development. They go on to note that in the USA, although the researchers are interested in oral discourse, they do not label it *oracy*. Researchers in the USA have conducted studies in the classroom to include oral group work, discussion and other forms of classroom talk. With young children, oral language takes place mainly in a social context. Children use language as a tool for socializing. The purpose of their paper is to review studies on children's oral language development within a social context. They conclude that spoken and written language experiences emphasize written communication skills, which help children to see the relationship between the spoken word and the written word. Children should be given opportunities to receive and express ideas, impressions and feelings in speak-ing and writing. In particular, they need to participate in activities that encourage them to learn written communication skills, where actual formal reading and writing skills unfold later. Thus, it is argued, the emphasis in the preschool years should be on oral language experiences, a prerequisite that will help children learn and under-stand the relationship between the spoken and the written language. They will learn to interpret ideas and impressions through reading; to listen and respond through speaking; and to convey their ideas, impressions and feelings through writing.

2. Developing metacognitive approaches to enhancing oracy

Here Deborah Jones's paper sets out a clear rationale for classroom actions to enhance speaking and listening. The importance of cooperation between adults and children, and children and their peers, is highlighted as integral to sound practice. This locates effective learning within a context of social interaction through the joint construction of meaning. She stresses the pivotal role taken by an adult in providing the necessary scaffolds for learning. Furthermore, the importance of conceiving language as a tool for collective meaning-making is acknowledged: speaking and listening, exploratory talk and reflection are fundamental to this process. Jones develops a perspective on the teacher's role and identifies four interlinked facets of professional action that aim to develop speaking and listening: dialogic teaching, promoting metacognitive awareness, planning and assessing. The emphasis on all four aspects is necessary. Her discussion of dialogic teaching and metacognitive awareness emphasizes the pedagogical imperatives for teachers who engage in the task of enhancing cognitive language schema through developing children's oral language skills. Supportive language environments require a collective focus on language tasks, reciprocity between teachers and pupils and the existence of risk-free situations in which ideas may be expressed openly and common understandings achieved. The arguments embrace the community in so far as the school should be prepared to derive benefit from the varied styles of communicative practice in culturally diverse social contexts and recognize the significance to children of code switching.

Flora Macleod, Philip Macmillan and Brahm Norwich take as their focus the improvement of oracy and literacy among childen who fall behind at school. Their paper reports on the effects of an intervention program that has been designed to help delayed readers. The program attempts to tap into a deficiency associated with learners being unable to deal with the association between speech at the level of individual sounds within words and their visual representations on a page of text. Many learners who display this deficiency when it comes to reading texts (written speech) are often fully competent in the production and perception of oral language. The central ingredient of the self-voice program, reported on here, is to enable children to hear the sound components of their own voice as it is normally heard by others but not themselves. This was made possible by using a Coomber 3902 tape recorder. This recorder is used extensively by those learning a new language as it allows the learner to hear their own voice as they speak, so that they can modify their accent. Learners wear headphones that allow their voice as they speak to play directly to their ears at a volume above their bone voice, thus suppressing it. In this way, learners are able to hear themselves speak, as it were, from the 'outside' (acoustically) rather than the 'inside'. The authors based the reported intervention strategy on the findings of a pilot study with delayed readers that investigated whether the self-voice feedback loop would facilitate phonemic awareness. Findings suggest that the delayed readers on which this device was trialled all developed a greater awareness of the sound to the sub-word components of written language. The authors report further that their initial work suggested that speech dysfluent children in clinical trails showed marked improvements in their oracy in terms of clarity of pronunciation and fluency.

Melanie Wilde and Rosemary Sage contribute an important perspective on developing the communicative competence and narrative thinking of 4- and 5-year-olds in educational settings. They explored the pivotal argument that for these facets of children's competences to develop effectively, certain conditions need to be created. Concerns for children's communicative competence at school entry are linked to the implication that it is more difficult for children to make the shift between informal language and a formal mode where the use of narrative skills to process large quantities of talk and produce a coherent response is essential. The research they report was intended to investigate how the narrative thinking and ability to communicate of a group of 4- and 5-year-olds could be developed further using the Communication Opportunity Group Scheme as an intervention. Their data indicate that improvements observed in children's narrative thinking and communicative competence was more likely to be due to the conditions provided by the intervention than the children's everyday educational settings. The authors argue that their findings provide a strong rationale for a less formal, prescriptive approach to the curriculum in England for 5- to 7-year-olds, especially as this seems to skew how teachers feel 4-year-olds should be taught as preparation for schooling.

Alastair Daniels opens the door to the world of the professional storyteller and explores the teacher's role as principal storyteller in the classroom—a teaching approach rich in potential for assisting children become effective learners. Storytelling is common to the history of all cultures and social groups and is traditionally the way in which significant features of a culture are preserved and handed down. Oral histories are indispensable features of cultural heritage, and storytellers are indeed celebrated for the traditions they have handed down. These require identifiable narrative strategies. Daniels argues that storytelling within the classroom can be an effective tool for helping children develop their own narrative forms through oral language. As pupils develop their own storytelling abilities, the teacher also needs to be aware of different strategies for remembering tales that can be employed by their pupils. Memorization is far from an isolated cognitive activity and there needs to be a recognition that effective memorization is not bound to one particular methodology, as much for the child-storyteller as for the teacher-storyteller. Daniels is clear that children need opportunities to experiment with different methods of memorizing that draw on a variety of stimuli (spatial, iconic, verbal and symbolic) in order to discover those strategies most useful to them; these can vary from simple visual cues to more complex verbal stimuli. Five fundamental aspects of classroom storytelling are developed, both in the telling of tales and teaching more generally. The author emphasizes that storytelling is a very different activity to story reading and that it arises each time the telling of a narrative idea is unmediated by a written text, which in itself is one of the fundamental aspects. Using a narrative style rich in classroom examples and exemplifications, Daniels provides a powerfully reflexive analysis of the way in which teachers may use storytelling to enhance critical aspects of children's oral language development. Interestingly, he recognizes that his structured approach possibly flies in the face of creativity. He, nevertheless, asserts that by maintaining a consistent and structured methodology, the teacher-storyteller is able to develop their own metacognitive skills in relation to narrative teaching. This framework for storytelling is one in which, therefore, the teacher takes on the role of principal storyteller in the classroom; it is from this position that a pattern of self-regulation can be set in narrative learning for the students without sacrificing the opportunities for creativity and imaginative play that are inherent in good storytelling.

The paper by Theodora Paptheodorou explores pedagogical approaches to mother tongue teaching of the Greek language to children living in communities outside of Greece. She compares the situation facing such communities with the kind of challenges faced by other ethnic minority groups hosted in a majority culture. In particular, the need to become acculturated to the host country and at the same time maintain their own language and cultural heritage. Although Greek community schools are well established in the UK there are concerns that gradually fewer and fewer children attend the schools and attendance patterns are irregular. Theodora observes that a complex set of interconnected factors contribute to this situation including, conflicting parental attitudes about the value of mother tongue learning, varying perceptions by children and parents about the status and utility of mother tongue and a lack of appropriate learning resources for teaching the mother tongue to young children. Against this background she describes the implementation of an innovative curriculum project designed to address some of these issues and explores the outcomes of subsequent evaluation. Among her conclusions she provides insights into appropriate pedagogical practices for children to engage with mother tongue learning but observes also that code mixing and interlingual lexicon may be seen as the cultural tools that evolve through the history of migrant communities and may be seen as appropriate means by which to communicate cognitive and conceptual frameworks of different cultures.

The final paper in this section is provided by Valkanova and Watts, who focus on the role of digital video in promoting oral language development through reflective self-learning (RSL) in seven-year-old children. In particular, they explore children's narratives and story-telling during the making of sound 'voice-over' tracks for their own video films. They provide evidence for Evan's evocation in the first part of this introductory paper that the development of oral language requires innovative pedagogical practices to stimulate dialogic learning, particularly those practices that fuel metacognitive—in this case reflective—approaches to oracy. Building on the notion that self-reflection is a central component in the building of self consciousness and self-conscious language, they describe a very contemporary research-based perspective of language acquisition and language learning in a specific context: early acculturation within school science.

References

Bruner, J. (1975) The ontongenesis of speech acts, *Journal of Child Language,* 2, 1–20.

Chomsky, N. (1957) *Syntactic structures* (The Hague, Mouton).

Chomsky, N. (1959) Review of B. F. Skinner's 'Verbal behaviour', *Language,* 35, 26–58.

Cromer, R. (1981) *Reconceptualising language acquisition and cognitive development,* in: R. L. Schiefelbusch & D. D. Bricker (Eds) *Early language: acquisition and intervention* (Baltimore, MD, University Park Press).

Descartes, R. (1637) *Discourse on method.*

Descartes, R. (1641) *Meditations on the first philosophy.*

Donaldson, M. (1978) *Children's thinking* (London, Fontana).

Francis, H. (1986) How do children learn to say what they mean? in: S. Burroughs & R. Evans (Eds) *Play language and socialization: perspectives on adult roles* (New York, Gordon & Breach).

Foucault, M. (1971) *The archaeology of knowledge* (London, Tavistock).

Kant, E. (1789) *Critique of practical reason.*

Locke, J. (1690) *Essay concerning human understanding.*

Russell, B. (1991) *A history of western philosophy* (London, Routledge); original work published 1946.

Vygotsky, L. S. (1978) *Mind in society* (Cambridge, MA, Harvard University Press).

Vygotsky, L. S. (1981) The genesis of higher mental functions, in: J. V. Wertsch (Ed.) *The concept of activity in Soviet psychology* (Armonk, NY, M.E. Sharp, Inc), 134–143.

Speaking, listening, planning and assessing: the teacher's role in developing metacognitive awareness

Deborah Jones

Introduction

There is a sense in which individuals are helped by articulating thoughts. It is often within the process of explaining or describing what we think that thoughts 'click' into place and we understand what we already know. In other words, making our implicit thoughts explicit through talk is a powerful learning tool for both adults and children. It may be assumed that because talk is interwoven into the fabric of the classroom and daily life in general, competency develops 'naturally' and without the need for explicit teaching. By contrast, this paper highlights the importance of rigorous planning for speaking and listening and the need to plan in specific and regular opportunities for assessing this area. In addition, the paper emphasizes the development of children's metacognitive awareness as integral to a powerful teaching and learning environment.

The UK context

Within the UK, the place of speaking and listening in the curriculum has had a chequered history. In 1988 the Cox Report (*English for ages 5–11*) stated that the value of talk as a means of learning was widely accepted as 1987 saw the establishing of the National Oracy Project to enhance the role of speaking and listening in the learning process. Although the English National Curriculum (1988, 2000) gave the same weighting to speaking and listening as to reading and writing, the National Literacy Strategy (DfEE, 1998) focused almost exclusively on reading and writing. However, UK studies have shown that children have few opportunities to engage in active enquiry through talk (Galton & Williamson, 1992). Equally, there has been concern in relation to the level of language competence exhibited by children on entrance to school (both in the UK and in other countries (Locke *et al.*, 2002; Riley *et al.*, 2004). In response to a perceived need from teachers, guidelines were developed in the UK (DfEE, 2000; DfES, 2003), in order to once again raise the profile of speaking and listening in the classroom.

A rationale for speaking and listening

It is important that a clear rationale for developing speaking and listening is established within classroom contexts, a rationale informed by key theories. The importance of cooperation between adults and children, and between children and their peers, has been highlighted as integral to sound classroom practice. Within the model of the 'zone of proximal development' (Vygotsky, 1978), learning takes place most effectively within a context of social interaction through the joint construction of meaning. The child is able to move towards new learning with the help of a more competent peer. Here the links between thought and language are stressed. In addition, the more experienced adult or peer may act as a scaffold for learning (Bruner, 1986). The pivotal role of the adult is to provide the necessary scaffolds for learning that develop children's knowledge, skills and understanding. Furthermore, the importance of the conception of 'language as a tool for collective sense-making, or "thinking together"' (Mercer *et al.*, 2003, p. 81) has been acknowledged. Speaking and listening, and exploratory talk and reflection, are fundamental to this process.

The teacher's role

The teacher's role in developing speaking and listening is crucial. Indeed 'the teacher's role in explaining, questioning, describing, organizing and evaluating in the classroom is mostly conducted through talk'. There are four clear, interlinked approaches that teachers can adopt to promote effective speaking and listening. This can be achieved through dialogic teaching, developing metacognitive awareness, planning and assessing.

Dialogic teaching

Teachers need to reflect on the kinds of speaking and listening they promote in the classroom. Their discourse is fundamental to the development of children's own talk (Coles, 2005; Myhill, 2006). Most classroom practice is characterised by initiation, response and feedback (IRF)—i.e. that is initiation though teacher questioning, response by the child and feedback, or closing down, by the teacher. In such instances, interactions between children and teachers are brief and contain closed questions, with the children focusing on the 'right' answer. Here, then, there is little speculative or exploratory talk; dialogic teaching has been promoted in order to counter this (Alexander, 2006). Alexander (2003) recommends a move to improving interactions through dialogic teaching, in which there are four conditions encouraging this:

- *Collective*: the focus here is on children and teachers addressing learning tasks together, whether as a group or whole class. The point is that no one works in isolation.
- *Reciprocal*: children and teachers listen to each other share ideas and consider alternative viewpoints.
- *Cumulative*: the importance of building on one anothers' ideas is highlighted.
- *Supportive*: children can articulate ideas in a risk-free environment and help on another to reach common understandings.

It is also important to note that the community outside the classroom presents a rich and varied picture of language use, evolving styles and differing communicative practices, where, for example, individuals switch between different languages and dialects. Classrooms should mirror this.

Developing metacognitive awareness

The teacher has an important function in developing children's metacognitive awareness. This lies at the heart of effective and powerful teaching. Metacognition refers to an individual's awareness of his/her cognitive processes and strategies (Flavell, 1979; Flavell *et al.*, 1995). It relates to the human capacity to be self-reflective, to consider *how* one thinks and knows; it directs attention to what has been assimilated and understood, and the ways in which this relates to the processes of learning. In addition, metacognition develops thinking as implicit understanding becomes explicit: Vygotsky (1962) has argued that when the process of learning is brought to a conscious level, children become aware of their own thought processes that helps them to gain control over *how* they learn. Talk is fundamental to this.

The development of metacognition demands understanding of different levels of awareness. The notion of different types of use can illustrate this (Fisher & Williams, 2002). *Tacit use* is characterized by children making decisions without really thinking about them. When children become consciously aware of a strategy or decision-making process marks *aware use*. The point at which children are able to select the best strategies for problem-solving is known as *strategic use*. In *reflective use* children reflect on their thinking before, during and after the learning and metacognitive process. As a result, they are able to evaluate progress and set targets for improvement.

Metacognition is a complex process whose development demands a variety of teaching skills, dependent on three key factors (Williams, 2006). First, the task must be worthy of serious thought. Clearly this necessitates planning which is both clear and appropriate. Secondly, the thinking and reasoning of pupils must be appreciated, requiring the establishment of a classroom ethos in which children can take risks without fear of reprisals and where a spirit of mutual respect and exploration is valued. Third, time needs to be granted to children in order to think about their thinking and to articulate thoughts about their learning. Strategies such as talking to teachers and peers in a structured way or keeping journals can facilitate this process. The role of the teacher in modelling the metacognitive process is central in asking questions that encourage children to consider how, for example, they solve problems; why they accept or reject particular ideas; or why, perhaps, they would undertake the process differently another time.

Planning

In addition, planning regarding both speaking and listening is a fundamental part of the teacher's role. When planning for talk, it is important to consider the *nature* of talk, and in so doing, to identify four discrete, but interdependent, aspects of speaking and listening:

1.   *social*: developing relationships;
2.   *communicative*: transferring meaning;
3.   *cultural*: different meanings may be adopted by different speech communities (among children this might be associated with popular culture);
4.   *cognitive*: using talk as a means of learning.

Teachers should plan to develop these aspects; indeed all are necessary of progress if a child is to become a well-rounded speaker. Children need to learn about the social elements of talk, the expression of feelings, the development of relationships and how additional aspects, such as body language, work together with talk in order to develop such relationships and affect or sharpen communication.

The cognitive aspect, however, is fundamental: in planning for effective speaking and listening opportunities, we are also planning for effective learning. An analysis of children's joint classroom work (Littleton *et al.*, 2005) has revealed three different types of talk in the classroom: *disputational*, unproductive disagreement; *cumulative*, or adding uncritically to what has been said; and *exploratory*, which demonstrates the active joint engagement of the children with one another's ideas (p. 169). Planning for effective learning is facilitated by focusing on exploratory talk. The National Oracy

Project (NOP) acknowledged that: 'learning is the product of the interaction between the old and the new, the known and the not known ... through talk it is possible to explore and clarify new meanings, review and revise old meanings, until there can be an accommodation between the two' (Norman, 1992, p. 41). Mercer (2000) highlighted the value of this kind of exploratory talk but notes that observational research indicates very little of it occurs naturally in the classroom.

However, further research (Cormack *et al.*, 1998) has indicated that, despite fears of teachers that children would not be focused, when children were provided with structured opportunities to work with their peers, they were able to use speaking and listening to:

- interrogate their own understanding;
- aid recall;
- instruct others;
- work on ideas and propositions;
- problematize;
- argue a personal point of view;
- rehearse subject-specific language;
- progressively shape knowledge;
- generate ideas;
- 'sponsor' learning.

Cormack *et al.* (1998) also highlighted that this effective use of speaking and listening for cognitive purposes was dependent on the clarity of the task—i.e. children knew what kind of talk was required—and an appropriate selection of topic, which allowed children to build on their previous knowledge and understanding.

In order to inform planning, teachers need to consider *audience*, *purpose* and *type of talk*. This approach is based on functional linguistics (Halliday, 1978), where the structure of the language used and the structure of the social action are mutually determining. As such, we vary what we say and how we say it, according to who we are with (the audience) and why we are speaking (the purpose). For children, development and progression in their speaking and listening skills is marked by an increasing confidence and competence in achieving these aims. Although children may implicitly be able to vary how they speak according to who they are with, the opportunities for extending their speaking and listening repertoire nevertheless need careful planning (Jones, 2006). Norman (1992) states that: 'the quality of children's talk is greatly affected by features not necessarily related to their oral ability' (p. 76). Studies have shown how gender, for example, impacts specifically on speaking and listening (Baxter, 1999; Hunter *et al.*, 2005), and literacy in general (Gambell & Hunter, 2000). Consideration of a wide range of factors, such as gender, group size, personality, confidence, self-esteem, competence in additional languages and use of non-standard dialects, needs to take place. In order to gain a comprehensive picture of the child's abilities in this regard, all these aspects then need to be considered, and it is part of teachers' roles to act in the light of any factors that may be impeding pupils' development and performance.

Assessing

Within the UK, National Curriculum assessment has undergone many changes since its introduction. Each year, handbooks of guidance (e.g. QCA, 2006) lay down the statutory assessment requirements for each key stage.[1] Both summative assessment, measuring attainment after teaching and learning, and formative assessment, informing the teaching and learning processes, is required.

There have been several important influences on the way assessment is approached. As a result of extensive research, the work of Black and Wiliam as recorded in *Assessment for Learning: Beyond the Black Box* (Assessment Reform Group, 1999) found that formative assessment strategies raise standards of attainment, and produced five key factors that improve learning through assessment:

- the provision of effective feedback to pupils;
- the active involvement of pupils in their own learning;
- adjusting teaching according to assessment results;
- recognizing the huge influence assessment has on pupil self-esteem and motivation;
- the need for pupils to be able to assess themselves and understand how to improve.

Other important factors for formative assessment were also noted:

- sharing learning goals with pupils;
- involving pupils in self-assessment;
- providing feedback which enables pupils to recognize and take their next steps.

Based on this research, Clarke (2004) has drawn out three additional aspects of formative assessment as follows:

1. Focusing feedback around learning intentions.
2. Organizing appropriate target setting.
3. Raising children's self-esteem throughout.

In 2002 the Assessment Reform Group produced *Assessment for learning: 10 principles*. In addition, QCA 'Assessment for Learning' materials have been provided for teacher support. Here an important distinction has been made, *assessment for learning* being defined as the process of classroom assessment to improve learning, whereas *assessment of learning* is defined as the measurement of what children can do.

All these initiatives have impacted greatly not only on how assessment is perceived, but also upon how assessment in schools is carried out. Implicit in the nature of formative assessment, as outlined above, is the development of metacognitive awareness which is required if pupils are to assess themselves and understand how to improve. The essence of target setting and self-assessment lies in the ability to know *how* one is learning.

Principles of assessment

There are certain principles that must inform assessment practice, whatever the curricular area (Jones, 2002). These will necessarily reflect the approach to teaching and learning, as assessment is inextricably linked to both of these. First, assessment should be continuous. Any assessments undertaken should take place over a period of time, in part, to give children the best possible chance of showing what they can do, and also in part, to build up a picture of the progression and development over time. Secondly, assessment should be curricular: assessment needs to be related to what children are currently learning and take place within a strong context of meaning, unlike some forms of traditional assessment that are bolt-on activities, unrelated to classroom work. Next assessment should be consultative. Assessment is not something that is applied to the child, but rather it should be a supportive, collaborative process and shared between a range of people. Input from children, parents/carers, teachers and other adults is a most useful part of practice. Finally, assessment should be communicative. Feedback by teachers to children or between peers, whether oral or written, should communicate clearly, as should assessment documentation. Feedback should be adapted to the audience, for example, reports for parents need to be jargon free. It is essential that shared understandings are established and maintained.

Involving children in their own learning

Central to the notion of children's self-assessment is the belief that we learn best through interacting with others. More specifically, this relates to Vygotsky's (1978) description of the 'zone of proximal development', which highlights the gap between what children can do on their own and what they can do with the help of a more competent individual. So, with assistance, children can reach a higher level of attainment than they could do alone. This involves the more competent adult (possibly a teacher, other adult or peer) interacting with children as a focused part of the teaching and learning process. Linked to this is the work of Sadler (1998), who noted that formative assessment is dependent on two elements. First the learner needs to understand the gap between a leaning goal and his or her current level, and secondly, there is a need for the learner to close up this gap. As Black *et al.* (2004) state, 'although the teacher can stimulate and guide this process, the learning has to be done by the student' (p. 14). This is not just about implementing strategies, this is about defining beliefs about teaching, learning and assessing, and setting up a classroom culture where pedagogy is clearly linked to those beliefs.

In practice, this means that planning and assessment need to be shared with children, so that they are 'let in' on the processes of teaching and learning. This is a crucial part of developing metacognitive awareness. As a result, learning intentions will be communicated to children in a language they can understand. Pupils need to know not only what activities they are required to do, but also why they need to do them and what the success criteria will be. These strategies will ensure that children are not learning in a vacuum. Rather, they will be certain of what they are doing, why they are doing it and how successful they are in the process. By identifying and sharing these aspects, any feedback/discussion of learning between teacher and pupil will have a clear framework. It is important that teachers explain to children what assessment is and why it needs to be done, equally, that it is a shared process (Jones, 2006). Setting up the classroom environment then, where children are free to make mistakes without recrimination and where errors will be viewed as part of the learning process, is essential. Risk-free environments are fundamental to dynamic teaching/learning/assessment contexts where children have shared control over their own learning.

To summarize, steps to follow in order to establish a successful teaching/learning/ assessing context are as follows:

- Set up a risk-free environment where children's self-esteem is built up.
- Explain what assessment is and why it is important.
- Share learning intentions in a language that children understand. This should include what is to be done and why.
- Describe the success criteria.
- Enable children to evaluate their work in relation to the success criteria.
- Have shared feedback between teacher and child.
- Set targets together.
- Reflect on the learning throughout.

Self-assessment and talk

Self-assessment and talk is a particularly sensitive area. The ways in which talk is carried out, the languages spoken or dialects used are part of identity and form a large part of who human beings are. As such, individuals can become very vulnerable when their talk is opened up for scrutiny. Children, in particular, need to know that assessment of their speaking and listening skills is part of a process designed to help them. They should know that formative assessment will enable them to express themselves more effectively, develop their repertoires of talk and expand their registers of talk, in ways which enable them to exercise control over situations. It is worth explaining to children that sometimes written assessments do not demonstrate real understanding of their capabilities because these are always mediated through writing. Being part of the assessment process and learning to assess themselves can be an enormously positive experience for children, an experience that not only involves them in their own learning, but also enhances their self-esteem. Making these aspects explicit to children and discussing the power of spoken language with them is a crucial part of the classroom where children are learning effectively not only about talk, but how to talk. In this area, more than any other, setting up a risk-free environment where self-esteem remains intact is of paramount importance (Koshy & Mitchell, 1993). Such a culture of collaboration is integral to the teaching and learning process (Underwood & Underwood, 1999). Children need to know that effective speakers and listeners can become powerful learners, teachers and citizens.

Closely aligned to self-assessment is peer assessment, where children can work together through several of the stages above. When setting up a system for peer assessment, ground rules should be clearly decided upon and established as part of a democratic classroom process; for example children need to respect each others' work, be clear on the learning intentions, carefully read/examine their work, and so on. Clearly the above requires some discussion and explanation, but this will help establish a climate where children can come to understand that the way in which we speak actually forms part of our identity as human beings, and as such, is not to be ridiculed or denigrated. This, as emphasized, is a sensitive area that will need constant reinforcement. Written and oral reflections on talk—the children's own and other people's—a vital way of moving children on in their learning. It is often within their reflections that children make explicit, for the first time, their developing understanding about the nature of talk and learning, and about their abilities in using it effectively.

Conclusion

To reiterate, planning, teaching, learning and assessing are parts of a cycle. All elements are interdependent, therefore it is vital that teachers have observed and assessed children's speaking and listening development in order to plan for progression. It is important that planning for teaching and planning for assessment should happen together. Fundamentally, speaking and listening should be embedded in the curriculum and not be a 'bolt-on', decontextualized activity. Teachers need to identify areas of the curriculum where the activities and the children's learning would be aided by speaking and listening. It is important to consider all curriculum areas, not just English, as talk is integral to all subjects. In addition, teachers should identify where aspects of speaking and listening should have an explicit focus as part of the English curriculum. Some speaking and listening activities may need to be planned for over an extended period of time, whereas others may constitute just a part of one lesson. All plans should:

- identify assessment objectives which are clearly linked to teaching and learning objectives/intentions. (*What*)
- specify which children (individuals/ groups) are to be assessed. (*Who*)
- indicate the method of assessment and recording mechanism. (*How*)
- timing, that is at which point assessment should take place and how long it should last. (*When*)

If assessment is to be effective, all these aspects must be considered.

A recent review by the UK Office for Standards in Education (Ofsted, 2005) claims that the weakest element of teaching is consistently the use of assessment. As a result, few pupils have an understanding of what it actually means to be good at speaking and listening; however, the integration of speaking and listening into planning for literacy should be both systematic and automatic. In this regard, there is much work to be done.

Speaking and listening are fundamental to learning and teaching. Talk is both a means of learning and an aspect to be developed and refined in its own right. It is also a powerful tool for communicating thoughts, expressing feelings, exercising power and generally developing identities as human beings. Within the classroom, both assessment of and through talk is vital. Assessing talk provides immediacy of access into the child's mind and a unique window into the learning process. Integral to this is the development of metacognitive awareness that provides the impetus not only for effective teachers, but also for effective learners.

Note

1. Handbooks on assessment guidance are produced annually for each key stage—see e.g. DfES & QCA (2006).

References

Alexander, R. J. (2003) *New perspectives on spoken English in the classroom* (London, QCA).

Alexander, R. J. (2006) *Towards dialogic teaching* (3rd edn) (Cambridge, Cambridge University Press/Dialogos).

Assessment Reform Group (1999) *Assessment for learning: beyond the black box* (Cambridge, University of Cambridge, School of Education).

Assessment Reform Group (2002) *Assessment for learning: 10 principles.* Available online at: http://www.assessment-reform-group.org.uk/publications.html (accessed 1 February 2006).

Baxter, J. (1999) Teaching girls to speak out: the female voice in public contexts, *Language and Education*, 13(2), 81–98.

Black, P., Harrison, C., Lee, C., Marshall, B. & Wiliam, D. (2003) *Assessment for learning* (Maidenhead, Open University Press).

Bruner, J. (1986) *Actual minds, possible worlds* (Cambridge, MA, Harvard University Press).

Clarke, S. (2004) *Unlocking formative assessment* (London, Hodder & Stoughton).

Coles, J. (2005) Strategic voices? Problems in developing oracy through 'interactive whole-class teaching', *Changing English*, 12(1), 113–123.

Cormack, Y. P., Wignell, P. & Nichols, S. (1998) *Classroom Discourse Project* (Canberra, Commonwealth Department of Employment).

Cox Report. Department of Education and Science (1988) *English for ages 5–11* (London, DES).

Department for Education and Employment (DfEE) (1998) *The National Literacy Strategy: framework for teaching* (London, HMSO).

Department for Education and Employment (DfEE) (2000) *English in the National Curriculum* (London, DfEE).

Department for Education and Skills & Qualifications and Curriculum Authority (DfES & QCA) (2003) *Speaking, listening, learning: working with children in key stages 1 and 2* (London, DfES).

Department for Education and Skills and Qualifications and CurriculumAuthority (DfES & QCA) (2006) *Assessment and reporting arrangements* (London, DfES).

Fisher, R. (1998) Thinking about thinking: developing metacognition in children, *Early Child Development and Care*, 141(1), 1–13.

Fisher, R. & Williams, M. (2002) *Unlocking writing* (London, David Fulton).

Flavell, J. (1979) Metacognition and cognitive monitoring: a new area of cognitive-developmental enquiry, *American Psychologist*, 34, 906–911.

Flavell, J., Green, F. & Flavell, E. (1995) *Young children's knowledge about thinking* (Monographs for the Society for Researching Child Development No. 60.1) (Chicago, University of Chicago Press).

Galton, M. & Williamson, J. (1992) *Group work in the primary classroom* (London, Routledge).

Gambell, T. & Hunter, D. (2000) Surveying gender differences in Canadian school literacy, *Journal of Curriculum Studies*, 32(5), 689–719.

Halliday, M. A. K. (1978) *Language and social semiotic: the social interpretation of language and meaning* (London, Heinemann).

Her Majesty's Inspectorate (HMI) (2005) *English 2000–05: a review of inspection evidence* (London, HMSO).

Hunter, D., Gambell, T. & Randhawa, B. (2005) Gender gaps in group listening and speaking: issues in social constructivist approaches to teaching and learning. *Educational Review,* 57, 329–355.

Jones, D. (2002) Keeping track: assessment in writing, in: M. Williams (Ed.) *Unlocking writing* (London, David Fulton).

Jones, D. (2006) Speaking and listening: planning and assessment, in: D. Jones & P. Hodson (Eds) *Unlocking speaking and listening* (London, David Fulton).

Koshy, V. & Mitchell, C. (1993) *Effective assessment* (London, Hodder & Stoughton).

Littleton, K., Mercer, N., Dawes, L., Wegerif, R., Rowe, D. & Sams, C. (2005) Talking and thinking togerher at key stage 1, *Early Years,* 25(2), 167–182.

Locke, A., Ginsberg, J. & Peers, I. (2002) Development and disadvantage: implications for the early years and beyond, *International Journal of Language and Communication Disorders,* 37(1), 229–247.

Mercer, N. (2000) *Words and minds: how we use language to think together* (London, Routledge).

Mercer, N., Fernandez, M., Dawes, L., Wegerif, R. & Sams, C. (2003) Talk about texts at the computer: using ICT to develop children's oral and literate abilities, *Reading, Literacy and Language,* 37(2), 81–89.

Myhill, D. (2006) Talk, talk, talk: teaching and learning in whole class discourse, *Research Papers in Education,* 21(1), 19–41.

Norman, K. (1992) *Thinking voices: the work of the National Oracy Project* (London, Hodder & Stoughton).

Ofsted (2005) *English 2002–2005: a review of inspection evidence* (London, Ofsted).

Qualifications and Curriculum Authority (QCA) (2006) *Assessment for learning.* Available online at: http//www.qca.org.uk/10009.html (accessed 8 March 2006).

Riley, J., Burrell, A. & McCallum, B. (2004) Developing the spoken language skills of reception class children in two multicultural, inner-city primary schools, *British Educational Research Journal,* 30(5), 658–672.

Sadler, R. (1998) Formative assessment and the design of instructional systems, *Instructional Science,* 18, 119–144.

Underwood, J. & Underwood, G. (1999) Task effects on co-operative and collaborative learning with computers, in: K. Littleton & P. Light (Eds) *Learning with computers: analysing productive interaction* (London, Routledge).

Vygotsky, L. S. (1962) *Thought and language* (Cambridge, MA, MIT Press).

Vygotsky, L. S. (1978) *Mind in society: the development of higher psychological processes* (Cambridge, MA, Harvard University Press).

Williams, M. (2006) Letting talents shine: developing oracy with gifted and talented pupils, in: D. Jones & P. Hodson (Eds) *Unlocking speaking and listening* (London, David Fulton).

Oral language development

Alice Sterling Honig

Language is a fantastic gift: it empowers humans to create new ways of speaking with, for and to others about any topic or experience. Language is a rule-governed, meaningful communication system. It is a symbol system, where a word or phrase stands for or represents something else that can be touched, thought about, seen, heard, felt, done, imagined, longed for, rejoiced or anguished about. Language can be used for many different goals, among others: to teach, to scold, to encourage, to express affection, to pray; or to deceive, to insult, to explain, to clarify, to declaim poetically, to ask for more information; or to describe a robbery, a soccer game or a love scene. Winston Churchill's magnificent oratorical eloquence was essential to galvanize Britain to withstand the onslaught of Nazi Germany during the Second World War. Other national leaders have used their oratorical powers to incite mobs to riot and kill.

Oral language proficiency with others is an awesome social skill that our ancestors developed less than 130,000 years ago. Language is also a mystery. Some years ago, Maria Montessori (1967) mused eloquently:

> Before man's arrival on earth language did not exist. And what is it? Barely a breath! A few noises strung together … It is a mystery impossible to fathom. (pp. 108–10).

Because reading and writing are so critical to positive achievements in school, the emphasis on enhancing language skills in classrooms has more frequently focused on teaching phoneme/grapheme correspondence and on strengthening reading fluency, reading for meaning and writing skills. Although in many families, 'elocution lessons' were popular a century ago, parents rarely 'teach' *oral language skills* to young children. For adolescents, in a few schools, debate societies do offer select students the chance to hone their oral skills on intramural debate teams with students from other communities.

Most people do not believe you have to teach children 'oral language'. After all, children entering kindergarten have approximately 14,000 words in their vocabularies. In addition, some theorists, such as Chomsky (1965), believe that language is hard-wired in the brain. And indeed, children in every culture learn to speak, many times quite without adult tuition. It is impressive that children raised in a variety of physical environments learn the relationship of verbal expressions to meanings. All cultures have oral language, although not all have written language:

> Virtually every child, without special training, exposed to surface structures of language in many interaction contexts, builds for himself—in a short period of time and at an early stage in his cognitive development—a deep-level, abstract, and highly complex system of linguistic structure. (Lindfors, 1987, p. 96)

Further, research confirms that one does not have to 'teach' babies language sounds. For the first ten or so months of life, a young infant hears and can differentiate among all the sounds of all the languages in the world. Babies in Hindu families respond to differences in English sounds, and English babies respond to sound differences in Hindi. A Japanese baby clearly responds to 'l' versus 'r' as different sounds early in the first year of life, but ceases to do so before the first birthday.

Despite our innate propensity at birth to be able to learn any language, the loving caregivers who socialize babies and young children are crucial for ensuring the power to *use language as a rich symbol system* that permits humans to share meaning with one another and to advance learning. Language learning depends on genetic potential *and* on social interactions (Bloom, 2002). Long years ago in Tsarist Russia, if usurpers staged a coup to overthrow the emperor, the infant heir in line to the throne would be put in a tower with a deaf-mute caregiver, to ensure that the baby would never grow up normally or ever become a threat to the usurpers.

Children learn amazing aspects of oral language, most likely without ever realizing how much they know. Subtle social skills in oral language are confirmed very early in children's lives. This becomes startlingly evident when two preschoolers tussle over a toy. One may call a peer in loud exasperation a 'poopy-head'. When visiting, grandpa expects polite behavior and self-control from the child. 'Poopy-head' is an appellation the preschooler knows that he/she must *never* direct to grandpa! Already, in their few short years of life, parents and caregivers have socialized the child to know when and with whom they can and cannot use social epithets even when upset.

Language beginnings in early communication patterns

Although mastering a wide variety of skills in oral language is a crowning human achievement, the earliest roots of language development lie in the communicative social interactions and games that caring adults play with babies who cannot yet 'talk'. A 3-month-old baby coos with throaty, open vowel sounds. Her delighted dad, cradling Natalie in arms as she faces him, responds with a broad smile and in a style called *parentese*. He uses a high-pitched voice, loving tones, drawn-out vowels and short, slow phrases: 'You're talking! I love to hear you talking, honey. Talk some more.' As dad pauses to let baby respond, baby stares at him and produces another throaty vowel sound with more earnest conviction. Dad's delight in her early vocalization seems to energize her determination to carry on a 'conversation' with him. This dialogue goes on for 16 cooing turns (as noted by papa who, as a developmental specialist and new father, of course has to write down his newborn daughter's accomplishment). The 'parentese' style of talking 'wires' connections in the baby's brain by sending cascades of rich chemical and electrical impulses coursing through the neurons of the brain. Such 'baby talk' is a fine way to stimulate infants' early interest in oral conversations and to focus their attention on words and dialogues.

Yet, the earliest 'dialogues' need not include vocalizations. Mutual loving gazing into each other's eyes, mutual harmonizing of a mother's ways of offering the breast and the baby's nursing style, or mutual settling into a peaceful snuggle in a rocking-chair while a parent sings to baby are other 'dialogues' that support the deep roots for later verbal mutual interactions. Decades later, these earliest dialogues blossom into intricate skills, such as intimate conversations between new lovers, or long neighborly exchanges of gossip over the garden fence or the office water-cooler, and even eloquent lectures by teachers!

Domains of oral language

As they grow, children learn aspects of the five domains of language as well as endless subtleties of high-level conversational skills. These domains are: phonology, syntax, semantics, morphology and pragmatics.

Phonemes

The sounds we produce in speaking are called *phonemes*. Babies progress from producing throaty vowel sounds, 'coos', to producing consonant clusters, such as 'dlth', and vowel combinations when only a few months old. The easiest consonants are labials, made by placing the lips together, as in 'mm' or 'bb'. Phonemes made by pressing the tongue against the upper palate, such as 'd' and 'n', are also easy. Babies then combine a consonant with a vowel sound. By about 6 months, babies duplicate these combinations to produce those phonemic combinations that prove such a delight to parents: 'mama' and 'papa' or 'dada', 'nana' (for grandma or nursey) and 'baba' for bottle or blanket. In several cultures in the world, parents often endow these early phonemes with the specific meaning of a family member: think of words for mother in other languages: 'maman' in French, 'madre' in Spanish, 'ima' (in Hebrew) and 'mat' (in Russian); and other examples include, in Mandarin, 'ma' (on the high tone, in this tonal language), signifying mother; 'babushka', grandmother, in Russian, and 'bubbie', grandmother, in Yiddish. Words for father in many languages also show this sensitivity to the early sounds that babies produce: 'apam' is 'father' in Hungarian, 'abba' in Hebrew and Arabic, 'pater' in Latin and 'padre' in Italian and Spanish.

At first, babies string together over and over the same consonant and vowel combination, as in 'bababa'. Later, they become proficient not only at these 'duplicated babbles' but at '*unreduplicated babbling*', or *jargon*, where a variety of consonants and vowels are strung together. Listen to a baby earnestly jabbering to a caregiver—so many different vowels and consonants—in an earnest attempt to communicate! The baby is even using *stress*, *pitch* and *juncture*, called 'suprasegmental elements' of language, in this complex jargon; and the baby looks up at his/her caregiver with a puzzled expression as he babbles with pauses, then he uses an upward inflection as if he/she were asking the adult a question. Or the baby points imperiously to the toy shelf and babbles with the commanding tone that signifies she wants something right away, mystifying as the content of the command may be for the adult. From about 10 months onward, the baby uses the pointer finger as well as babbling to share wishes, events, worries and joys with caring adults.

This *joint attention* and shared regard for an activity, topic, or event is critical for boosting early conversational skills: teacher holds Ofira in her arms at the window as they both watch the bird-feeder outside, where the children have often helped to pour in birdseed. 'Look at the birdie', exclaims the teacher. Ofira grins and affirms, 't'eet-t'eet'.

How important is early babbling? Adults need to treat these early attempts at oral language with interest and courtesy. They are the babies' first attempts to use language to communicate meaning with their special adults. Yet many adults do not realize that these precursors of words are worthy of attention and adult effort to respond as the toddler struggles to share information and desires. We have much to do in society to help some loving family members realize what powerful oral language boosters they can be for children and how they can actualize their powers (see Honig, 2001).

Some young children wrestle with coordinating their tongue, lips, pharynx, larynx, palate and teeth in order to pronounce words such that an adult can understand them. They omit a difficult-to-pronounce phoneme, for example, and ask to play 'te'pho' rather than telephone. Children learn to pronounce both voiced and unvoiced pairs of consonants: e.g. 'v' versus 'f'; 'b' versus 'p'; and 'd' versus 't'. If a teacher asks children to touch their Adam's apple while pronouncing these phonemes, then the children are able to feel the vibrations for a voiced, in contrast to an unvoiced, consonant.

Sometimes children do hear the way a sound should be pronounced but they cannot yet manage to produce this phoneme:

> Standing at the goldfish tank with four-year-old Jackie, I shared his delight as we watched the fish flick their golden tails while swimming. 'Shishies', Jackie announced in delight while pointing at them. 'Pretty golden shishies', I responded enthusiastically (I was trying to find out whether he could hear but not yet pronounce the correct sound). Jackie frowned! 'No shishies, teacha! Shishies!' he corrected me, indignantly. Jackie could hear the sound of 'f' in fishes, but not pronounce it.

Some phonemes are particularly difficult for children to pronounce. A five year old may still say 'lellow' for 'yellow'. 'R' is a difficult sound for many children. Children may *substitute phonemes* even into kindergarten, as they talk about how they enjoy petting the class 'bunny wabbit!'. Sounds like 'ng' may not be mastered until 6 years of age. Some consonant clusters, as 'str' in 'street', remain difficult for children well into the school years. Other children early on are able to produce sounds easy for adults to understand:

> While diapering Maija, Ms Kathryn heard a scream. Turning, she saw Leslie staring at another toddler who was crying. Leslie was prone to hit peers to take away a toy. 'No hitting, Leslie', Ms Kathryn called out. 'I did not hit her. I bit her', retorted Leslie, clear as a bell.

Syntax or grammar

Syntax refers to the orderly grammar rules a given language requires for the construction of acceptable sentences. Syntax rules differ for different languages. Usually, in English, an adjective precedes a noun, as in 'the white house'; adjective and noun are reversed in the Spanish 'la casa blanca'. English grammar rules do not permit double negatives. In French, however, a child quite correctly says 'Je n'ai pas d'argent' ('I don't have any money', but literally translatable as 'I don't have no money').

Since toddlers often have only two or three words to express themselves, caregivers need to be aware of what speech categories toddlers are able to use. Toddlers omit the little functional words that adult speech requires, such as 'a' or 'the', so their talk is often called 'telegraphic speech'. Yet basic grammatical categories of topic and comment and modifier are present, even in these early toddler phrases. Despite the short 'telegraphic speech' that toddlers use, they are quite sensitive to violations of grammar rules (Honig, 2001).

A researcher asked two year olds a series of questions in which grammatical morphemes were replaced with other words:

> Directed to 'find the dog for me', 85% of toddlers could point to the correct animal picture. When the phrase was 'find was dog for me', toddlers pointed to the dog 55% of the time. Only 40% of toddlers pointed correctly when directed, 'find gub dog for me'. (Honig *et al.*, 2001, p. 386)

Semantics

Children learn that concepts have semantic features and meanings. A sister is a female person and a child of the same parent. Talking about the 'bachelor's wife' will make some kids giggle. They already know that a semantic property of the term 'bachelor' refers to a man who is *not* married. Semantic understandings grow gradually. Ask a three year old whether he has a nose or toes, and he can triumphantly point to them and say their names. 'I got dat!' said one little child to me with great satisfaction! But they cannot explain what the component features of a nose are, such as where a nose is found, what is does or how it is shaped. Toddlers may not grasp the fact that two different words can have the same meaning. Talk about a moon as a crescent. A preschooler may pronounce the word after the adult, and still go on using only the word 'moon', even when the crescent sliver is clearly visible in the sky.

Deictic terms are too difficult for toddlers. Using terms such as 'this one' and 'that one' requires that the speaker becomes the point of reference from which the terms can be understood. Thus, when speaking with young children, an adult needs to use specific terms. Saying 'put these blocks over there and those blocks over here' is frustrating for the child. Labelling long versus short blocks and specifying the exact shelf on which to store the blocks will be very helpful in gaining children's cooperation at clean-up time.

The first symbolic concepts babies learn are related to the personally important people, events and activities in their lives. Children begin to attach labels or words to those concepts. Because a small child has a limited vocabulary and even more limited powers of explanation, it is often difficult to assess a child's semantic competence, that is whether a child *really* understand what a word means (Bloom, 1990). Some tests give a clue that the child does understand the concept but does not have the adult terminology yet. Ask a preschooler where a pig lives and she may answer 'a pig house'. *Semantic transparency* characterizes that child's responses; the child has semantic competence but has not learned the special words 'pigpen' or 'pigsty' that denote a pig's residence. Ask about what we call the child of a mommy pig, and a toddler may reply 'Piggy' or 'pig baby' rather than 'piglet'. Many toddlers have already learned to add a 'y' or 'ie' ending (doggie, horsy, kitty) as the semantic symbol for 'little one'. The child clearly has the conceptual understanding of the question but not the technical terminology specific to the *lexicon* (dictionary words) of his speech community.

Semantic relations are expressed in early toddler grammatical formulations

'Telegraphic speech' categories reveal how many semantic relations that toddlers have already acquired, even when they are using just two or three words together. Adults need to listen for and use all their creative adult skills to decode the meanings revealed in early telegraphic speech:

Agent—action:	Doggy run! ('A dog is running outside the center play yard', or 'I love to play with Fido and watch him run in our yard'.)
Agent—object:	Mama shoe. ('Mama is putting on my shoe' or 'Mama is holding the shoe' or 'Mama bought me new shoes'.)
Action—object:	Eat soup. F'ow ball. ('Teacher is throwing the ball' or maybe 'I want to throw the ball'.)
Possession:	My ball! Mommy sock.
Negation:	No nigh'nigh ('No sleep time right now!')
Wishes:	Want dat!
Object—location:	Book dere. Cup table.
Action—location:	Go, Chucky-cheese. Sit car.
Object—description:	Tove hot! ('Hot stove!'). P'itty d'ess. ('Pretty dress.')
Disappearance:	Allgone juice. [comment on emptied juice cup]
Questions:	Who dat?; Whazzat?; How do dat?
Recurrence:	More tickle. More cookie.
Object—use:	Cut Kni'. ('Cut with a knife.')
Feelings:	Me yike nana ('I like bananas.')
Imperative:	Thtay dere! ('Stay there!') Daddy, up! ('Daddy, pick me up in your arms!')
Invitations/requests:	Want p'ay? ('Do you want to play?')
Entity—attribute:	Dat kitty ('That is a kitty.')

Note that the 'Why' question is very difficult for a young child to decode. A preschooler may ask an adult: 'Why', over and over, even when the adult has patiently tried to answer the 'why' question until he is weary! 'Why' is a rare example of a verbal behaviour that young children learn to say early, but their understanding of the meaning comes much later. A three year old asked her mystified father: 'Why the garage door?' Far more usual is the situation that *receptive* language (listening to and understanding words and sentences) precedes *expressive* language.

Morphemes

Morphemes are the smallest units of meaning in a language. 'Elephant', 'the' and 'bug' are words; they are also morphemes. These are called *unbound morphemes* because they do stand alone as words. Some morphemes are *bound*, and they do not stand alone. They can only be used to modify the meaning of a word. Some negation morphemes radically change the meaning of a word: 'kind' versus '*un*kind; 'comfort' versus 'discomfort'; or 'complete' versus '*in*complete'. The bound morpheme 'ing' is learned early in toddlerhood and signifies ongoing action. 'Papa s'immin me!', announced an 18-month-old girl, very pleased at being able to relate her special adventure of going swimming at a local pool with her father.

Some bound morphemes are affixed as prefixes, as in '*circum*navigate'. Some occur as word endings that change the meaning, for example, from an adjective to an adverb ('sad' versus 'sad*ly*'). Some morphemes signify an agent as the 'er' in 'teach*er*'. A kindergarten child once told me with great relish that his mom was the best 'cooker' in the world. A lovely compliment by an appreciative son, despite his not yet understanding that the word 'cook' as a noun requires no extra morpheme!

When several different morphemes have the same meaning but different phonology, they are called *allomorphs*. The rule for forming plurals usually requires adding the sounds 's' as in 'cats' or 'z' as in 'dogs' or 'ez' as in 'glasses'. However, pluralization rules for other nouns differ from the standard. 'Alumnae', 'foci' and 'fish' are examples of such rule exceptions that older children need to learn specifically through adult tuition and reading. Other sounds also used in English to indicate 'more than one', are: 'ren' in 'children', 'ez' in 'judges' and 'a' in 'errata'. All these different sounds meaning 'more than one' are allomorphs.

In some languages, such as Hebrew and Turkish, morphemes are appended to the beginnings and endings of words, for example, to represent articles such as 'the'. Some languages are highly inflected. In Latin, nouns have case endings, depending on the relationship of the noun to the verb. Thus, Virgil's splendid poem on the Trojan War, the *Aeneid*, begins: 'Arma virumque cano' ('Of arms and the man I sing'). 'Arma' ('arms') begins the sentence because a Latin speaker knows that the poet is using arms as a plural in the accusative case, and as the object of the verb 'I sing' that occurs as the third Latin word in the poem.

Similarly, a Russian child learns that noun endings refer to different cases. She learns to say not just 'stol' (the word for 'table'), but additional words such as: 'stola, stoloo, stolye', for example, in order to express the genitive, the dative and the ablative cases in which the noun may be used. Morphemes are essential to specify meanings in highly inflected languages.

Sometimes the morphemes required for correct usage have not been used in a particular community; and children come into school and grow up using morphemes unique to their linguistic/culture group. After a conference in a southern US community, a preschool aide once asked me whether she would be getting a 'certificary' (rather than 'certificate').

Rich oral language opportunities are critical for children not only to enlarge vocabulary, but also to learn the myriad morphemes requisite in specific situations to modify words the children know. For example, children will learn that although both morphemes express a negative, in English speech one says '*dys*functional' and '*im*possible'. Switching the prefixes around is not permissible in standard English. Poets are allowed more leeway! A baby goat is called a 'kid', but in one lovely Christmas song, the composer refers to 'One goatling from the far hills, one white, white bird', among the gifts brought to Bethlehem.

Some dialects and some languages tend to omit clusters of sounds or omit morphemes that signify a specific meaning. Among children who grow up in households where Black English is spoken, plural morphemes may not be required. 'He got fi'cen' ('He has five cents') said a teenager to her friend in the grocery store as she pointed to her brother. In standard Mandarin, there are no specific morphemes as markers for the plural or the past tense. 'Haidze' can mean child or children. Yet, the Mandarin speaker easily indicates plurality or past tense by the sequenced way that spoken symbols are linked together.

Researches have established that for English language speakers, there is an orderly progression in the first 14 morphemes a child acquires (Brown, 1973):

1. present progressive inflection ('hugging');
2. prepositions 'in';
3. preposition 'on';
4. plural;
5. irregular past tense ('sang'; 'rode');
6. possessive ('Ian's hat');
7. uncontractible copula ('Right you are'; 'The giraffe is tall');
8. articles 'a' and 'the';
9. regular past tense ('played');
10. regular third-person present tense ('plays');
11. irregular third-person present tense ('has');
12. uncontractible auxiliary ('I do so want to play');
13. contractible copula ('He's a puppy'; 'I'm happy');
14. contractible auxiliary ('I'd like to play too').

In order to assess whether a child knows a morpheme and can use it correctly, Gleason (2005) developed the *WUGS test*. Nonsense syllables are used to encourage the child to state the answer. For example, the examiner shows sketches of first one and then two plump bird-like creatures, and says: 'Here is a wug. Now there are two of them. There are two——' Can the child produce the correct plural morpheme? Or the examiner shows a stick figure whirling something on a string: 'This man likes to bod. Yesterday he——' Can the child produce the correct past tense?

Pragmatics

The system of oral social rules that children learn in order to be considered 'nice' or 'naughty' is called pragmatics. Children learn early in many families that unless they say 'please' parents will not give them a cookie. In some cultures they learn to call grandparents by honorific names. Children learn that professionals, such as medical specialists, are referred to with initial titles of respect, such as 'Dr Smith' and not as 'Johnny'. They are taught to say 'thank you' when offered a sweet or other gift.

In Japanese, a person may be required to use different words to address an employer or 'superior' compared with kin or friends. In France, a child learns to use 'tu' as the familiar 'you' word for intimate others, and 'vous' more formally. In Russian, this distinction is also strong. In Pushkin's *Eugene Onegin*, the passionate lover Lenski, about to engage in a deadly duel, sings of his longing for his beloved Olga: 'Ya vas lyubil' ('I loved you'). In Tchaikovsky's opera, Lenski uses the formal word 'vas' for 'you'. Yet one would expect in a tender Russian love song rather to hear the intimate word for *you* as in 'Ya tebya lyublyu' ('I love you').

Greeting and parting words often show the clear way in which children have been socialized. Older children may be taught to greet elderly strangers with the formal, 'How are you?'. To friends they may say, 'What's up?' or 'How ya doin'?'. They also learn stock phrases which are pragmatically required in certain social situations, but which the speaker may not believe, such as 'I do hope that we see each other again soon. It has been a pleasure meeting you'.

How language develops

Given the five domains of language that children must learn, how does a child acquire ever more subtle, loquacious and sophisticated oral ability?

First words

Although differences in oral language skills are evident by 3 years of age, the 'window' for normal oral language production is quite wide. Some babies say their first words before 9–10 months; others say their earliest words when nearly 2 years old. A baby tends to use a single word where an older child would use sentences. Linguists call the earliest sounds that babies seem to be using more or less consistently for a specific person or object *protowords*. If adults confirm that the infant clearly and exclusively uses that word only in a special context, or for a special object or person, then the expression may be considered a word. If a baby calls out 'num-num' and bangs on his high chair with a spoon as he sees a caregiver approaching with food and does not use that expression in any other context, we may infer that 'num-num' is the child's word for his meal. First word learning is often slow:

> I was sitting in a restaurant with a 13–14-month-old baby who had not yet expressed a word. While mom chatted with the other guests, the server brought some rolls to the table. I kept tearing off tiny bits of bread and delightedly exclaiming 'bread' as I offered delectable morsels of bread to the hungry baby in the high chair near me. After a half-hour, when I enthusiastically held out a tiny bit of the bread and asked 'Want some bread, lovey? Bread?', the baby said 'b'ead' to my rapturous delight (and that of his mom). Sometimes achieving the first word takes a lot of teaching effort!

First words are often nouns that represent familiar aspects of the infant's environment, such as foods, parts of the body (nose, eye, etc.), clothing, toys, animals and dear persons. In a northern city, snowbound and dark all winter, one baby's first word was "li" for light, which had to be turned on early every evening. Another baby, carried in mama's arms every day to visit a nearby pond and throw breadcrumbs for the ducks swimming there said her first word: 'Duh', for duck.

Many parents simplify early word learning by giving the baby an easier noun, such as 'Nana' for nursey, 'baba' for blanket or bottle, or 'pee-pee' for urine. To determine what words babies do understand and say, researchers at the MacArthur Foundation created a scale based on the presence of baby gestures (such as 'bye' or 'up'), words and phrases. Mothers completed a checklist that contained 396 words, to find out which words babies understood (*receptive vocabulary*) and which they understood and could say (*expressive vocabulary*). At 10 months, some babies understood about 11 words. The top 10% of babies understood about 154 words. By 16 months, babies in the bottom 10% understood 92 words and babies in the top 10% understood 321 words. The difference in spoken words was even greater: 180 words for the top 10% and 40 words for the bottom 10%. Yet babies do go on to become equally competent language learners. When should a teacher be worried? Experts say that if children neither understand nor say any words by 18 months, if they avoid eye contact, rarely babble, do not respond to a whisper and show little interest in baby communications, such as 'hi' or 'bye', then professional help should be sought (Golinkoff & Hirsh-Pasek, 1999).

Some infants not only have a large single-word vocabulary, but have rich meaningful associations with the words they are producing, however garbled the pronunciation:

> Caring for a 13-month-old who was not yet walking, I chose a picture-book and tried to settle on a couch to read with the little boy. The family dog kept jumping up and wanting to be petted. "Oh', I muttered, 'I wish I had a bone for you. Then I could read a book to Roy.' 'Bone?' asked the baby, looking up at me. 'Yes, if the doggie had a bone, he could chew on it and then we could read our book', I explained. Roy padded off on all four paws. He went around a corner and through three rooms. He headed for the dog's dish under the sink, purposefully picked up the leather dog bone lying on the floor nearby, held it tightly in one hand, and padded back to the room. We were able to read peacefully together. Despite using only one word at a time, Roy had a very clear concept of what a dog bone was, where it was to be found and to what use it would be put!

Vocabulary spurt

Although infants produce one word at a time, toddlers are learning 8–11 words each month. By the time toddlers have a vocabulary between 50 and 100 words, a 'vocabulary spurt' occurs—a geometric increase in the number of words said. No longer can doting parents manage to write down all the words that their amazing toddler is saying. When does this vocabulary spurt appear? Sometime during the second half of the second year of life, toddlers often demonstrate this explosive period of vocabulary growth. This *vocabulary spurt* shows a wide window of occurrence: Some children show this spurt at 14 months and some not until 2.5 years. Sometimes toddlers produce nine new words per day! And sometimes these are scatological words that the parents have been using freely up to now. When the vocabulary spurt arrives, parents may need to discontinue using swearwords that seem so salient to the toddler, who learns them from adults expressing strong emotions:

> In the days when we used record players rather than CDs in childcare, I was trying to put on a record that had a scratch, and the record would not play. With a worried face, one angelic 3-year-old explained to me earnestly: 'Teacher, weco'd player all fuck' up!'

How do advances in cognitive abilities relate to this vocabulary spurt? Researchers note that the vocabulary spurt occurs about the same time that toddlers are able to sort items into two groups, such as cars/trucks/buses versus teddy-bears and other soft animals. Piagetian theory has posited that cognitive competence precedes language competence. It seems that when toddlers can create *mental categories* of two different kinds of toys, then they are more able to label categories of objects verbally, and are more likely to exhibit the vocabulary spurt.

Overextension and underextension

Babies with single words will often use them to denote vast numbers of other items or creatures. Some young children call all men 'Daddy'. Many babies initially will call an animal by the sound the animal makes conventionally in that culture. 'Quack-quack', 'bah-bah' and 'tweet-tweet' are words that an 18-month-old English-speaking child might produce for visiting grandparents if asked to do so by parents proud of their daughter's verbal accomplishments.

Travelling with a baby in the countryside, parents become exhausted to hear their toddler call out 'Doggie' every time a cow, horse or sheep appears in a meadow. Sometimes, despite a parent's best intentions to teach the toddler that a cow is much bigger than a doggie, is eating grass, and says 'Moo', not 'woof-woof', the child may happily continue to name every animal a doggie. The child *extends* the word for one type of creature to cover many others. Yet, if asked to point to the cow in a picture where a doggie picture is also available, the toddler may point accurately. Receptive understanding precedes expressive competence. Young children create overextensions that startle a parent with poetic imagery. One toddler said 'olive' as he pointed to each round, dark eye of the family poodle:

> While living in France in a cold-water flat with our toddler, I had noticed a delay in his producing words even as I was proud of how accurately Larry understood and carried out requests made in either French or English. As I pushed the stroller over a bridge crossing the River Seine, the toddler looked down and exclaimed joyously 'Juice!'. He knew that

juice was the liquid he loved to drink for breakfast. Here was a whole bunch of juice flowing by below the bridge!

Some *overextensions* reflect the growing power of grammatical knowledge of young children:

> Standing at the candy machine in the hallway, the preschooler waited in happy anticipation of the candy bar she would receive after putting several coins in the machine. As the tiny bar slid out, the child exclaimed with indignation to her mom: 'They highered the money and they smallered the candy bar!'

The little girl had learned that '-ed' endings were often required to express the past tense. Thus, some children may have been using the accepted past tense 'fell' imitatively. But once they understand that the morpheme '-ed' is usually required to create the past tense, they use this new knowledge to *regularize* the verb 'to fall' and the verb 'to hurt'. Having taken a tumble in the playground, a child exclaimed to his teacher: 'I fallded down and hurted myself.' Teachers need to feel proud of the learning that this 'mistake' represents. The preschooler's oral language is now reflecting *internalization* of morphological and grammatical rules, which do, of course, have so many exceptions. This internalization of rules can also be seen when preschoolers refer to 'mouses' or 'footses' instead of 'mice' or 'feet'. In this case, a *morphophonemic* change is required in English to replace the internal sound in the singular word with a different sound in order to form the plural; and, of course, for some plurals the rule is to add no extra morpheme, as for 'deer'. When preschoolers make regularization mistakes, cheerfully provide the standard English word required—but do admire the linguistic advances inherent in the young child's creative expressions!

Underextension is common in early oral language. Sometimes children will use a word to mean far less than an adult realizes. 'Doggie' to a young toddler may mean only Rex, the family dog. By 'car', the child is referring only the family's stationwagon instead of all cars. Teachers need to tune in to a child's use of words in these special ways.

Fast mapping

Fast-mapping ability means that a toddler can learn where and when to apply a newly heard name for an event or object after hearing the novel label only one time. Despite different family experiences with words, toddlers become adept at learning new words quickly:

> While living in Paris in an apartment house, I spent some days caring for Daniel, an 18-month-old grandchild who had always lived in a one-family home. As I held his hand and took him out into the hallway to take the elevator down to the first floor, I explained that we would go into an *elevator* in order to go downstairs and then outdoors to take a walk together. When the elevator came, the toddler entered with me, smiling, and exclaimed 'Abileelee' as we rode down. Later, on our return from the walk, Daniel immediately and zestfully identified the elevator as 'Abileelee' as soon as we re-entered the elevator to go back to the apartment. His command of the sounds of this new word was not very precise, but he certainly tried hard and got down pat the importance of three syllables in that new word, as well as a speedy ability to apply the new word correctly.

How do toddlers learn new words so quickly? Researchers hypothesize that novel names map to categories that are heretofore unnamed for them. They have also found that this fast mapping occurs only when the child is on the verge of the vocabulary spurt. Suppose you show a child who has reached the vocabulary spurt a new and unfamiliar toy (such as a toy eggbeater the child has never seen) and call that toy by a made-up name—such as 'Dax'. Now place three familiar toys and that one odd object in front of the toddler. First, ask the child for a familiar object such as a toy car. Say 'Thank you' and replace that familiar toy in the row of toys. Then ask, 'Now, please give me the Dax'. The toddler is quite likely to hand you the unknown toy, even though you have named it just once clearly for her. Fast mapping is an awesome skill that facilitates oral language learning for children just about the time they are reaching or have reached their vocabulary spurt.

The importance of rhymes

Babies often practice words while lying in their cots. Toddlers often create nonsense sounds that rhyme. The ability to hear and produce rhymes in oral language is a positive predictor of success in learning to read. The Dr Seuss books for children are superbly replete with nonsense rhymes of daunting, tongue-twisting complexity that rejoice a child's heart, as well as challenge the oral skills of the adult reading to that child.

Adults can play many giggly games to increase preschoolers' and kindergarten-age children's enjoyment in listening for, searching for and creating rhyming words. A teacher playing rhyming games grins and chants: 'I have a big fat cat. On her head she wears a ...' The children shout out 'hat' triumphantly as the teacher pantomimes putting something on her head. *Pantomime* is a supportive technique for helping children search for a rhyme. The use of puppets helps also in promoting rhyming games.

Singing songs with rhyming couplets is another technique to facilitate rhyming skills. The English folk song: 'Mr Froggy went a courting and he did ride, um hum, um hum. /A sword and pistol by his side, um hum, um hum', has dozens of couplet verses that rhyme and the melody is easy for children to learn (Honig, 2005). A wonderful aspect of singing long narrative songs with easy-to-learn melodies is that children can themselves participate in creating new rhyming couplets. For Mr Froggy, one child created, 'Then into the feast flew Mr Moth, um hum, um hum./And he did bring the wedding tablecloth, um hum, um hum'.

Poetry adds zest to oral language learning. Children love *onomatopoeia*, when words represent the sounds referred to, as in the 'buzz of the bees'. Poetic imagery, use of dance and musical cadences present playful strategies that captivate children and extend their motivation for oral language learning (Katz & Thomas, 2004).

Different strategies in oral language learning

Researchers have noted that, by 19 months of age, children seem to adopt one of two distinct strategies for learning oral language. Nelson (1981) called one strategy 'referential' where children acquire a large vocabulary of nouns fairly early; they name objects and use language to refer to things happening around them. The other strategy she called 'expressive' where children tend more to use pronouns and repeat many formulaic phrases:

> A college student, enrolled in a course in early language development, was required to listen to preschoolers talking during play. While he was taking notes of conversations in the preschool classroom, one little girl came up and asked: 'Can you do me a favour?' The student put down his notebook and asked: 'What can I do for you?' The girl looked up puzzled and said 'Huh?'. She had learned this entire sociable phrase, but she had no idea of its specific meaning or how to respond once the kindly student answered her.

Sometimes a social phrase has been learned well but the child's command of pronunciation may make it difficult for a teacher to decode. Feeling exasperated with his teacher telling him not to snatch toys one morning, a boy started to walk out of the classroom announcing 'I fi'ta go'. This expression 'I am fixing to go' was a social phrase he had heard often at home. It took all his teacher's skill to decode his meaning and cheerfully redirect him to an interesting activity inside the classroom. Nelson (1991) has reflected that mothers of referential children speak about objects and name them more, while mothers of expressive children talk more about persons and social scenarios. Both parental strategies result in successful language learning; but teachers will want to tune into the strategy that a particular child has learned to use.

Dialect differences

Dialect differences are found in all countries. A classic example from the musical comedy *My Fair Lady*, is Eliza Doolittle's superb rendition of Cockney dialect with its dropping of 'h' sounds and its nasalizing of some vowels. 'Just you wait 'enry 'iggins, just you wait!' Eliza says angrily. After Professor Henry Higgins takes Eliza into his home and works with her, he transforms her dialect characteristics. Now she graciously converses in society by remarking, 'The rain in Spain stays mainly on the plain', with an upper-class British pronunciation.

Dialectal differences are sometimes noted as changes in phoneme pronunciation. In the southern United States, for example, 'pan' may be pronounced as a diphthong 'pay-un'. That dialect may also permit syntactic combinations not permitted in mainstream oral talk, such as: 'I hit him upside da head', rather than 'I hit him on the head'. Russian standard speech and a black English dialect permit deletion of a present-tense form of the verb 'to be' the *copula* ('he my brudder' for 'he is my brother').

Some dialects allow deletion of final post-vocalic consonants in oral language. Teachers can always ask a child to use a word he has pronounced in a sentence so that they are able to discover the child's understanding. Using his word 'bol' in a sentence, one child said, 'I ate a bowl of cereal'. Another said, 'That guy were a bol' warrior', while a third child offered: 'That guy shot with a bow and arrow.' Teachers who serve children from different dialect communities will want to ask children to use a word in a sentence such that the adult can more accurately figure out what the dialectic rule is for that child. One professional mom whose teenager spoke a dialect at home in the Bronx told me she asked her daughter to pretend that learning standard English rules, such as agreement of nouns and verbs, was just like the girl's learning rules for Spanish, which the teenager was studying in one of her classes. This advice worked for her teen daughter!

The ability to *code switch* is very important for youngsters to learn if they speak a dialect as their first language. This is particularly urgent if some aspects of a dialect ('I ain't got no time') are marked as 'unacceptable' in the later work world or in higher educational settings. It is interesting that, in early gangster films, thugs often used dialect ('You got some money wid you?'). Their use of dialect as well as their nefarious activities confirmed that they were the 'bad guys' in that film. Youth who have learned to code switch and use accepted oral language rules in one environment and shift back into the comfort of dialect at home and in the neighbourhood have a powerful tool at their command!

Gender differences

Studies show that girls tend to talk earlier than boys:

> They reach each of the [language] milestones earlier than boys—but only by a little bit …
> Biological theorists argue that because girls mature earlier, the part of their brains devoted
> to language becomes specialized sooner. (Golinkoff & Hirsh-Opasek, 1999, p. 139)

Girls lead boys on number of words produced, number of words understood, number of words used in combinations, sentence complexity and maximum sentence length.

But perhaps socialization practices of parents and caregivers also tend to account for some of these gender differences. Researches show that girls linger longer with moms dropping them off at childcare. Boys often gallop into the playroom right away, and they may not get a chance to hear as many goodbye, loving words and parental wishes or small conversational exchanges as girls get to hear.

As preschoolers, children begin to use special ways of talking either more characteristic of males or of females, referred to as *genderlects*. For example, a girl may make an oblique request where a boy will ask directly. Boys use more vernacular than girls and they use swearwords more than girls. Genderlects are learned through socialization in families, educational settings and in playgroups.

Birth order

Parents who have had more than one child tend to have talked more to the oldest child, to whom they have given undivided attention. Thus it is understandable that first-born tend to talk earlier than later-born children. But these differences may well disappear when later-born children experience rich, personalized language interactions in their childcare classrooms. Parents can give a boost to language learning of later-born children by taking advantage of special opportunities, such as settling-to-sleep time, diapering time or bath-time to engage in extended conversational talk (Honig, 1982a, 1982b; Honig & Brophy, 1996).

Learning complex oral language rules

Complex changes occur in children's *expression of negation* from toddler to preschool age. Toddlers tend to put such a negation word at the beginning or at the end of a sentence. At a birthday party where a toddler had already seen one balloon burst by a peer, she hid her own balloon behind her back and shouted out: 'Baby balloon other bite no!' The syntax was certainly 'creative' but the semantic meaning was very clear! A toddler announced at lunchtime: 'No me want pisgetti.' But during the next few years, he learnt to transport a negation word into the body of the sentence as he politely said to his Grandma, 'No, thank you, I don't want any spaghetti'.

Older toddlers only gradually become aware that self and other terms must be switched in responding conversationally. Visiting for several hours in a childcare room, I asked a 15-month-old girl: 'Would you like to climb up in my lap and I will read you a story?' She agreed happily: 'Want to climb up on mine's lap!' (rather than saying 'your lap').

As children grow older they learn more and more complex language rules. They learn that there is an obligatory 'flip-flop' rule for pronoun–verb location in creating some questions. They then switch from saying, 'Where I can go?' to 'Where can I go?'. They also learn that, in certain circumstances, the 'flip-flop' rule is not obligatory. Sophisticated in using an embedded phrase, the older child asks a parent: 'I wonder whether I can go to play at Tamar's house after lunch?'

As they grow in oral language skills, children learn to answer a question such as 'Don't you want that candy?' with 'Yes, I *do* want that one', rather than with the toddler expression 'Want dat'. Instead of saying 'Why he dooed dat?', children learn to insert the auxiliary word 'did' and ask: 'Why did he do that?'

Children learn to *embed* 'Wh' questions in sentences such as: 'I wonder when we can go to the zoo?' Embedding is a skill that children delight in as they chant old nursery rhymes such as: 'This is the house that Jack built.' Children love chants with never-ending clauses, such as 'The bear went over the mountain to see what he could see', or the chant: 'The farmer takes a wife, the farmer takes a wife. Hi ho the derrio, the farmer takes a wife.'

Interactive play is much richer from preschool years onwards (Otto, 2002). Children now have oral language skills as well as imaginative mental skills to specify roles and activities in the play scenario. 'You be the fireman; I'll be the fire chief', says Ahmed to his friend, as they don yellow oilcloth firefighters' coats in the dressing-up area.

Many materials are available to help teachers devise interactions that enhance oral language skills (Honig, 1982a; Van Allen & Allen, 1982). Jalongo (2003) suggests that integrated approaches work best:

> A children's librarian planned a preschool story hour with a camping theme that included storytelling, story reading, singing, and watching a film. First, she rolled up brown construction paper into log shapes and decorated them with orange and yellow crêpe paper streamer 'flames'. When the children arrived, they were seated in a circle around the 'campfire'. The librarian started the session by assessing children's prior knowledge with questions such as: 'What is camping?' 'Have any of you ever been camping?' 'What are some of the things you do when you camp out?' (p. 196)

Further enriching this lesson, the teacher read several stories, including 'Bailey goes camping'; she read 'Sophie's knapsack', while unpacking a real knapsack filled with camping items.

Adults need to tune into whether oral language is elaborated or stereotyped in children's dramatic play scenarios. Some children at play frequently use words such as: 'I'm a monster and I'm gonna get you!' The other children run away with shrieks as they are chased in this stereotyped game. Teachers need to think up particularly ingenious ways to extend a child's conversational options when the child habitually engages only in rigidly scripted dramatic play scenarios or in scenarios that habitually exclude some peers. Suppose children in the housekeeping area are busy pretend cooking. As they play family roles, some children tend to exclude a socially shy or inept child from participation, with a dismissive explanation: 'You can't play. We already have a mommy and a daddy.' The teacher then enthusiastically remarks that Jerome can be the deliveryman with a special package for the family. He needs to come in so that they can sign for the package. Then, maybe they can invite him to stay for some tea and a snack. When such teacher extensions are not carried out intrusively, they support an increase in prosocial play themes while also increasing children's language and social skills.

By school age, children learn that *indirect requests* by adults have the same power and requirements as direct requests. A parents no longer says, 'Please pick up your toys', but simply exclaims: 'My, what a mess of toys all over the living room!' Children understand the meaning of this *indirect parental request* for them to clean up their toys.

Children become more sophisticated in realizing that even when two sentences sound much alike, they may be radically different in designating the subject of the action. Two typical examples are: 'Toby is eager to please' and 'Toby is easy to please'. In the first phrase Toby is the subject, and in the second, Toby is the object of others' actions and they are trying to please him.

Passives are difficult for young children and may remain baffling for years. Most preschoolers are unable to decode the passive verb form. If asked to show a 'toy car bashing the truck' or the 'car being bashed by the truck', they are likely to tune into the first noun mentioned and then take the toy car each time and bash the toy truck. School-age children become adept at transforming basic declarative kernels to create complex questions, conditionals, past and future forms, as well as passives

Chomsky's (1965) theory of *transformational grammar* posits that skills to recast sentences are hard-wired in, even as the child's mental ability matures throughout the school years. Older children become adept at taking a *kernel idea* (Chomsky's 'deep structure'), such as a 'cat chases a rat' and transforming that kernel into an awesome variety of 'surface structures' that the child can produce and understand: 'Will the cat chase the rat?'; 'Has the cat been chasing the rat?'; 'Will the rat be chased by the cat?'; 'Would the cat have chased the rat?'; 'Did the rat get chased by the cat?' ; 'Was the cat chasing the rat?''; 'Had the rat not been chased by the cat?' ; 'The rat will have been chased by the cat, won't it?'; 'Hadn't the cat chased the rat?'; 'Is the cat not chasing the rat?'; and 'Shouldn't the cat be chasing the rat?'

Over time, children not only become powerfully adept at transforming a kernel idea into a variety of grammatical forms, called *surface structures*, but also learn *transport rules*:

> Jeff saw Tabitha, a shy child, hanging about near the edge of groups of children busy play-ing at building garages for cars and for spaceships. He was not sure whether he had heard her murmur in a low voice, 'I wanna play'. Jeff, a warm and sociable child, called out in an inviting tone: 'Do you want to play with us?' The 'do' in that sentence had to be added to the verb 'want' and transported to the beginning in order to create the question. An admirable feat in early oral language mastery!

Children also learn to listen for confusing sentences, when a surface structure may have *more than one kernel of meaning*:

- Visiting relatives can be a nuisance. (The meaning of this sentence may refer to the activity or to the persons.)
- They are eating apples. (Persons or the type of apples may be referred to.)
- Time flies like an arrow; fruit flies like a banana. ('Flies' is a verb in one case, but a noun in the other.)

Knowledge and ability to express subtle shades of meaning and complex semantic features grow throughout the school years. While cooking with an adult, children learn that 'slicing' and 'dicing' are not the same. Dicing means that one cuts the food into tiny bits compared with slicing. Children learn more formal as well as more slang words for given actions. They learn nuanced expressions for a basic concept. Semantic distinc-tions for locomotion include: 'walk', 'amble', 'stride', 'shuffle along', 'strut', 'prance', 'trudge', 'hobble along', 'march', 'stroll' and the slang 'get a move on'. Children learn that they can say butter and ice 'melt' but that sugar does not melt in water. It dissolves.

Semantic distinctions are critical for understanding and successfully navigating the social world of peers and friendships. In schools, children become alert to words that are slights. They recognize and, alas, sometimes use backhanded 'compliments' that are really 'put-downs': 'Oh, you aced the algebra test? Well, we all know that nerds always do well in mathematics.'

Humour, riddles and oral language

Children create humour quite early in their language learning (Honig, 1988). Young babies, towards the end of the first year, find *fricatives* funny. Try 'fo-foo' or 'physicist' to delight an eight month old. Toddler humour is sometimes based on phonological play. A toddler grins as she murmurs: 'Oogy, woogy, poogy, shmoogy', while bounc-ing along holding on to a parent's hand.

A Russian psychologist reported that his two year old came in smiling and said to him, 'Daddy, 'oggies meow-meow! The father replied: 'Oh no, honey, doggies say woof-woof.' Crestfallen, the toddler tried again. On her third try, her father suddenly understood that his daughter was using her limited oral language skills to create a joke. 'Oh sure, and kitties say "bow-wow"', he said to her, with a broad grin. Under-stood at last, the toddler broke into happy laughter.

Young children do love the *format* of 'knock-knock' jokes. They often laugh out loud but still do not understand the meaning of the 'joke', nor how to create a 'knock-knock' joke with an amusing punch line, although they repeat the formulaic initial words.

Help children early to decode humour in oral language in order to sharpen thinking skills, as well as to add zest to oral language learning. School-age children enjoy *ricochet* words, in which the repeated element is modified: roly-poly, shilly-shally, chit-chat (Steinmetz & Kipfer, 2006).

A clever eight year old, who was overly loquacious in class, complained to me that his teacher picked on him. Then he brightened and added in a joking tone: 'She will probably even tell me that I make my 11s backwards!' A nine-year-old Australian youngster asked me whether I knew what one gets by pouring very hot water down a rabbit hole. He grinned when I gave up, and he announced: 'Hot cross bunnies!'

Adults use analogies and similes both in clichéd and in imaginative ways. A parent complains to a child: 'You are as slow as molasses!' or exclaims that 'Time sure does fly when I am very busy.' Having been exposed to a rich use of analogies and metaphors, kindergarten children may be able to enjoy jokes with simple dual meanings to be grasped, as in the riddle: 'Why did the boy throw his alarm clock out of the window?' Answer: 'To see time fly.' School-age children easily grasp a joke that represents an absurdity, such as: 'How can you make a dog stop barking in the back seat?' Answer: 'Put him in the front seat.'

Preschool children have difficulties with jokes that require specialized knowledge, such as: 'Why did the boy tiptoe past the medicine cabinet?' Answer: 'So he would not wake the sleeping pills.' They may have difficulty too understanding jokes that require pulling apart several morphemes within a word. Some jokes require the listener to become aware of the different semantic meanings of morphemes that must be considered, as in the joke: 'Why can't you ever starve in a desert?' Answer: 'Because of the sandwiches there.'

Remember that preschoolers and even kindergarten-age children may still give literal interpretations to analogies and to expressions that require a child to understand analogies and metaphors as non-literal symbols. Walking into a classroom, I spied an adorable toddler with curly hair and a round tummy. Smiling, I greeted with him tenderly with: 'Hi, bunny rabbit.' Solemnly, he replied, 'I not a bunny wabbit. I a boy.' Where a child has heard many loving expressions such as 'Sugarplum', 'Honeybunch', 'Sweetpea' or 'Pumpkin' from caregivers, a young child is more likely to have learned that these appellations are expressions of adult affection for the child and are not meant literally:

> During a home visit, I overheard Joey's mother talking on the phone to her husband. She hung up the phone and reported to her son in a disappointed voice, 'Sweetie, Daddy won't be able to eat supper with us tonight. He is all tied up at the office.' The preschooler burst into terrified tears. He obviously had visions of his beloved daddy tied up with ropes by bad robbers!

Once children have learned the power of morphemes to change words, they may well enjoy creative combinations of morphemes. Teachers can engage older youth to think of how to combine morphemes to create humorous sayings. Offer syntactically correct constructions, such as 'disbarred' for lawyers who behave illegally and 'defrocked' for ministers of religion who do so. Then ask the children to create other categories based on the morphemic use of 'de-'. Can they think of and discuss why the following questions are absurd: can musicians be 'denoted', electricians 'delighted', dry cleaners 'depressed', cowboys 'deranged', models deposed' and tree surgeons 'debarked'?

Teachers can further engage older children in reflecting on semantic complexity by using jokes and puns and asking children to talk about what is funny and why. Here are some puns to ask older youngsters to read, discuss, explain and enjoy:

- When a clock is hungry it goes back four seconds.
- A chicken crossing the road is poultry in motion.
- A bicycle cannot stand alone because it is two-tyred.
- You feel stuck with your debt if you can't budge it.
- What is the definition of a will? It is a dead giveaway.
- The short fortune-teller who escaped from prison was a small medium at large.
- Is a pig that loses its voice disgruntled?
- Santa's helpers are subordinate clauses.
- A boiled egg in the morning is hard to beat.
- Bakers trade bread recipes on a knead to know basis.

School-age children love mischievous verses, puns, songs and sayings. They may particularly enjoy discussing the adage: 'Those who get too big for their britches will be exposed in the end.' Children may be challenged to think hard about how clever were the four brothers in business together, when they named their cattle ranch: 'Where the sun's rays meet.' Engage the class in a discussion about why a 'wise guy' and a 'wise man' are opposites.

The *Washington Post* holds a yearly *neologism* contest where readers are asked to supply alternate meanings for common words. This is a wonderful challenge for older youngsters. Can they coin new word meanings and come up with some linguistic zingers, such as these recent winners?

- Coffee—a person upon whom one coughs.
- Flabbergasted—appalled over how much weight you have gained.
- Caterpallor—the color you turn after finding half a grub in the fruit you are eating.
- Negligent—absentmindedly answering the door in your nightgown.
- Lymph—to walk with a lisp.
- Sarchasm—the gulf between the author of a witty remark and the person who doesn't get the joke.

When youngsters are allowed to change spellings slightly, as in some of the above examples, they can conjure up even more exuberant linguistic twists.

Proverbs

Elementary school age children may still have difficulty understanding the humour in jokes that require sophisticated semantic knowledge of multiple word meanings and knowledge of historical events or human foibles. Because of limited experience, some children equally have difficulties explaining adages and wise sayings. For example the Spanish proverb: 'Quien no se aventura no pasa el mar', literally means: 'If you don't venture, you will not get across the sea.' It resembles the English proverb 'Nothing ventured, nothing gained'. Children need experience with metaphors and deeper meanings in order to be able to tell a teacher what a proverb means. Teach proverbs and talk about them with children to give a boost to their oral language skills and to their mental representation skills. In some Hispanic culture groups, *dichas* (proverbs) are frequently used to instruct children in proper social behaviours.

Teachers deepen oral language skills with older children as they challenge their students to struggle with oral explanations of philosophical sayings or thought-provoking brief selections from authors. Give out a thought-provoking quote. Ask the youngsters to come to class prepared to share examples, ideas and feelings about the quotes. Try the dark musings of Alexander Solzhenitsyn, in *The Gulag Archipelago*, about life in Soviet labour camps. The author wrote:

> If it were all so simple: if only there were evil people somewhere insidiously committing evil deeds, and it were necessary only to separate them from the rest of us and destroy them. But the line dividing good and evil cuts through the heart of every human being.

How do youths feel about that message? Does it comport with their life experiences so far? How does it relate to what they view on TV, or know about world suffering and wars?

Suprasegmental elements

Adolescents enjoy jokes that require knowledge of phonological variations and several semantic meanings for the same sound. However, they can also enjoy humour that depends on subtleties of stress, pitch and juncture, which were used by babbling babies to indicate their intent at garbled narrations, question asking or imperatives. For example, one older student uses these three elements to say provocatively: 'Woman without her man is nothing!' Another student grins and retorts, 'Woman! Without her, man is nothing!' *Suprasegmental* elements, emphasized in different ways, make a vast difference in the oral presentation of this phrase and in the interpretation and belief system underlying the oral delivery!

Introduce the idea of absurdities in discussions about *oxymorons*. Choose some songs that use the contradictions inherent in oxymorons to alert children to absurdities. In the song 'I am going to Alabama with my banjo on my knee', the protagonist sings: 'It rained so hard the day I left, the weather it was dry. /The sun so hot I froze to death; Suzannah don't you cry.'

Storytelling, story reading and discussion

Teachers have scheduled oral storytelling 'show and tell' times in classrooms for generations. Korn (1998) reminds us that:

> Encouraging children to tell stories is important not only for its role in enhancing communication skills, but also for its part in helping children develop a sense of who they are as active participants in the world and as social beings in culturally significant interactions with others ... Teachers can mediate young children's learning and further the development of empathic understanding by helping children distinguish between their own perspectives and those of others ... Conversation in the classroom and outside, offers children opportunity to reflect out loud on their experiences and on their own subjective reactions to events, and to engage with other children's experiences as well. (p. 225)

Encouraging storytelling is particularly urgent when there are children from many cultures in a classroom. Children construct stories of who they are in relationship with family members and culturally significant others. By eliciting children's stories, teachers give a strong message that stories from every household and every culture group are welcomed:

> At the round lunch table, where hot dogs had been served, the teacher asked each child to tell about how their families served hot dogs. Tim announced proudly that his dad let him have ketchup *and* mustard with his hot dog. Jose happily reported that his mama served frijoles with hot dogs. Each child used oral language to share with the group and to affirm the cultural uniqueness of their eating experiences as well as the similarities.

Teacher Vivien Paley (1986) chooses a child daily from whom she takes dictation. She carefully writes down the child's theme and scenario. Each child gets a chance to relate his or her unique story that will be acted out later in a special place in the classroom. The child storyteller gets to choose the children who will play each character in the playlet. Such a technique promotes oral-language storytelling skills. Giving this special attention to children who are withdrawn or worried about separation from family, or unskilled at entry bids that can open up play opportunities with others, promotes not only oral language, but also enhances social skills, feelings of belonging in the group and feelings of empowerment.

Socratic questions

Using open-ended questions during conversation times with children may elicit more oral language than the use of convergent questions that just require a 'yes/no' answer or one, single 'correct' reply to a question such as: What colour is the sky?' Yet, in a study in dozens of childcare settings, over 80% of teacher questions to toddlers in childcare were convergent (Honig & Wittmer, 1982). Open-ended questions arouse children's feeling of expertise as they respond to their teachers.

These questions are particularly important for teachers of school-age children who have a special agenda, such as arousing children's awareness of important social issues. With Socratic questions, teachers encourage children to think about the difficult lives of some children who live in refugee camps, shelters for homeless families or in families without money for warm clothing or food; teachers need to draw on children's 'everyday, lived knowledge and experiences to examine issues such as poverty' (Chafel *et al.*, 2007, p. 80).

Story reading and discussion

Research evidence shows that core oral-language functions are important for later reading success (McGinness, 2006). And conversely, shared story reading with young children is an excellent way to enhance their oral language skills (Whitehurst *et al.*, 1994). In a toddler classroom, teachers read aloud the book *Hiding* by Shirley Hughes (see Rosenquist, 2002). The teachers initiated conversations to explore the vivid mental images in the book; they planned activities by drawing upon words and illustrations from the book and had the children verbally recall images and text. To extend concept awareness, they had the children act out aspects of the story. Teachers encouraged children to point out bugs hiding under leaves or squirrels hiding in the cracks of trees. In classroom talk, they incorporated new words and descriptive phrases from the story to enhance children's vocabulary development.

Socioeconomic influences in language learning

Studies over decades have shown that the number of words a child hears and how often he is immersed in the rich auditory 'soup' of language best predicts that child will have a richer vocabulary and more complex sentences by 3 years of age. Almost half a century ago, research revealed socioeconomic status (SES) differences in children's oral language. Bernstein (1964) noted that British working-class children, when asked to describe pictures, responded with a *restricted code*. They used few adjectives and adverbs, and used pronouns rather than nouns. In contrast, he reported that middle-class children used an *elaborated code*. They used a greater variety of syntactic forms and modifiers and described more about the pictures. Have these differences changed over the years?

Thirty years ago, in her observational studies in New York City, Schachter (1979) reported that 50% of the speech of low SES mothers to toddlers, but only 30% of the speech of high SES mothers, consisted of directives. No ethnic differences between black and white mothers were found. But SES differences were marked. Low SES mothers' speech had 25% 'don'ts'. High SES mothers had 10%. Educated mothers were three times more likely than low SES mothers to *respond to a prior communication of the child*.

But what if these SES differences depend on who is assessing the child or what the testing situation is like? Children may be reluctant to talk when in the presence of a strange adult, particularly if that adult is from a different social or cultural background. Also, some children are much shyer temperamentally than others.

Inuit children in northern Canada, when interviewed by fluent speakers in their own language, provided very short responses (Genesee, 2006). Their cultural mores did not make them feel comfortable speaking with strange adults, even those adults who used the children's native language.

Sensitive to just such issues, Tough (1977) studied oral language differences of three year olds from higher and lower SES families in England. Rather than using language tests, Tough recorded the children at play with a chosen companion and a collection of interesting toys. Even under these more natural play conditions, Tough reported:

> At the age of 3 the children in the disadvantaged groups were not using language sponta-
> neously for purposes that were already evident in the talk of the children in the advantaged
> groups. The disadvantaged groups showed little evidence of the use of language for: recall-
> ing and giving details of past experience; reasoning about present and recalled experience;
> anticipating future events and predicting the outcome; recognizing and offering solutions
> to problems; planning and surveying alternatives for possible courses of action; projecting
> into the experiences and feelings of other people; using the imagination to build scenes
> through the use of language for their play. (p. 169)

More recently, data from observational research carried out over several years in the homes of 42 families at different educational/economic levels confirmed with startling clarity how different the social world of language continues to be for many children living in more difficult socioeconomic circumstances (Hart & Risley, 1995). Mothers in welfare families gave many more directives to children. They talked much less to their young children (616 words per hour) compared with working-class parents (1,251 words per hours) or professional parents (2,153) words per hour. Social class differences have implications for differential development of child language power.

Further, these researchers reported that a child in a professional family received 32 positives and 5 prohibitions per hour. The working-class family provided 12 positives and 7 prohibitions per hour. The welfare child received 5 positives and 11 prohibitions per hour. Language inputs to children seem linked with emotional and motivational talk that may have impact on children's language skills and cognitive performance. The researchers speculated that such differences would impact on children's language skills and intellectual attainments well into the school years. Some decades ago, Schachter and Strage (1982) reflected that:

> Not only language but also self-confidence in one's ability to be a good learner may be
> influenced by these SES differences in speech patterns. Active learning requires self-confi-
> dence and faith in one's own efforts. The response style of high-education mothers would
> seem to support the growing autonomy and independence of the language-learning child
> and engender the kind of self-confidence that active learning requires. (p. 89)

Do we have evidence from research that such differences in provision of oral language actually make a difference for later child language and school achievement? A study of low-income African-American families followed the learning careers of a preschool child (24 to 42 months old) and an older school-age sibling. Successful older siblings were performing well on the *Gray oral reading test* in second grade. What were the differences in home language environments? The parents of the successful older siblings spent a fourfold greater percentage of time supplying encouragement compared to discouragement, and they gave more explanations. Older siblings with lower *Gray oral reading test* scores had received about equal amounts of encouraging as discouraging talk. In the successful families, the preschoolers produced more intelligible and longer utterances. They initiated verbal interactions significantly more with their parents. The critical nature of parent verbal input was further revealed when the preschoolers in these low-income families were followed into the 2nd grade. Those preschoolers who were now successful readers in the 2nd grade turned out to be children who had received seven times more encouragement than discouragement. The unsuccessful readers had received 1.5 times as much discouragement as encouragement in verbal interactions that they had initiated as preschoolers with their parents (Norman-Jackson, 1982).

Does low SES mostly predict lower language and academic achievement? Not necessarily. Swan and Stavros (1973) asked kindergarten teachers to identify low-income children doing very well in the classroom. The teachers described these children as asking meaningful and appropriate questions and able to describe their experiences colorfully as well as express a noticeable sense of humour. These low-income families, as might be expected, showed the classic pattern of support for positive early child language development:

> The parents expressed a genuine interest in the children's activities and felt secure and positive about their parenting skills. They talked a lot with their children and engaged in animated mealtime conversation. (Honig, 1982b, p. 62)

This important research reveals just how critical it is to create home-visitation and teacher-outreach programs to encourage parents to enrich and encourage child oral language skills. These researches confirm that although language does depend on hard wiring in the brain, teachers and families are extremely important language partners to enhance children's ability to master high-level oral language skills.

Learning other languages

Bilingualism

Given the ever-growing needs for global commerce and communication, researchers in early childhood have puzzled over how to help children develop oral language skills in several languages. In Europe many children exchange vacation times and go to live with children in families in nearby countries. In addition, they often begin second language learning in early grades. Researchers have established that if a child learns a new language prior to about 10 years of age, then the child succeeds in pronouncing words like a native speaker. After that age, a person may be fluent, but will have difficulties with phoneme pronunciation in the new language. A French-speaking adult may be able to lecture in English, but may continue to say 'zis' instead of 'this', since the 'th' sound is not pronounced in French. An English-speaking person may never learn how to roll the 'r' to say 'ferrocarril' ('railroad') in impeccable Spanish, nor to pronounce the throaty 'ch' sound to say 'Channukah' when referring to the Jewish holiday.

Babies are easily able to learn two languages. One research revealed that when a Spanish-speaking father spent about a half-hour each day at the crib talking with baby, then that infant had a large Spanish receptive vocabulary at 1 year of age, and later on easily came to converse in both languages. Some little children do frequent *code-mixing* when brought up in two languages. They may substitute a word in one language while speaking the second language. 'What's this?' I asked, holding up a fork to show a child from a German-speaking family. 'That's a guppel!' she announced, mixing English and German in her response. The rule for optimal dual language learning from birth onward seems to be: have one speaker use one language and another speaker use the other language so that the baby grows up with oral language skills in both languages with no trouble in figuring out which language to use with which caregiver:

> Visiting a friend in Paris, I spied her preschool-aged grandson standing at the door. That child lived with his parents in London. Mom spoke to him in French. Papa spoke only in English. The child stood there, hesitating whether to enter the room. Grandma spoke French to him. She told him that I was an American visitor who spoke English and French. The child readily came in and spoke with me in English and I told him that I knew French also and that was why I was speaking French with his French-speaking grandma. Apparently, he had felt shy. If I had been a French lady, then he had already learned that he would have had to give me a more formal and elaborate greeting!

Immersion

The importance of *immersion* as the best facilitator of second language learning has been promoted widely (Snow, 1990). Children learn about 50% of their classroom lessons exclusively in the second language. This concept is based on the technique of bilingual immersion for French and English as promulgated in St Lambert, Canada. Immersion has been adopted in Singapore to ensure early learning of English by school children. It has been adopted in China as a late immersion program (Qiang & Zhao, 2000). In Singapore, obstacles to the success of immersion programs have occurred when teachers themselves were lacking in English language skills. Teachers did benefit from training sessions that focused on enhancing their teaching strategies. When the immersion classroom teachers were taught to use *integrated thematic approaches* and *communicative language teaching principles*, then children's second language learning improved (Lim, 2004).

Teachers in schools that serve youth from many different cultures have noted that, in forming friendships, youths will use mixed patterns of language use. Rampton (1995) calls this *language crossing*. In a London school teenagers of British, Punjabi, Caribbean and Bangladeshi descent were sharing expressions in each other's languages. The youth had created a multiethnic way of talking and interacting. Their oral language crossing creativity permitted the boys to strengthen their friendships, as well as it reflected the multicultural diversity of their lives.

Language delays and difficulties

A wide variety of developmental atypicalities is associated with language delays and difficulties (Greenspan, 2001). Teachers aware of the many factors that impede oral language learning can more sensitively respond to behaviours that are baffling. Such knowledge also lessens feelings of frustration and discouragement as the adult tries hard in individual responsive interactions to encourage oral language. Teaching sign language to children with oral language delays has been of help.

Severe retardation

Mental retardation, when severe, can result in inability to learn oral language. Dedicated teachers may use Bliss symbols (which resemble Mahjongg tiles on a stand) to teach severely retarded youngsters to recognize and use nouns. But severely retarded youngsters still have a deep struggle to learn a verb such as 'to sit', even when bodily actions and stick drawings are used to illustrate the concept.

Deafness

Some children are born deaf. When that baby looks at a toy or a kitten playing with yarn, or his older sibling building with blocks, 'he receives none of the mood music that accompanies the social experiences of the hearing baby' (Wood *et al.*, 1986, p. 22). Unfortunately, infant deafness is often missed during routine medical examinations during the first year of life, unless the baby is put in a special chamber and given a specialized hearing test.

Spencer Tracy, a famous actor of the last century, had a baby who was profoundly deaf. Yet no paediatrician had noticed the problem. The mother only realized the baby was deaf when he was about 1 year old, lying awake in his carriage on the porch. She noticed that her baby did not startle or respond at all as she was going outside to care for him and had slammed the nearby porch door with a loud bang.

Sometimes artificial amplification of speech sounds through hearing-aids may boost residual hearing for a deaf child. But beyond a loss of 55 dB, the ability to hear speech sounds and learn *oral* language is severely impaired. The child hears more vowels than consonants and adult speech will be unintelligible for the child.

Clinicians differ in their beliefs as to which systems of support are best to help deaf children learn language. Some emphasize the importance of cochlear implants that will permit interactions with hearing children. Some deaf parents do not want their deaf children to have these implants, lest the child lose intimate contact with the world of deaf culture that communicates exclusively with sign language. Whether finger spelling, lip-reading or signing, or use of all three techniques, results in more optimal learning outcomes for deaf children is still being debated.

It is important to help deaf parents understand that their normal hearing children will not learn oral language just from being placed in front of a television set. Language learning depends crucially on rich social interactions.

Hearing loss

Some children suffer *temporary hearing impairment* from repeated bouts of *otitis media*, infection in the middle ear where fluid buildup has caused blockage:

Walking with a neighbour as we both pushed her 10-month-old in a stroller, I watched as the baby happily pulled off his socks. 'You sure know how to pull off your socks and wiggle your pretty toes', I called to the baby, barely a couple of feet in front of us. There was no bodily or vocal response at all from the baby. I quietly asked the mom about ear infections and found that her child had experienced *otitis media* repeatedly over the past months. A physician subsequently inserted drainage tubes in his ears. This made it possible for this normally born child to begin to hear and respond more to oral language; however, he still struggled with oral language in kindergarten.

Middle ear infections are likely to be more frequent for very young children attending group care. Teachers need to be alert to how oral language is influenced by these recurring infections. The children have difficulty in hearing morphological markers, such as 'ed' or plural 's' or differences in speech intonations. Harris (1990) has expressed concern that a parent, teacher or therapist will become discouraged by the child's 'inattentiveness, distractibility, difficulty in understanding speech in group settings, frequently asking for questions to be repeated, confusion with multi-stage commands, difficulty in recalling verbally presented material, and inappropriate responses to questions and commands' (p. 211).

To facilitate oral language development, Harris (1990, p. 212) recommends the following:

- Seat the child where she is in a position to see and hear the teacher or the therapist at the front of any group.
- Ensure that the child is attending before speaking.
- Encourage the child to look at the speaker.
- Check the child's understanding of what has been said.
- Encourage the child to ask for clarification.
- Where possible, provide visual aids.
- Pace the rate at which speech is delivered.
- Give the child time to interpret and respond to what has been said.
- If necessary, provide the child with a study area free of distracting noise.

Visually impaired children

Clinical research with children who are born blind shows that they too struggle to learn oral language skills. The blind child has *discrete and unrelated experiences* of sound, smell and touch, Providing tactile exploration and locomotion possibilities and responding to the child's cues from such explorations is crucial to helping language develop. This child does not have joint gaze or other communicative tools, such as pointing to get an adult to bring an object near. Teachers need to signal their presence by *touching the child and speaking.* Teachers need to *recognize the motions and location of the child's hands,* rather than seeking facial cues as one does when addressing a sighted baby.

For children with some limited vision, teachers will find it useful to use *verbal prompts* along with large colourful pictures: 'Here is a picture of a girl with a brush. She is brushing her——'.

Play games where the adult and visually limited child do not share visual information. Set up a screen between the adult and child. Provide each with a separate array of toys and objects. The child with visual difficulties can still respond to and with oral language. Suppose the adult asks: 'Do you have a comb? Please give me a comb.' The visually impaired child feels each object on her side of the screen. Then she replies, 'I do not have a comb here. Can you ask for something else?'

Autism

Autistic children have a range of difficulties. One of the most marked is a lack of interest in communicating and a lack of coordinated social behaviours with others, such as signalling an intention to a peer or adult. Autistic children exhibit stereotyped behaviours and insistence on following rigid routines. They may have oral language in infancy that diminishes over the next years. Some have *echolalia*, a repetition of words just heard:

> Working on a puzzle with a lovable 5-year-old autistic boy who was sitting comfortably on his mama's lap, I encouraged him enthusiastically, 'Show Dr Honig how you put the piece down into the puzzle.' I made a palm-down gesture to encourage his cooperation. He picked up the puzzle piece and tried hard to fit it in the square hole, while echoing: 'Show Dr Honig how you put the piece down in the puzzle.'

Echoing the speech of others, abnormalities of speech rhythms, problems of word meanings, inability to make eye contact, stereotyped prolonged body rocking and hand twirling are characteristic of some autistic children. Lengthy one-on-one social interactions and clear and exaggerated language articulation are important adult skills that enhance oral language with autistic children. Encouraging a child to move rhythmically to the familiar tunes of children's songs can be helpful.

Use of sign language has boosted language learning for many autistic children. Since many classrooms integrate children with handicaps, it is important for teachers to try a variety of communication techniques to help a child become able to socialize more positively with peers. Increase the use of rhythmic songs. Adults have a more powerful teaching tool when they help children learn songs by *combining words, movement, and melody* in order to motivate language-delayed children to want to sing and sway along to the song.

Other oral language delays

Some children have normal hearing and intelligence but are delayed in language production. Sometimes these troubles are due to muscular or neuromuscular disorders, such as cleft palate, *dysarthria* and *apraxia*. Dysarthria comes from difficulties with controlling speech musculature. Drooling, abnormal tongue protrusions, and lack of muscular coordination make pronunciation of consonant clusters difficult. In apraxia, a child has normal chewing, sucking and swallowing movements but shows articulation errors, additions, reversals, distortions and substitutions. Comprehension may be normal. A teacher needs to be aware that the expressive language difficulties of some children, especially with consonants, may be a sign that they need a referral for assessment of possible apraxia.

Some children use oral language, but have difficulties producing initial or final sounds of words. Parents and teachers can use verbal materials in interactive language games that alert children to differences in initial and ending sounds (Honig, 1982a; Honig & Brophy, 1996). Can the child listen for the word with the different beginning sound, if you say: 'pick, pig, big, pack'?

Some children talk, but they have poorly developed understanding of the following principles of conversation.

Cooperation and topic relevance.   Each member participating in the conversation should show the same general idea of the topic and the direction of the conversation. This is difficult for some preschoolers. Piaget wrote down preschool conversations in Geneva where one child talked about an owl and then the child who was presumably listening cheerfully rejoined by chattering away about her new bedroom slippers! If they are going to talk about different subjects, children gradually realize that first they have to alert the first speaker to the fact that they want to change the topic.

Speakers who have learned the rules for oral conversations take turns and wait for the other person to finish talking before taking a turn. Bloom (1993) studied the proportion of a child's utterances built on prior conversational talk. This proportion grew from 20% to 30% at 25 months and to almost 50% by the time a child was using three- and four-word sentences.

Quality and quantity.   Even toddlers can describe important personal events. Loving grandparents were minding Madeleine, a toddler whose parents had gone off for a vacation trip. Auntie Terry came to visit and was conversing with the toddler. Madeleine did not yet understand what a 'vacation' is, but she enthusiastically described: 'Mama, papa up in da sky, in airp'ane.' She raised her hands way up high to describe physically what she had seen while she watched from the airport viewing platform as the plane carrying her parents had lifted off on its journey.

Description skills.   Caregivers need to strengthen their support for *elaborative child descriptive language power.* If an adult asks a child what he did over the weekend and he says 'went in car', the child is providing very little and vague information. He had gone in a car with his dad and mom and siblings. They met uncles and aunts for a family picnic in a park where they all played ball, went on swings, and ate hamburgers that Uncle Jo barbecued on a grill. Although they cannot persistently question a child (the child will feel uncomfortable), adult conversational partners can encourage children to provide more specific descriptions of plans, goals and action sequences in which events important to the child occurred:

We all got in the car. Then mama said we forgot the pickles and mustard for the picnic basket. Then we all had to wait in the car while she ran back in the house to pick those up.

How can adults help children develop this power? First, give the child undivided attention. Look into the child's eyes. Wait for the child to formulate phrases. Do not correct word pronunciations. This frustrates children. From time to time, nod and say 'uh-huh' to let the child know that you are following the details of his or her narrative. When there does seem to be a gap in the story, then use a Socratic question to encourage the child to 'fill in the gaps' ('How did your Uncle Jo manage to get the ball back when it bounced into those bushes?'). Show that you are really listening and personally interested in what the child has to say. If the child has trouble continuing, you may want to ask gently: 'What happened right after you got to the park and got out of the car?' The most important single gift a teacher gives each child is his or her personalized, genuinely interested attentiveness as well as encouragement.

Conclusion

Caregivers and teachers are crucial supporters for oral language flowering (Honig, 2001). Since the social context is so critical for rich oral language acquisition, parents and teachers need to become aware of their own understandings about how language is organized and what the different aspects of language are. These *metalinguistic* skills permit talk *about* all rules, aspects and stages of language development. They permit recognition of oral language progress as adults expand and elaborate on early speech and encourage children to develop complex and eloquent ways to express themselves.

Caregivers in families and in schools need well-honed skills for tuning into the level of linguistic complexity in each child's oral language An adult then is more ingeniously and creatively able to 'scaffold' (in Vygotsky's felicitous term) oral language activities to ensure each child's chances not only for school learning success, but for ability to flourish in negotiations in peer play, friendship patterns, multicultural understandings and team activities. Teachers strengthen children's ability to convey personal narratives. They motivate youngsters to try new ways of expressing their own personal stories in rich conversations. Alert to language levels for each child, teachers more accurately figure out how best to prepare and individualize activities and interactions. They know how to engage each child in rich conversations about that child's particular interests. They use poetry, painting, collages, song, dance and other art forms to boost oral language learning and to lengthen and strengthen children's oral language skills. At the same time as they provide precious language gifts, teachers fulfil their own specialized classroom goals as educators. They optimize children's cognitive competence even as they are advancing children's oral language learning skills.

References

Bernstein, B. (1964) Elaborated and restricted codes: their social origins and some consequences, *American Anthropologist*, 6(2), 55–69.

Bloom, L. (1990) *Language development from two to three* (New York, Cambridge University Press).

Bloom, L. (1993) *The transition from infancy to language* (Cambridge, Cambridge University Press).

Bloom, P. (2002) *How children learn the meaning of words* (Cambridge, MA, MIT Press).

Brown, R. (1973) *A first language* (Cambridge, MA, Harvard University Press).

Chafel, J. A., Flint, A. S., Hamel, J. & Pomeroy, A. H. (2007) Young children, social issues, and critical literacy, *Young Children*, 62(1), 73–80.

Chomsky, N. (1965) *Aspects of the theory of syntax* (Cambridge, MA, MIT Press).

Genesee, F., Paradis, J. & Crago, M. B. (2006) *Dual language development and disorders: a handbook on bilingualism and second language learning* (Baltimore, MD, Paul H. Brookes).

Gleason, J. B. (2005) *The development of language* (6th edn) (Needham Heights, MA, Allyn & Bacon).

Golinkoff, R. M. & Hirsh-Pasek, K. (1999) *How babies talk* (Harmondsworth, Penguin).

Greenspan, S. I. (2001) Working with children who have language difficulties, *Scholastic: Early Childhood Today*, 2, 21.

Harris, J. (1990) *Early language development: implications for clinical and educational practice* (London, Routledge).

Hart, B. & Risley, T. (1995) *Meaningful differences in the everyday experiences of young American children* (Baltimore, MD, Paul H. Brookes).

Honig, A. S. (1982a) *Playtime learning games for young children* (Syracuse, NY, Syracuse University Press).

Honig, A. S. (1982b) Research in review: language environments for young children, *Young Children*, 38(1), 56–67.

Honig, A. S. (1988) Research in review; humor development in children, *Young Children*, 43(4), 60–73.

Honig, A. S. (2001) Language flowering; language empowering, *Montessori Life,*Fall, 31–35.

Honig, A. S. (2005) The language of lullabies, *Young Children*, 60(5), 30–36.

Honig, A. S. & Brophy, H. E. (1996) *Talking with your baby: family as the first school* (Syracuse, NY, Syracuse University Press).

Honig, A. S., Fitzgerald, H. E. & Brophy-Herb, H. E. (Eds) (2001) *Encyclopedia of infancy in America* (Santa Barbara, CA, ABC-Clio Press).

Honig, A. S. & Wittmer, D. S. (1982) Teacher questions to male and female toddlers, *Early Child Development and Care*, 9(1), 19–32.

Jalongo, M. R. (2003) *Early childhood language arts* (3rd edn) (New York, Pearson).

Katz, S. A. & Thomas, J. A. (2004) *The word in play: language, music, and movement in the classroom* (2nd edn) (Baltimore, MD, Paul H. Brookes).

Korn, C. (1998) How young children make sense of their life stories, *Early Childhood Education Journal*, 25(4), 223–228.

Lim, S. E. A. (2004) Enhancing Hong Kong preschool English language teachers' strategies in providing early learning experiences, in: C. S. S. Leung & S. C. Wong (Eds) *Current studies on reading research and the teaching of reading* (Hong Kong, Hong Kong Reading Association).

Lindfors, J. W. (1987) *Children's language and learning* (2nd edn) (Englewood Cliffs, NJ, Prentice-Hall).

McGinness, D. (2006) *Language development and learning to read: the scientific study of how language development affects reading skills* (Cambridge, MA, MIT Press).

Montessori, M. (1967) *The absorbent mind* (New York, Dell).

Nelson, K. (1981) Individual differences in language development: implications for development and language, *Developmental Psychology*, 17, 170–187.

Norman-Jackson, J. (1982) Family interactions, language development and primary reading achievement of black children in families of low income, *Child Development*, 53, 349–358.

Otto, B. (2002) *Language development in early childhood* (Upper Saddle River, NJ, Pearson Education).

Paley, V. (1986) *Boys and girls: superheroes in the doll corner* (Chicago, University of Chicago Press).

Qiang, H. & Zao, L. (2000) Canadian second language immersion and application in China, *Comparative Education*, 4, 38–41.

Rampton, B. (1995) Language crossing and the problematisation of ethnicity and socialization, *Pragmatics*, 5(4), 480–513.

Rosenquist, B. B. (2002) Literacy-based planning and pedagogy that supports toddler language development, *Early Childhood Education Journal*, Summer, 241–249.

Schachter, F. F. (1979) *Everyday mother talk to toddlers: early intervention* (New York, Academic Press).

Schachter, F. F. & Strage, A. A. (1982) Adults' talk and children's language development, in: S. G. Moore & C. R. Cooper (Eds) *Young child: reviews of research*, Vol. 3 (Washington, DC, National Association for the Education of Young Children).

Snow, M. A. (1990) Instructional methodology in immersion foreign language education, in: A. M. Padilla, H .H. Fairchild & C. M. Valdez (Eds) *Foreign language education: issues and strategies* (Newbury, CA, Sage), 156–171.

Steinmetz, S. & Kipfer, B. A. (2006) *The life of language* (New York, Random House).

Swan, R.W. & Stavros, H. (1973) Child-rearing practices associated with the development of cognitive skills of children in low socioeconomic areas, *Early Child Development and Care*, 2, 23–38.

Tough, J. (1977) *The development of meaning* (New York, Halstead Press).

Van Allen, R. & Allen, C. (1982) *Language experience activities* (2nd edn) (Boston, MA, Houghton-Mifflin).

Whitehurst, G. J., Arnold, D. S., Epstein, J. N., Angell, A. L., Smith, M. & Fischel, J. E. (1994) A picture book reading intervention in day care and homes for children from low-income families, *Developmental Psychology*, 86(5), 679–689.

Wood, D. J., Wood, H. A., Griffiths, A. & Howorth, J. (1986) *Teaching and talking with deaf children* (Chichester, Wiley).

Dialogic teaching: developing thinking and metacognition through philosophical discussion

Robert Fisher

Why dialogue is important

'Why is speaking and listening important?' I asked a group of nine year olds during my recent Philosophy in Primary Schools research project. 'It helps you to think', said Andrea. 'It helps to build your brain', said Dan. 'You learn more', said Pat. They are surely right. Human intelligence is primarily developed through speaking and listening. The quality of our lives depends on the quality of our thinking and on our ability to communicate and discuss what we think with others. Talk is intrinsic to literacy and to our ability to form relationships with others. It is the foundation of both verbal and emotional intelligence.

Dialogue is important because it is the primary means for developing intelligence in the human species. It is through the capacity to verbalize that consciousness and understanding develop. Tomasello *et al.* claim that consciousness originates in 'a species-unique motivation to share emotions, experience, and activities with other persons' (Tomasello *et al.*, 2004). They refer to this as a 'dialogic' capacity, and claim that it is more fundamental than language or tool use. It is through dialogue that we develop consciousness, learn control over internal mental processes and develop conceptual tools for thinking.

Bakhtin claims that the basis of being human (or 'human being') is not self-identity, but the opening of dialogue, an opening that always implies the simultaneous inter-animation of more than one voice (Sidorkin, 1999). As Vygotsky (1978) noted, 'all the higher mental functions originate as actual relations between human individuals'. We internalize those voices and develop the mental functions that we learn through dialogue with others. Hobson (2002) argues that both a child's self-awareness and ability to think creatively are internalized from the dialogic bond formed between mother (or other primary caregiver) and child. These dialogues begin pre-verbally, beginning with 'peek-a-boo' games in the cradle, and open up 'mental space', and a dialogic space of multiple perspectives through which things become thinkable for the first time. A child's consciousness and repertoire of concepts is expanded through talk with significant others such as parents and peers. Research shows that the opportunities for speaking and listening that children experience before they enter school vary greatly in terms of potency and quality. Children's early experiences of dialogue clearly put some children at a disadvantage and empower the learning potential of others (Hart & Risley, 1996).

Dialogic teaching: what classroom research says

In school the teacher is the primary mediator of children's cognition and metacognitive awareness, supported by other adults. There children learn to see things from at least two perspectives at once: their own point of view and that of their teacher or other adults. Bakhtin points out that people do not take words from a dictionary, but from the mouths of other speakers, and so they carry with them the voices of those who have used them before. For him dialogic talk consists of an 'inter-animation' or 'inter-illumination' of voices (Bakhtin, 1981). The world for us, and the process of making meaning, is essentially dialogic. Meaning is created through dialogue; it has no fixed or stable identity, but is the product of different voices. Children need to be exposed to and involved in enquiry with different voices, ideas and perspectives, for example, through responding to three equally important questions:

- 'What do I say?'
- 'What do you say?'
- 'What do other people say?'

Research on children's experience in schools, in the UK, shows that the quality of classroom talk has the power to enable or inhibit cognition and learning (Alexander, 2006). The forms of instruction and learning conversations that stimulate thinking can be described as 'dialogic'. Dialogic teaching refers therefore to the kinds of verbal interaction that provide cognitive stimulus, expand consciousness and enlarge the dialogic space for thinking in children's minds.

The concept of 'dialogic teaching' builds upon a long tradition of theoretical and empirical research into the role of talk in learning and teaching. This research has included the work of cognitive and cultural psychologists (Vygotsky, 1978; Bruner, 1996), discourse analysts (Dillon, 1990; Coulthard, 1990, 1992), psycholinguists (Halliday, 1993; Wells, 1999), sociocultural linguists (Barnes, 1995) and philosophers (Bakhtin, 1981, 1986; Lipman, 2003), as well as many classroom researchers (Galton *et al.*, 1980; Alexander, 2000) who have provided influential perspectives on the role of dialogue in learning.

The fruits of this research have not always permeated into classroom practice. Research has found that children's experience of speaking and listening in the classroom is not dialogic and does lead to learning or stimulates cognitive response (Wegerif, 2002). Such research shows that schools and teachers often do not fully exploit the learning potential of talk for learning in the classroom. This, to summarize Alexander (2006), is because they often:

- view talk only as a means for learning and not an aim of learning;
- fail to use talk to cognitively challenge children;
- focus on the social and affective functions of talk rather than the cognitive;
- not plan for sustained and effective group dialogue;
- not teach children the ground rules for effective dialogue;
- rely on written and ignore oral learning tasks and modes of assessment;
- use feedback to praise and support rather than diagnose and inform;
- employ teacher questions but not questions from pupils;
- use closed questions inviting recall, rather than challenging questions inviting speculation;
- not allow children enough time for of thinking, reasoning and enquiry.

Researchers claim that children's talk in group work often lacks cognitive challenge (Mercer, 1995, 2000). Children do not naturally engage in sustained intellectual enquiry. Getting children, individually or in group activities, to speak and listen together, often advocated in curriculum guidance (as in DfES/QCA, 2003) is not enough. Speaking and listening does not necessarily lead to learning. Classroom research shows that children talking together does not often evidence what Habermas (1991) called 'communicative rationality' or cognitive challenge (Fisher 2003, 2005a, 2005b). There is therefore a need to identify the elements of effective dialogue and other kinds of talk used in school if the potential for speaking and listening to promote and accelerate children's learning is to be fully realized.

Forms of talk

Talk in classrooms can take many forms; these include:

- *instruction*: telling the pupil what to do, and/or imparting information;
- *recitation*: teaching through questions designed to test or stimulate recall;
- *monologue*: one person speaking, without engagement with others;
- *conversation*: talk with others characterized by uncritical sharing, lacking depth and challenge, speaking and listening at a low level of cognitive demand;
- *discussion*: exchanging ideas with others, to share information or solve problems;
- *argument*: where individuals views compete and monologic viewpoints are aired;
- *dialogue*: exploratory talk with others, cooperative enquiry with dialogic space to agree/disagree, challenge, question, appeal to reason and allowing possible self-correction.

Traditional teaching, and many interactions between parents and children, is characterized by the familiar rote-learning routines of instruction and recitation. These are dominated by teacher talk and one-sided discussion is characterised by what Edwards (2005; Edwards & Westgate, 1994) calls 'unequal communicative rights'. Most teachers and parents, though by no means all, extend this repertoire through the use of discussion to share and exchange ideas and dialogue that scaffolds understanding through the use of open questions. All these kinds of talk serve useful purposes and have their place in learning conversations.

In traditional classrooms it is the teacher's voice that is authoritative and persuasive. Wertsch (1991) describes the process of appropriating the voices of others, such as the teacher; by children as a process he calls 'ventriloquation'. This is evidenced, for example, when children try to guess what the teacher wants them to say. However, in dialogic talk we listen to the voices expressed by the child. Dialogic talk challenges children to voice their thoughts. The practice of dialogue is an essential element in their development as future independent learners and active citizens.

Talk is important when it empowers children socially as well as cognitively, and helps them to acquire the capacity to narrate, explain, instruct, ask different kinds of question, listen to and build upon answers, analyse and solve problems, speculate and imagine, discuss, argue, reason, negotiate, explore and evaluate ideas. To do this effectively with others they need to be trained in the skills of dialogue. This means learning to be able and willing to:

- listen to and be receptive to alternative viewpoints;
- ask effective questions;
- think critically and creatively about the issues under review;
- exercise good judgement in what they think and do.

Several research studies have now demonstrated that teaching children how to talk together effectively improves their thinking and learning (see e.g. Mercer, 2000). Such studies show that good talk does not always just happen—it needs to be planned. Good questioning promotes children's understanding and does not merely test their recall of information. Such questioning can improve comprehension in reading and writing, as well as in talk. Research shows that the quality of children's talk is greatly enhanced if children are given *time* to think (Fisher, 2005a, 2005b). Thinking time and talking time before an activity, during an activity and after an activity will help extend children's thinking, and provides the oral groundwork for learning. Talk is also a powerful tool for raising the confidence of children, especially those with special needs and those with low self-esteem.

Children enjoy and are stimulated by well-structured oral lessons. But they need cognitive challenge to turn mere talk into talk for thinking and to develop their dialogic skills. One well-grounded approach to introducing young children to dialogic thinking is 'Philosophy for Children'.

Talk for thinking using 'Philosophy for Children'

The Philosophy in Primary Schools project used a special form of 'talking to think' based on an approach called 'Philosophy for Children'. 'Philosophy for Children' is a programme for teaching thinking developed by Matthew Lipman (Lipman, 1981); it has since been adapted and developed for use in many countries (Fisher, 2003). It is a form of dialogic teaching that emphasizes the development of critical and creative thinking through questioning and dialogue between children and teachers and between children and children. Researchers have reported striking cognitive gains through this approach in the classroom (Trickey & Topping, 2004). 'Philosophy for Children' can help enhance communicative skills, as well as develop habits of intelligent behaviour, through aspects listed as follows:

- *Curious*: asking deep and interesting questions.
- *Collaborative*: engaging in thoughtful discussion.
- *Critical*: giving reasons and evidence.
- *Creative*: generating and building on ideas.
- *Caring*: developing awareness of self and care of others.

Philosophical dialogue develops the kinds of thinking that children may not use in other lessons, including *philosophical intelligence*—the capacity to ask and seek answers to existential questions (Fisher, in press). Philosophy begins in wonder and in the capacity for curiosity. Curiosity is more important than knowledge since it is needed to generate knowledge. Philosophic enquiry develops questioning skills and builds on children's natural curiosity. It also provides a means for children to develop *discussion skills*—the capacity to engage in thoughtful conversations with others. Discussion of complex objects of intellectual enquiry such as stories provides cognitive challenge and enhances *critical thinking* and verbal reasoning—capacity to draw inferences and deductions from all kinds of texts, and helps develop *creative thinking*—the capacity to generate hypotheses and build on the ideas of others. Philosophy with children helps develop *emotional intelligence*—the capacity to be self-aware and caring towards others, providing essential practice in *active citizenship* and participative democracy. It also provides a context for developing 'me-cognition', the beginnings of metacognition.

Being curious: asking open questions

What research on 'Philosophy for Children' (P4C) has shown is that even young children have the capacity to engage in philosophic questioning, like Tom, aged 5, who asked: 'Where does time go when it stops?' Tom may not, of course, fully understand his question, but he is full of curiosity and wonder. This capacity to question lies at the heart of intelligent behaviour. But as he gets older it is likely that Tom will ask fewer questions in school. However, the practice of P4C would help to sustain and develop his ability to question and interrogate the world. It has a well-researched pedagogy called 'community of enquiry' and teaching programmes through which the habits of intelligent behaviour can be developed. These habits will help them face the conceptual problems and conflicts that facethem in an uncertain world. An eight year old expressed the problem we all face:

> The trouble is people are telling you different things, and sometimes your mind tells you to do different things too!

The following are some of the questions raised by a group of seven–eight year olds who had asked if they could discuss God at their next philosophy session in the community of enquiry (Winyard, 2005). The questions reflect the breadth of their vision and imagination:

- Who made God?
- Who is God?
- How was God made? How old is God?
- How did God make the world?
- Why was God made?
- Is God real?
- How did He make us?
- What does Heaven look like?
- Why is God so special?
- Why does God make thunder?
- Why did God make us?
- Why did God make the devil?
- Why does God kill us?
- Why did God make swear-words?

Teaching for thinking requires a community approach to enquiry in the classroom, not one or two voices many voices creating single viewpoints but many voices creating multiple viewpoints within a dialogic space. The community of enquiry is sustained by the use of complex open-ended questions and elaborate explanatory responses— by teachers as well as children. For example, a teacher using a story that includes the theme of truth (such as Aesop's fable of 'Mercury and the Axe'[1]) might prepare a number of open-ended prompt questions to encourage children to discuss the nature of truth. The following presents a list of such questions that have been used in many primary classes.

Thinking about telling the truth

Key question: What is truth?

1. Do you think this is a true story? Why?
2. What do we mean when we say something is true?
3. What do we call something that is not true? What does 'false' mean?
4. What is a lie?
5. What do we call a story that is not true? What is fiction/a fable/a fairytale?
6. Which character in the story was honest? What does 'honest' mean?
7. Which character in the story was a liar? What does 'liar' mean?
8. Is it better to tell the truth or lies? Why?
9. Have you ever told a lie? Can you say when or why?
10. Is it ever right to tell a lie? Is it ever wrong to tell the truth?

Here is an excerpt from one such classroom discussion, prompted by the teacher using questions like those listed above:

Child 1: Sometimes you say something you think is true. It's not a lie if you think it is true.

Child 2: I disagree with that because you could think something was true and say it was true when it was not true.

Teacher: Can you give an example?

Child 2: Well, if you could say it is raining because you thought it was raining and it was only birds on the roof. You can say something you think is true, although in fact it is not true.

Child 3: You can only tell if something is true if you or somebody sees it with their own eyes and ears. That is why there are many people think things are true, like ghosts or witches, that sort of thing. But you might be wrong, so you have to check it first before you say it's true.

Child 4: It's not true because you say it is, but it might be.

The unique value of 'Philosophy for Children' is that it is the only well-researched thinking approach that focuses specifically on developing questioning and, in particular, the kinds of questioning that enable children to think and act with philosophical intelligence.

Collaborating in thoughtful discussion

Teaching children the skills of dialogue is an end in itself and an essential thinking and communicative skill that provides a foundation for other skills such as creativity, reasoning and metacognition. The keys to success in children solving problems through discussion lies, as with adults, in them learning to listen to each other, responding to the ideas of others and being willing to change their thinking in the light of the thinking of others. These habits move dialogue away from merely 'saying what I think' towards building on the ideas of others in the shared space of the dialogue. Every dialogue creates a space of possibility for shared thinking. But it requires ground rules. These need to be made explicit if children are to internalize them as habits of behaviour when in discussion with others.

The ground rules for discussion need to be agreed, preferably by the children, with help from the teacher. Research shows how important the agreeing, implementing and reviewing of ground rules is in creating the conditions for successful discussion. One study describes how teaching the ground rules for effective discussion helped children do better at non-verbal reasoning test problems than control classes who had not been taught rules for discussion (Wegerif, 2002). Simply learning how to discuss in reasonable and reflective ways seems to help improve children's reasoning and problem-solving skills.

In the Philosophy in Primary Schools Project the most commonly agreed rules for successful discussion identified by primary children (sometimes differently expressed) were:

- Only one speaks at a time.
- We all listen carefully to others.
- We think before we speak.
- We say what we mean.
- We think about what other people say.
- We give reasons for what we say.
- We can disagree and ask 'why?'.
- We show respect to others.

One teacher did this by listing and discussing with the children all the 'talking' words they could think of, such as 'argument, 'discussion' and 'reason'. The children in groups then discussed and agreed the meaning of each word (with the help of dictionaries and thesauruses). Then they discussed in groups 'the most important rules that people talking in groups should follow' and were asked to come up with no more than six of these. They then discussed as a class the different sets of rules and agreed a final list to display in the classroom.

Each session begins with a review of the ground rules. Children can stop the discussion if they see any ground rules being broken. At the end of the lesson there is a plenary in which the discussion and ground rules are reviewed, with questions such as:

- Did we have a good discussion today?
- What was good about our discussion?
- What could have been better? How?
- What do we need to remember next time?

Being critical and creative

Critical thinking can be summed up as the use of reasoning to draw inferences and make deductions. For young children it means being challenged to give reasons for opinions. Creative dialogue can be summed up as 'playful talk' (Wegerif, 2005), what I have termed 'Menippean dialogue' in classrooms (Fisher, in press), which is being playful with ideas and suggesting divergent possibilities. For young children it means applying imagination to their thinking, and trying alternative explanations and ideas. Dialogue as shared enquiry needs to be mediated by the teacher by processes of playful speculation (creative thinking) and by applying criteria of judgement (giving reasons).

What philosophical enquiry offers is a tried and tested strategy for helping children to apply critical and creative reasoning to stories and other texts. The teaching strategy, which is based on whole-class discussion, is called 'community of enquiry'. It is not a new strategy, but one that is gaining popularity, because it works in making children more reflective and critical thinkers (Burgh *et al.*, 2006).

How does it work in the classroom? Ideally the group sits in a circle or horseshoe, the aim being that everyone can see everyone else. The following are typical stages in a lesson; for other descriptions of the stages of a philosophy with children lessons see Haynes (2002), Cleghorn (2002) and Fisher (1996, 1999).

A 'Philosophy for Children' lesson format

Focusing exercise: sharing the learning objectives, reminding the agreed rules, and using a relaxation exercise or thinking game to ensure alert yet relaxed attention.

Sharing a stimulus: presenting a story, poem, picture or other stimulus for thinking.

Thinking time: children think of what is strange, interesting or unusual about the stimulus and share their thoughts with a partner.

Questioning: children ask their own (or partner's) questions which are written on a board, these are discussed, clarified and grouped, then one is chosen to start the enquiry.

Discussion: children are asked to respond, building on one another's ideas, with the teacher probing for reasons, examples and alternative viewpoints.

Plenary: children are asked to summarize what has been said, review the discussion (e.g. using a graphic map), and reflect on what they have learnt.

Children tend to expect to have their questions unequivocally answered by adults, not discussed by other children. They are often not used to having their attention focused on a particular issue for a length of time, to discuss questions in a systematic and sustained way or to consider things from a variety of viewpoints. But if they have a stimulus, for example, a story, then even young children can respond to questions in ways that can be called philosophical. This may mean helping them to move from the concrete and literal aspects of the story to the conceptual and the abstract, moving the discussion from *what* happened in the story and *why* to thinking about *what it means*.

Discussion can be moved to philosophical levels through use of Socratic questions (Fisher, 2003). Socratic questioning means using a series of questions to progressively engage higher levels of thinking—including literal, analytical and conceptual levels of thinking. The following are examples of questions that engage these three levels of thinking:

1. *Literal (or factual) questions ask for information*:
   'What is this about?'
   'Can you remember what happened?'
   'What do you have to do?'

2. *Analytic questions call for critical and creative thinking*:
   'What question(s) do you have?'
   'What reasons can you give?'
   'What are the problems/possible solutions here?'

3. *Conceptual questions call for abstract thinking*:

   'What is the key concept (strategy or rule) here and what does it mean?'
   'What criteria are we using to judge this (or test if it is true)?'
   'How might we further investigate this concept (strategy or hypothesis)?'

The following extract of a discussion of the story 'The Monkey and her Baby' (Fisher, 1999) with six–seven year olds shows the teacher trying to move the children's thinking on through a Socratic questioning:

Teacher:	Why did the mother think that her baby was best?
Child:	Because it was beautiful. She thought it was beautiful.
Child:	She thought it was beautiful because she was the mother.
Teacher:	What does it mean to be beautiful?
Child:	It means someone thinks you are lovely.
Child:	You are perfect ...
Child:	Good to look at.
Teacher:	Can you be beautiful even if no one thinks you are lovely?
Child:	No. You can't be beautiful if no one thinks you are beautiful.
Child:	You can be beautiful inside, you can *feel* beautiful ...

Paul, a reluctant reader, aged 8, suddenly sees the point of it all during a philosophical discussion of a story:

Oh, I get it. We're not supposed to just read the story. We're supposed to think about it.

For him it is a revelation. Although still struggling with the mechanics of reading, he finds he is able to make a personal response, to question, to discuss inferences and meanings using challenging texts during the shared reading session. For John, aged 10, philosophy not only gives him time to think in a serious, structured and sustained way, but also:

It helps you ask questions. It shows you there can be many answers to one question [and] it makes you think that everything must have a reason.

For Michelle, aged 10, the community of enquiry gives you a chance to self-correct your thinking:

In philosophy lessons you can say what you really think and sometimes you change your mind.

P4C is not only about developing thinking and discussion skills through the use of stories, but also about being 'reasonable', which means being more than rational. To be reasonable we need to be mindful of self and others.

Caring: being mindful of self and others

The two sets of dispositions or attitudes which philosophy for children aims to foster are being mindful of oneself and of others. Both derive from the dialogical nature of the process, developing social skills through cooperative activity. Discussion in a community of enquiry requires the group to develop trust and the ability to cooperate, and to respect the views of others. Lipman (2003) calls these aspects 'caring' thinking. Caring thinking involves learning to collaborate with others in a community of enquiry, developing empathy and respect for others. It means being guided by questions such as:

- What do others think?
- Can I understand what they think?
- Can I learn from what they think?

By taking part in a community of enquiry, children develop and strengthen what Goleman calls 'emotional intelligence': studies that show that a youngster's life chances are at least as much affected by emotional intelligence as they are by other aspects of intelligence (Goleman, 1997). Emotional intelligence includes:

- *Self-awareness*: knowing how/what you are feeling and how it impinges on your work, having a realistic awareness of one's abilities.
- *Self-regulation*: handling emotions so they facilitate the task in hand, being conscientious.
- *Resilience*: sustaining motivation, persevering in the face of set-backs, striving to improve.
- *Empathy*: sensing what other people are feeling, and using that information in our dealings with them, being able to have a rapport with a wide range of people.
- *Social skills*: reading social situations, using skills to persuade, lead and negotiate.

Philosophical discussion can develop all these personal qualities. It does so by making thinking relevant to children's personal needs and quest for answers. It is less a curriculum and more a way of life. It has more to do with what the Greeks called *phronesis* (practical wisdom) than it has to do with *tekne* (skills), more to do with the intellectual behaviour than competence. It is to do with the dispositions to behave intelligently when confronted with problems, uncertainties and puzzling questions. It is about persisting on a task, sustaining the enquiry, pursuing the question. It is about encouraging mindfulness and resisting impulsivity, thinking before acting, allowing others their say. It is about listening with understanding and empathy, devoting mental energy to attending to what others say, perceiving other points of view and sensing others' emotions. It is about the metacognitive capacity to know oneself, to be aware of one's own thoughts and feelings and their effects on others.

The exercise of philosophical enquiry is, like any educative practice, most effective when it is participatory, proactive, communal, collaborative and given over to constructing meanings rather than receiving them. With its emphasis on inclusive, democratic practice philosophy with children provides a powerful means for children to share experience and explore meaning. They can learn to express their views with confidence, to raise doubts and questions, and to challenge the thinking of others. Through engaging in a community of enquiry children learn how to:

- ask their own questions and raise issues for discussion;
- explore and develop their own ideas, views and theories;
- give reasons for what they think and believe;
- explain and argue their point of view with others;
- listen to and consider the views and ideas of others;
- change their ideas in the light of good reasons and evidence.

Dialogue is crucial to its radical democratic role. Children are soaked with written and visual information. They need to be given a voice, a voice to question, to challenge, to construct and deconstruct the meanings around them. As Jason, aged 10, said:

> Everyone is telling you things and not getting you to think things through.

'Philosophy for Children' (P4C) provides a way through which children engage critically with their given world and find a space to think things through. Like other groups in society, such as women, ethnic minorities and the poor, children's views have been marginalized and their claims to knowledge and reason devalued. It opens up a space for thinking, for sharing beliefs and for creating knowledge, as in the following excerpt from a discussion by a group of nine year olds on whether it is right for parents to smack their children:

> Child: I think Sophie's was a good idea why smacking children is wrong.
> Teacher: What was the idea?
> Child: Well she said it was wrong because smacking you doesn't tell you why it was wrong, it just tells you that if you do it you will get smacked. That means you'll do it again if you can get away with it and not be smacked. But if you are told why it is wrong ... whatever it is ... then you are less likely to do it again. Because you know why it is wrong. If you understand the reason ...

P4C has been shown to be effective in teaching democratic community values (Burgh et al., 2006). It gives children a voice and a vote in deciding the focus and the course of the enquiry. It offers an arena for the free flow of their views, a space for creativity and dialogue.

'Philsophy for Children' does not provide just a 'talking shop', or an exercise in free-flowing discussion. Research suggests that programmes that promote thinking skills have positive effects on academic achievement (McGuiness, 1999). The research evidence from a wide range of small-scale studies across the world indicates that the philosophy for children programmes can make a difference to various aspects of a child's academic performance. Findings from my Philosophy in Primary Schools research project echo worldwide research into P4C programmes and show positive effects on:

- pupils' achievements in academic tests;
- children's self-esteem and self-concept as thinkers and learners;
- the fluency and quality of children's questioning;
- the quality of their creative thinking and verbal reasoning;
- their ability to listen to others and engage effectively in class discussion.

Research shows the positive effects of philosophical discussion extend across the curriculum. Jemma, aged 10, said:

> Philosophy can help in all your lessons, no matter what you're learning.

Teachers generally feel that philosophical discussion adds a new dimension to their teaching and the way their pupils think. One teacher put it as follows:

> We need to teach the habits of good thinking and through using 'Stories for Thinking' we can do just that ... children become more ready to ask questions, to challenge each other and to explain what they mean.

Kim, aged nine, said:

> The important thing is not to agree or disagree but to say why.

Children too value what philosophical discussion has to offer not only as a stimulus to learning in the classroom, but as a life skill. Camilla, aged 10, said:

> Philosophy helps you make the most of your mind.

The best way to teach the habits of good thinking and discussion skills is for the teacher to model these behaviours and, in particular, the heart of dialogic teaching which is cognitive challenge. The following are some strategies to provide cognitive challenge in dialogue with children:

- *Questioning and challenging*:
  Asking why, how, what if?
  Posing unusual questions or problems.
  Asking for reasons.

- *Making connections, seeing relationships*:
  Sharing previous knowledge or experience.
  Agreeing, disagreeing and saying why.
  Giving examples.

- *Exploring and building on ideas*:
  Imagining and seeing things in the mind's eye.
  Asking: 'what if?' and 'what if not?'.
  Playing with and building on ideas.

- *Reflecting on ideas*:
  Reviewing progress of the discussion.

Reflecting critically about the process of discussion.
Thinking about our thinking and the thinking of others.

It is through this process of reflection, thinking about our thinking and the thinking of others, that metacognitive awareness develops. The foundation for metacognition in young children lies in developing 'me-cognition'.

Developing 'me-cognition': the foundations for metacognition

There has been a growing recognition that metacognition or self-awareness, including awareness of ourselves as learners, helps us to learn more effectively (Fisher, 1998). The term 'metacognition' was introduced by Flavell in 1976 to refer to 'the individual's own awareness and consideration of his or her cognitive processes and strategies' (Flavell, 1979). It refers to that uniquely human capacity of people to be self-reflexive, not just to think and know but to think about their own thinking and knowing. Flavell argued that if we can bring the process of learning to a conscious level, we can help children to be more aware of their own thought processes and help them to gain control or mastery over the organization of their learning (Flavell *et al.*, 1995).

Vygotsky (1962) was one of the first to realize that conscious reflective control and deliberate mastery were essential factors in school learning. He suggested there were two factors involved in gaining knowledge. At first it is unconsciously acquired, followed by a gradual increase in active *conscious control* over that knowledge. This essentially reflects the difference between cognitive and metacognitive aspects of learning. Metacognition is not thinking *about*, but thinking *above* (above cognition), and becoming consciously aware of how one thinks and learns.

Metacognitive awareness builds autonomy by helping children become more self-aware and self-evaluative. It contributes to self-understanding and emotional intelligence. The challenge for teachers, support staff and carers is to help children see themselves as agents of their own thinking.

Metacognitive awareness develops with age. Older children are more successful learners partly because they have internalized a greater quantity of metacognitive information, but metacognitive development relates not just to age, but also to experience. Teachers can help even young children to develop some of the metacognitive strategies that underpin successful learning (Fisher, 1998).

One way of thinking about the beginnings of metacognitive awareness in young children is to help them see the 'me' in cognition. Much of their cognitive activity in learning is about doing, remembering and responding to others. Metacognition is about reminding them of the *me*-thinking, in thinking about what *I* think and how *I* learn. It is this aspect of metacognition I call me-cognition (Fisher, 2006).

'Me-cognition' is about what I know, think and feel about myself. It involves applying our thinking skills and emotional awareness to self-understanding. Me-cognition involves being aware of what one can and cannot do and ways to do what one wants to do or learn. Asking children about their personal lives, hopes and fears make good starters for thinking, for it focuses on what they think, know and have experienced. Many kinds of questions can encourage children to think about themselves and their lives. As Tom, aged 10, said:

> You don't really know what you think until someone asks.

For example, by finding answers to questions, such as:

- What do I think about myself?
- What do I know about myself?
- What do I feel about myself?
- What makes me different from other people?
- What makes me special?
- What makes 'me' me?

Such questions have challenged philosophers, psychologists and scientists down the centuries. Outside the oracle at Delphi was the injunction: 'know thyself.' For the ancient Greeks this was the hardest challenge to thinking and the highest form of wisdom.

'Me-cognition' is a capacity for self-understanding that all humans possess. It is a form of personal intelligence that Gardner (1999) calls 'intra-personal intelligence'. It is expressed in a child's ability to be aware of what they think and feel and of their personal preferences. It activates processes of metacognition, which is thinking about one's own thinking. The skills of me-cognition are developed when the individual learner is given a voice and a choice in what they think about themselves and their lives. Such self-reflection lies at the heart of personalized learning. As Joel, aged nine, put it:

> A good teacher makes what you think matters.

Conclusion

This paper has explored the important relationship between dialogue and cognitive and metacognitive development in young children. It concludes that dialogic enquiry is a primary thinking skill from which other skills follow, that 'Philosophy for Children' approaches provide effective methods for dialogic teaching that can support and develop children's capacities for cognition and metacognition.

When children develop the habits of intelligent behaviour, the results can be unpredictable. When they learn how to interrogate ideas within texts and in the world, they will also learn to interrogate you and what you say. Talking for thinking with children is an intellectual adventure, full of unexpected challenges.

Note

1. For the story 'Mercury and the Axe', and further questions and suggestions on ways of using the story to create a community of enquiry see Fisher (1996, 1999).

References

Alexander, R. J. (2000) *Culture and pedagogy* (Oxford, Blackwell).

Alexander, R. J. (2006) *Towards dialogic teaching* (3rd edn) (Cambridge, Cambridge University Press/Dialogos).

Bakhtin, M. (1981) *The dialogic imagination* (Austin, TX, University of Texas Press).

Bakhtin, M. (1986) *Speech genres and other late essays* (Austin, TX, University of Texas Press).

Barnes, D. (1995) *Communication and learning revisited* (London, Heinemann).

Bruner, J. (1996) *The culture of education* (Cambridge, MA, Harvard University Press).

Burgh, G., Field, T., Freakley, M. *et al.* (2006) *Ethics and the community of enquiry* (Melbourne, Thomson).

Cleghorn, P. (2002) *Thinking through philosophy* (Blackburn, Education Printing Services).

Coulthard, M (1992) *Advances in spoken discourse analysis* (London, Routledge).

Daniels, H. (2001) *Vygotsky and pedagogy* (London, Routledge).

Dillon, J. T. (1990) *The practice of questioning* (London, Routledge).

Dillon, J. T. (1994) *Using discussion in classrooms* (Buckingham, Open University Press).

Department for Education and Skills & Qualifications and Curriculum Authority (DfES & QCA) (2003) *Speaking, listening, learning: working with children in key stages 1 and 2* (London, DfES).

Edwards, A. (2005) 'Let's get beyond community and practice': the many meanings of learning by participating, *Curriculum Journal*, 16(1), 49–65.

Edwards, A. D. & Westgate, D. P. G. (1994) *Investigating classroom talk* (Lewes, Falmer).

Fisher, R. (1996) *Stories for thinking* (Oxford, Nash Pollock).

Fisher, R. (1998) Thinking about thinking: developing metacognition in children, *Early Child Development and Care*, 14(1), 1–15.

Fisher, R. (1999) *First stories for thinking* (Oxford, Nash Pollock).

Fisher, R. (2003) *Teaching thinking: philosophical enquiry in the classroom* (2nd edn) (London, Continuum).

Fisher, R. (2005a) *Teaching children to think* (2nd edn) (Cheltenham, Nelson Thornes).

Fisher, R. (2005b) *Teaching children to learn* (2nd edn) (Cheltenham, Nelson Thornes).

Fisher, R. (2006) Thinking about me: me-cognition, *Teaching Thinking*, 20(1), 50–55.

Fisher, R. (in press) 'Dancing minds: the use of Socratic and Menippean dialogue in philosophical enquiry, *Gifted Education International Journal*, 22(2–3).

Fisher, R. (forthcoming) *Philosophical intelligence.*

Flavell, J. (1979) Metacognition and cognitive monitoring: a new area of cognitive-developmental enquiry, *American Psychologist*, 34, 906–911.

Flavell, J., Green, F. & Flavell, E. (1995) *Young children's knowledge about thinking* (Monographs for the Society for Research in Child Development No. 60.1) (Chicago, University of Chicago Press).

Galton, M. & Simon, B. (1980) *Inside the primary classroom* (London, Routledge).

Gardner, H. (1999) *Intelligence reframed* (New York, Basic Books).

Goleman, D. (1997) *Emotional intelligence: why it can matter more than IQ* (New York, Bantam Books).

Habermas, J. (1991) *The theory of communicative action*, Vol. 1 (Cambridge, Polity Press).

Halliday, M. A. K. (1993) Towards a language-based theory of learning, *Linguistics in Education*, 5, 93–116.

Hart, B. & Risley, T. R. (1996) *Meaningful differences in the everyday experiences of young American children* (Baltimore, MD, Brookes).

Haynes, J. (2002) *Children as philosophers* (London, Routledge Falmer).

Hobson, P. (2002) *The cradle of thought: exploring the origins of thinking* (London, Macmillan).

Lipman, M. (1981) 'Philosophy for Children' in: A. L. Costa (Ed.) *Developing minds: programs for teaching thinking* (Alexandria, VA, Association for Supervision and Curriculum Development).

Lipman, M. (2003) *Thinking in education* (Cambridge, Cambridge University Press).

McGuiness, C. (1999) *From thinking skills to thinking classrooms: a review and evaluation of approaches for developing pupils' thinking* (Research Report No. 115) (London, DfES).

Mercer, N. (1995) The guided construction of knowledge: talk amongst teachers and learners (Clevedon, Multilingual Matters).

Mercer, N. (2000) *Words and minds: how we use language to think together* (London, Routledge).

Sidorkin, A. M. (1999) *Beyond discourse: education, the self and dialogue* (New York, State University of New York Press).

Tomasello, M., Carpenter, M., Call, J., Behne, T. & Moll, H. (2004) Understanding and sharing intentions: the origins of cultural cognition, *Behavioral and Brain Sciences*, 28(5), 720–721.

Trickey, S. & Topping, K. J. (2004) 'Philosophy for children: a systematic review', *Research Papers in Education*, 19(3), 365–380.

Vygotsky, L. S. (1962) *Thought and language* (Cambridge, MA, MIT Press).

Vygotsky, L. S. (1978) *Mind in society: the development of higher order processes* (Cambridge, MA, Harvard University Press).

Wegerif, R. (2002) The importance of intelligent conversations, *Teaching Thinking*, 9, 46–49.

Wegerif, R. (2005) Reason and creativity in classroom dialogues, *Language and Education*, 19(3), 223–237.

Wells, G. (1999) *Dialogic enquiry: towards a socio-cultural practice and theory of education* (Cambridge, Cambridge University Press).

Wertsch, J. V. (1991) *Voices of the mind* (New York, Harvester).

Wertsch, J. V. (1998) *Mind as action* (New York, Oxford University Press).

Winyard, J. (2005) Cunning little vixens, *Teaching Thinking and Creativity*, Spring, 30–36.

'Listening to myself': improving oracy and literacy among children who fall behind

Flora J. Macleod, Philip Macmillan and Brahm Norwich

The controversies over which is the best way to teach beginning and delayed readers have, unfortunately, on occasions, produced more heat than light (Stanovich, 1990; Smith, 1994). As a result, theories of how reading should be best taught have not always been tested through the mechanisms of rigorous scientific empirical enquiry or rationale debate. Many individuals have ended their school days with a reading level that prohibits, or makes difficult, full access to all that contemporary society has to offer in economic, cultural and other areas of personal development. This is a problem not only for the individual, but for society at large. It has become a major issue for governments of advanced nations, and one that causes them to seek ways to improve the literacy standards of their populations. For example, Adams (1990), Snow *et al.* (1996) and the National Reading Panel (2000) were all reports funded by the US Federal Government, and the Bullock Report (1975) and the research that underpinned the National Literacy Strategy (DfEE, 1998) and Rose Report (2005) were funded by the UK government

Children, and particularly those who have fallen behind their peers in reading, cannot be left to their own devices. Intervention of one sort or another is essential. The paper reports on the effects of an intervention programme that has been designed to help delayed readers. The programme attempts to tap into a deficiency associated with learners being unable to deal with the association between speech at the level of individual sounds within words and their visual representations on a page of text. Many learners who display this deficiency when it comes to reading texts (written speech) are often fully competent in the production and perception of oral language. The central ingredient of the self-voice programme reported here is to enable children to hear the sound components of their own voice as it is normally heard by others but not themselves. This was made possible by using a Coomber 3902 tape recorder. This recorder is used extensively by those learning a new language as it allows learners to hear their own voice as they speak, so that they can modify their accent. The learner wears headphones that allow the voice as they speak to play directly to their ears at a volume above their bone voice, thus suppressing it. In this way, the learner is able to hear themselves speak, as it were, from the 'outside' (acoustically) rather than the 'inside'.

To clarify, our articulatory properties refer to the way in which we form our speech into distinct sounds, syllables or words using our vocal chords. In the normal course of events, we receive (hear) the sounds of our own speech through the bones in our head, whereas, we receive (hear) other people's speech acoustically. Their voices are transmitted to us through the air. As we receive our own speech not in reference to its acoustic properties as we do other people's speech, but in reference to its articulatory properties, we do not normally hear ourselves as others hear us. The main advantage of the Coomber 3902 is that allows learners to hear themselves speak as others would hear them, while speaking. In the case of foreign language teaching this is an important facility as it gives the learner a mechanism whereby they receive immediate feedback on their articulations (pronunciations). In effect, the Coomber 3902 acts as a mechanistic 'accent modifier'.

We had used this equipment in exploratory trials in the UK and North America with delayed readers to see if the 'self-voice feedback loop' used by second language learners would facilitate phonic awareness. We hypothesized that it would increase learners' awareness of the association between the visual squiggles that make up words and the sounds they make. We found that the delayed readers on which we trialled this device all developed a greater awareness of the sound to the sub-word components of written language. This led to an increased awareness of how to integrate sounds (phonemes) with letters (graphemic representations). We also noted that, once equipped with these enhanced sensitivities, our delayed readers were more able to read words when tested using before-and-after standarized tests after a relatively short intensive intervention period. There was also a suggestion that speech dysfluent children in our clinical trails were showing marked improvements in their oracy in terms of clarity of pronunciation and fluency.

Encouraged by these early findings, we set about investigating the effectiveness of the intervention in a range of classroom and school settings. We were interested in the extent to which the self-voice intervention would produce measurable improvements using word recognition tests. We were particularly interested in whether the self-voice intervention would work within normal classrooms and schools without undue upheaval and within normal budget constraints. This chapter reports on what we found when we transferred it into normal classrooms. First, we briefly review the theoretical principles that underpin the programme.

Reading development and reading delay

Reading delay may well have many causes, including the neurological and the genetic. Perhaps sometime in the future new neurological and genetic remedies will be constructed. Until such time, from a teacher's perspective, the answer to reading delay lies in developing teaching methods and curricula that are generally effective in promoting reading development. Teachers are thus reliant for their remedies on using theoretical developments and evidence-based practices.

The current theoretical consensus concerning reading development and reading delay makes direct links between oracy and literacy. Writing is written speech. At its simplest level, when we write in English, we use a code and a set of rules, so that the reader can re-create the original speech. Although we speak in syllables, the writing code in English, at least, is based on phonemes. In order to read written speech, the reader needs to make an association between the visual symbol on the page (e.g. 't') and the phoneme or sound that it makes ('t'). Readers have to work out how the squiggles on the page relate to the sounds that they know from speaking and listening. For example, the reader needs to know that 'cat' has three separate phoneme sounds '/k/ ... /ae/ ... /t/' which are represented by the letters c, a and t. This is what is known as phonological awareness in the reading literature. Phonological awareness is considered to be central to being able to read successfully (e.g. Adams, 1990; Swan & Goswami, 1997).

Phonological awareness training is now an established part of the reading curriculum in the UK (DfEE, 1998; DfES, 2006). It is about raising the learner's awareness of the sound structure of language. The learner is asked to listen to a spoken word and perform the required segmentation, such as 'cat', '/k/ ... /ae/ ... /t/', and so on. Through activities such as this, the learner is being helped to develop their knowledge of the correspondence between letters and their pronunciations, such as between speech sound 'ch' and what the letters 'ch' look like when written.

Although phonological awareness is now accepted as a necessary condition of success in reading, it is not considered to be a sufficient condition. Bus and Van Ijzendoorn (1999) came to this conclusion after conducting a meta-analysis of 52 phonological awareness training studies. They evidenced that the development of letter recognition and orthographic (alphabetic) coding skills were also important. Although Bus and Van Ijzondoorn's work concerned the beginning stages of reading, it is reasonable to extrapolate from their findings to argue that this also applies to interventions with delayed readers. Besides, there is evidence that delayed readers not only experience difficulty acquiring grapheme-to-phoneme (letter to sound) correspondence rules, they also have difficulty deciphering the alphabetic (sound to letter) code (Byrne & Fielding-Barnsley, 1989).

Thus, training in phonics, which is the reverse of phonological awareness training, is also now an established part of the reading curriculum in the UK (DfES, 2005, 2006). This is about training learners in the application of knowledge of grapheme-to-phoneme (letter to sound) correspondence rules. For example, when a reader sees the written from 'ch', they have to work out it how it sounds when spoken. Thus, while phonological awareness training is about working from sound to text, training in phonics is working from text to sound. Both types of training are essential in the learning to read process and are in complementary relationship with one another (see for a comprehensive review of this area Adams, 1990).

If a learner's visual coding is inadequate, then it will be more difficult for them to learn the association between, for example, the consistent visual symbol 'ch' and the phoneme or sound they know from speech '/ch/'. Likewise, if their auditory coding is inadequate, then it will be more difficult for them to learn the reverse association, that is mapping the sub-word sounds from speech to their visual counterparts. This means that it is essential for teachers to tap into the mechanisms associated with early visual coding of letters within words and early auditory coding of the sub-word components of spoken language (e.g. Ehri *et al.*, 2001; DfES, 2005).

When addressing the problem of delayed readers, the question arises as to why some learners appear to be less sensitive to the configuration of internal components (or symbol strings) of words. In the reading literature this is generally put down to complications arising from the co-articulation process of speech (e.g. Bradley & Bryant, 1985; Liberman, 1985, 1997; Goswami & Bryant, 1990). The argument goes that, because we speak in syllables not phonemes, some learners experience problems separating syllables into their constituent phonemes (sounds). This is because when we speak, each constituent sound is affected by those that follow. This happens because when our speech production mechanism is producing the first sound in a word, it is getting ready to produce the second, and so on. This makes it difficult for the listener to recover single phonemes from a stream of speech, which, in turn, makes it difficult for some learners to rapidly and securely acquire phoneme/grapheme correspondences. These learners have difficulty in developing their ability to separate out (segment) phoneme sounds that make up words or syllables within words, so that they can match these against their visual counterparts. Since word recognition is conditional on the successful segregation and integration of the components (letters) that make up words, the result is poorly developed word recognition skills.

There is now general agreement in the reading literature that it is this mismatch between the formation of the sound and the sound itself that makes it difficult for some children to acquire reading attainment adequate to their needs. There is also a consensus that this deficiency can be ameliorated by explicit phonic awareness instruction complemented by phonological awareness training (e.g. Snowling, 1996; Tunmer & Chapman, 1998; Stainthorp & Tomlinson, 2002).

The self-voice intervention

As indicated earlier, an important feature of the recording equipment that we used in our exploratory trials was that when the learner was making a taped lesson, the voice they heard was their own, but coming to them via the air from the outside rather than via the bone from the inside. The learner, as it were, was thus able to hear themselves as they speak from the outside in. A second important feature on the Coomber 3902 from the teacher's point of view, was the 'joggle' facility on the rewind control. This is a facility that was originally developed for studio recording purposes as it controls the amount of tape that can be rewound per button press. This made it easier to edit out mistakes.

In our early trials we used this facility to edit out reading mistakes 'on the fly' (contemporaneously with the recording). This meant we could edit out mistakes as we went along, rather than after the recording had been completed. We found this approach had several advantages. It was economical with time and required less effort from the learner and the teacher. It was also more in keeping with normal teaching practices and routines to correct errors as the lesson progressed rather than when it had finished. We therefore adopted this approach in the classroom situation.

The teaching materials were not constructed specially for the intervention. Their earlier development had been based on the theoretical ideas underpinning reading development and reading delay reviewed in the previous section. To recap, the materials were derived from the theoretical notion that speech is coded to print through the phoneme device and the addition of a set of orthographic rules that deal with levels of organization beyond basic letter/sound correspondences or phonics. Singly there are 26 letter sounds in the English alphabet but these combine to give 43 or 44 different sounds or phonemes.[1] English is a syllable-stressed language. This means that when a different stress is laid on a syllable in a multi-syllabic word, the meaning of the word can alter, for example, con*tract* (to shorten) and *con*tract (an agreement).

The teaching materials were designed in such a way that, when a tape was being made, both analytic and synthetic phonics were being used. Analytic phonics involves the segmenting of words. Every word is seen, said and segmented. Synthetic phonics involves synthesis or pronouncing segmented words as full words. These full words were then read within the context of a sentence. Finally, the full sentence in which the target word appears in context had to be written out.

Implementing the programme within schools

Given the current restrictions on teaching oracy and literacy in English state schools imposed by government policy, we were particularly interested in exploring whether our programme could be transferred into ordinary classrooms at this time. Since 1998, the teaching of reading in state school classrooms in England is set entirely within the National Literacy Framework (DfEE, 1998), and now contained within the Primary National Strategy (DfES, 2006) for literacy teaching. As well as setting out teaching objectives for the whole of the primary school (key stages 1 and 2) to enable pupils to become fully literate, the framework gives guidance on how and when this teaching is to take place. It is highly prescriptive in terms of day-to-day literacy teaching. The daily routine involves an hour of literacy teaching, broken down into a 15-minute-whole class teaching session followed by a 15-minute whole-class activity. This is then followed by 15–20 minutes of group work, culminating in a 10-minute plenary.

An additional literacy support element within the framework of the literacy hour is designed to help pupils aged 7–11 years (key stage 2) who have failed to keep up with their peers in reading and other related literacy skills and competencies. These are the pupils who would not otherwise receive extra support in this area. The additional practice work, designed specifically for these pupils, is administered during the allocated 15–20 minutes; group work in one-to-one or small-group sessions. The bulk of this work is taught by non-qualified teachers, under the guidance of qualified teachers. It was these teaching assistants who we trained to deliver our programme.

We considered training essential to ensure intervention integrity as well as consistency across tutors and schools. All the training was carried out by an educational psychologist, one of the authors (P.M.) and who was already known to all participating schools. Although the training took place in individual schools at different points in time, the format and content of the sessions were always the same. They involved 15 hours spread over three consecutive days, one half-day session followed by two full-day sessions. The first half-day session provided an introduction to the programme including the theoretical principles on which it was based. During the following two days, the teaching strategy was explained and modelled. Demonstrations, role play and hands-on workshops were used to enable the trainees to practise on each other and on pupils who were not part of the study. Training materials were designed to take the trainees back to their own learning-to-read experiences. Special emphasis was put on the fostering of letter-to-sound and sound-to-letter links. These activities helped to engender a supportive learning atmosphere.

After training, each participating pupil received 20 sessions of input made up of two sessions a week for 10 weeks. Each training session took place during the 15–20 minute group work allocated time within the literacy hour. These were one-to-one sessions with a teaching assistant where the task was to help the pupils make a tape recording of themselves reading a list of words. The teaching assistant then edited the tape to make it error free before it was given to the pupil to practice on. A fresh tape was made at each of these twice-weekly, one-to-one sessions using progressively more difficult words. In between tape-making sessions the pupils had five 15-minute sessions where they required to practice independently using the tape that had been made at the preceding tape-making session. In these practice sessions the pupils read a list of words while simultaneously listening to the words being spoken by themselves. At the end of each practice session, the pupils were required to read the list of words without the tape and to correct themselves if they made a mistake.

The pupil participants

A total of 159 pupils aged between 6 and 13 years took part. They were drawn from across seven schools and had a reading age that was at least one year behind their chronological age. The seven participating schools were made up of five state primary schools, one private primary (preparatory) school and one state secondary school. All were located in the south-west of England. The scores of pupils who missed three or more teaching sessions were eliminated from the analysis.

Measuring the effectiveness of the programme

We were interested in exploring whether the programme produced measurable gains in the pupils' reading recognition abilities compared to other pupils not receiving the programme and compared to the participating pupils own reading recognition gains before they began the programme. We used a pre- and post-test quasi-experimental design over three data collection phases. In phase 1 we compared the self-voice intervention with a control group who followed their normal classroom routine.

Two-word recognition tests were used for pre- and post-testing, the *Boder test of reading–spelling patterns* (Boder & Jarrico, 1982) and the *Neale analysis of reading* (3rd edn) (Neale, 1999). All pre- and post-testing was done by the teaching assistants and took place during the week immediately before the programme began, and during the week immediately after the programme had finished. The whole programme, including pre- and post-testing, took place over a 12-week period.

In the initial phase we found that the self-voice group made greater gains, on average, between pre- and post-testing than the normal classroom routine group. The 22 pupils in the self-voice group gained, on average, 1.56 months (standard deviation = 0.66) compared to the 22 pupils in the normal classroom routine group who had a mean gain of 0.37 months (standard deviation = 0.35). This difference was statistically significant ($t = 7.6$, $df = 43$, $p = 0.0001$).

Encouraged by this outcome, in the next phase we introduced a further control group which was similar to the self-voice, in many respects, but had another person's voice on the tape. We thus compared the reading gains made over the 10-week intervention period of pupils who had received the 'self-voice' intervention with pupils who had received 'another-voice' intervention and with pupils who had followed their 'normal classroom routine'. The purpose of the 'other-voice' intervention was to introduce a more carefully matched comparison condition to avoid Hawthorne effects which are known to inflate experimental results because of the special attention being paid to participants. The 'other voice' group followed a similar routine to the self-voice group and practised on the same word lists. They did not, however, make a tape of their own voice reading these words and practised instead by listening to a tape of the words being read by another person's voice. The voice on the tape saying the words on their list was that of an adult female who was not known to them.

We found that, in this second data collection phase, the 37 pupils in the self-voice group gained more, on average, than the 36 pupils in the 'other-voice' group and than the 35 pupils in the normal classroom routine group. The self-voice group gained, on average, 1.1 months (standard deviation = 0.42) compared to 0.34 months (standard deviation = 0.22) in the normal classroom routine group and 0.42 (standard deviation = 0.42). Again, these differences were found to be statistically significant ($F = 43.9$, $df = 107$, $p = 0.001$).

In the third and final data collection phase, we compared the scores of the 59 pupils who were waiting in line, in the normal classroom routine conditions, in both phases 1 ($n = 22$) and 2 ($n = 37$) with their scores after taking part in the self-voice intervention. We found that they made greater gains in the self-voice condition than they did when they were waiting in line in the normal classroom routine condition. In the self-voice condition, they gained, on average, 1.25 months (standard deviation = 0.57) compared to 0.35 months (standard deviation = 0.27) when they followed their normal classroom routine over a similar period. This difference was found to be statistically significant ($t = 10.96$, $df = 116$, $p = 0.001$).

We thus found that, at all group-level comparisons, pupils who were given the self-voice intervention programme made greater gains than those who were not given it. We also found that the same pupils made greater gains when they were participating in the self-voice intervention than when they were following their normal classroom routine in a similar period immediately prior to the self-voice intervention.

Closer scrutiny of these results showed that the standard deviations for those in the self-voice condition were higher across the board than for those in the comparison groups. This meant that there was a greater spread of gains within that self-voice group compared to other groups. This suggested that relying on group-level comparison only may be misleading. To counteract this possibility and to get a greater insight into how and when the intervention worked or did not work, group-level comparisons were supplemented by sub-group comparisons and individual-level comparisons. We surmised that consistency in findings across contexts and within-pupil differences would be useful in drawing conclusions about the generalizability of the self-voice intervention.

Our sub-group comparisons involved compared gains made by girls and boys. We also looked at how pupils from different schools performed relative to one another: we compared younger pupils' gains with those of older pupils; we considered whether initial reading age, relative to chronological age, made a difference. In these subgroup comparisons we found that, although girls gained slightly more than boys in all three data collection phases, these differences never reached statistical significance. While we found that pupils with higher initial reading ages gained more than those with lower initial reading ages, when initial reading age relative to chronological age was taken into account, these difference disappeared. There was, however, some evidence that older pupils benefited more from the self-voice intervention than younger pupils. Their teachers put this down to more mature pupils being better equipped to cope with the self-voice intervention because it demanded an ability to work independently. There was also some suggestion that pupils attending one state primary school made greater gains than those attending the six other schools in our sample. None of these sub-group level comparisons, however, reached statistical significance.

We then compared individual learners by identifying outliers, that is those who gained the most or gained the least from the self-voice intervention. We found that the typical pupil who gained the most from the intervention was female, older (10+) with an initial reading age of just over one year behind their chronological age. On the other hand, the typical pupils who gained the least from the self-voice intervention were male, younger (7–8) and most likely to be pupils at the only non-state school in our sample. These findings concurred with the findings from our sub-group comparisons.

Discussion

Mean gain scores showed that those pupils who participated in the self-voice intervention did indeed make greater gains in their ability to recognize words than those in similar groups who did not experience this intervention, or they themselves when similar periods of teaching and practice were compared.

But to what extent can we generalize from these results? As we found no significant interactions between the effects of the self-voice intervention and a number of contextual and individual variables, our results support the contention that the intervention effect can be generalized across a range of schools, teachers and girls and boys of different chronological and reading ages when used to support readers who have fallen behind. While the evidence presented here does not extend to children whose reading ages are the same as or above their chronological ages, theoretically we would argue that the same effect, that is the acceleration of word recognition, would have been obtained by any group in the initial stage of learning to read. Extrapolating from our findings, it is reasonable to argue that, used as a preventative measure for those who do not spontaneously discover the connection between graphemes and phonemes, the self-voice could explicitly teach this connection. This is especially important given that prevention interventions have been found to be more effective than remedial interventions (Ehri *et al.*, 2001).

The effects reported in this chapter were attained at the immediate end of the intervention programme and investigations as to the longevity of this effect are ongoing. However, in considering the longer-term value of the intervention programme for those who received it, a key question is whether the improvements noted at word-level oral reading leads on to mastery and use of both metacognitive (self-monitoring, self-regulation) and cognitive (rereading, activating background knowledge, adjusting reading speed) strategies that facilitate text comprehension. The question of transferability to everyday reading tasks within and beyond the classroom is an important one which leads on to the issue of whether the theoretical rationale for the self-voice intervention has been upheld by our findings.

On theoretical grounds, our explanation for stronger word recognition performance of the self-voice condition relative to the other-voice and the normal classroom routine condition was that those in the self-voice feedback group were better equipped to make a direct link between the pronunciation of words and the visual (letter) cues on the page. This was because they could hear their own voice saying the words as they spoke them on to the tape, and on which they later practised. We interpreted these results as revealing that hearing their own articulated voice (as opposed to the bone voice they normally hear) helped them to understand the internal structure of spoken words. This, in turn, gave them a better understanding of the alphabetic code that underpins words written down. Before the learner can read, they must be able to figure out the graphic symbols on the pages and map them on to their auditory counterparts. The tape, we would argue, provided pupils with a direct and immediate means of connecting words (letter strings) on the page to their pronunciations.

In addressing the question of the extent to which the positive results reported in this paper validate the theoretical principles underpinning the programme, the strongest evidence comes from the phase 2 data, which had a carefully matched control on all aspects except the voice on the tape used to practice on between the twice-weekly tape-making sessions. While there are plausible grounds for optimism about the effectiveness of the programme, it is less clear whether the positive results were due to the theoretical basis of the intervention or some other factor, or set of factors.

During the making of the tape, there were numerous opportunities for metacognitive exchanges and modelling on a one-to-one basis with a specially trained and experienced classroom assistant. The tape also provided opportunities to practise independently. Both the self-voice and the other-voice groups had their work regularly (twice-weekly) monitored and, no doubt, in these sessions feedback was offered. Both the self-voice and the other-voice conditions may have gone some way to fostering the learner's agency over their own learning, including responsibility for their own learning. So, then, we must ask why was listening to one's own voice a more powerful learning experience? It is possible that listening to one's own voice helped learners see how letter sounds fit into words and encouraged them to explicitly consider word sounds. This, in turn, should make them better able to isolate phonemes within words.

However, another equally plausible explanation for the results comes from the self-as-model hypothesis. This hypothesis derives from a body of literature within psychology that indicates that using oneself as a model can be an effective means of ameliorating academic failure (see for a review Hitchcock *et al.*, 2003). Generally, self-as-model refers to the observation of images of oneself engaged in the behaviour one is seeking to modify. Images can be high tech, low tech or no tech. They can be video tapes, audio tapes, still photographs or an imaged visualization. According to Vygotsky (1978), observing or listening to a superior performance would indicate future mastery as a transformation, facilitated through the guidance of a more skilled person, takes place within the zone of proximal development. But what if that more skilled person is a view of one's own (future) mastery? Would not the image be more powerful? There is some evidence to suggest that the self is the ideal model because it maximizes the degree of observer identification (e.g. Clark *et al.*, 1992). An important aspect of the self-voice intervention was the editing out of mistakes so that the practice tape provided a perfectly mastered self-model of reading behaviour. Not only would the audio tape have provided a flawless model of (future) mastery, but a model of oneself performing successfully. From a social learning theoretical perspective, it is reasonable to argue that this would strengthen their belief in their own capacity to become a successful reader (Bandura, 1997). Self-awareness through self-observation may have an important role in facilitating other metacognitive factors, such as self-belief and self-efficacy among children, and particularly those who fall behind their peers.

Conclusion

Although the delayed readers who were in the self-voice intervention groups in our study made greater grains in their word recognition scores than those in the other-voice and normal classroom routine groups, caution is needed in jumping to the conclusion that this is the sole result of the intervention. Although this may be the case, we must also consider the possibility that factors other than the theoretical assumed processes might have influenced the outcome. Further comparative evaluations are therefore necessary to examine how the intervention works procedurally, and how we can map these operations theoretically. This will involve a programme of research focusing on different ways of setting up the intervention. For example, the nature of the link between what is being learned in the self-voice condition as opposed to the other-voice condition should be explored in further intervention research.

Note

1. The difference in phoneme numbers, 43 or 44, is due to differences in how the 'wh' phoneme is pronounced. Some pronounce it as 'wh' by aspirating before voicing, and others as 'w', which makes a different sound.

References

Adams, M. J. (1990) *Beginning to read* (Cambridge, MA, MIT Press).

Bandura, A. (1997) *Self-efficacy: the exercise of control* (New York, W. H. Freeman).

Boder, E. & Jarrico, S. (1982) *The* Boder test of reading and spelling patterns (New York, Grune & Stratton).

Bradley, L. & Bryant, P. (1985) *Rhyme and reason in reading and spelling* (Ann Arbor, MI, University of Michigan Press).

Bullock Report. Department of Education and Science (1975) *A language for life* (London, DES).

Bus, A. G. & van Ijzendoorn, M. H. (1999) Phonological awareness and early reading: a meta-analysis of experimental training studies, *Journal of Educational Psychology*, 91, 403–414.

Byrne, B. & Fielding-Barnsley, R. (1989) Phonic awareness and letter knowledge in the child's acquisition of the alphabetic principle, *Journal of Educational Psychology*, 81(3), 313–321.

Clarke, E., Kehle, T. J., Jenson, W. R. & Beck, D. E. (1992) Evaluation of the parameters of self-modeling interventions, *School Psychology Review*, 21, 246–254.

Department for Education and Employment (DfEE) (1998) *National Literacy Strategy: framework for teaching* (London, DfEE).

Department for Education and Skills (DfES) (2006) *Primary National Strategy: draft framework for teaching literacy. Consultation document* (London, DfES).

Ehri, L. C., Nunes, S. R., Willows, D. M., Schuster, B. V., Yaghoub-Zadeh, Z. & Shanahan, T. (2001) Phonemic awareness instruction helps children learn to read: evidence from the National Reading Panel's meta-analysis, *Reading Research Quarterly*, 36(3), 250–228.

Goswami, U. & Bryant, P. (1990) *Phonological skills and learning to read* (Hove, Lawrence Erlbaum).

Hitchcock, C. H., Dowrick, P. W. & Prater, M. A. (2003) Video self-modeling intervention in school-based settings: a review, *Remedial and Special Education*, 24(1), 36–46.

Liberman, A. M. (1997) How theories of speech affect research in reading and writing, in: B. Blachman (Ed.) *Foundations of reading acquisition and dyslexia* (Mawah, NJ, Lawrence Erlbaum).

Liberman, A. M. & Mattingly, I. G. (1985) The motor theory of speech perception revisited, *Cognition*, 21(1), 1–36.

National Reading Panel Report (2000) *Teaching to read: an evidence-based assessment of the scientific research literature and its implications for reading instruction* (Washington, DC, NICHD Clearing House).

Neale, M. D. (1999) *Neale analysis of reading ability: manual* (3rd edn) (Melbourne, Australian Council for Educational Research).

Rose Report. Department for Education and Skills (2005) *Review of early reading* (London, DfES).

Smith, F. (1994) *Understanding reading* (5th edn) (Hillsdale, NJ, Lawrence Erlbaum).

Snow, C., Burns, S. H. & Griffing, P. (Eds) (1996) *Preventing reading difficulties in young children* (Washington, DC, National Academy Press).

Snowling, M. J. (1996) Annotation: contemporary approaches to the teaching of reading, *Journal of Child Psychology and Psychiatry*, 37, 139–148.

Stainthorp, R. & Tomlinson, P. (Eds) (2002) *Learning and teaching reading* (British Journal of Educational Psychology Monograph series II: Psychological aspects of education: current trends) (Leicester, British Psychological Society).

Stanovich, K. E. (1990) A call for an end to the paradigm wars in reading research, *Journal of Reading Behaviour*, 22, 221–231.

Swan, D. & Goswami, U. (1997) Picture naming deficits in developmental dyslexia: the phonological representations hypothesis, *Brain and Language*, 56(3), 334–353.

Tunmer, W. E. & Chapman, J. W. (1998) Language prediction skill, phonological recoding ability and beginning reading, in: M. Joshi & C. Hume (Eds) *Reading and spelling: development and disorders* (Hillside, NJ, Lawrence Erlbaum).

Vygotsky, L. S. (1978) Interaction between learning and development, in: M. Cole, V. John-Steiner, S. Scribner & E. Souberman (Eds) *Mind in society: the development of higher psychological processes* (Cambridge, MA, Harvard University Press), 79–91.

Narrative learning, EAL and metacognitive development

Martin Cortazzi and Lixian Jin

In this paper, we elaborate on some aspects of narrative learning in relation to children in schools who are developing English as an additional language (EAL). 'Narrative learning' refers to learning from, about and through stories, and learning through reflecting on the experience of narrating and the narrating of experience. We introduce a framework for a classroom approach to oral narratives with such pupils that highlights this reflexive aspect of developing awareness of stories and metacognitive reflection. While our focus is primarily on pupils who use EAL, we believe the insights and approach are valuable for all learners.

We first make some points about EAL and metacognition, before considering some basic principles for language development for EAL learners in relation to classroom interaction. We then discuss stories as narrative, narrative development and some uses of narrative to develop language and other skills for EAL learners. We also give an extended example from a classroom of a narrative approach which uses keywords and story maps to develop language and some metacognitive skills; it includes the suggestion that if EAL pupils are supported to tell their personal stories, this may help their linguistic and metacognitive development and give credibility to the voice of their experience. The framework introduced here should be valuable for teachers and teaching assistants in classrooms and for speech and language therapists and others who work with children to help them develop oral fluency.

English as an additional language

There are a number of terms used to refer to those children within the English-speaking school system in the UK, or similarly in many other countries, who as recent migrant arrivals or longer-term residents speak another language as a first or dominant language and whose use of English is not at the same level as those using English as a first language. Terms such as pupils with 'limited English proficiency' (LEP) or 'English as a second language' (ESL or E2L) are now generally discarded in Britain for their negative connotations or their failure to acknowledge the bilingual—often multilingual—skills these pupils bring with them. Instead, reference is currently made to pupils learning and using 'English as an additional language' (EAL) or to 'bilingual learners'. These last terms draw attention to how, for these pupils, English is one developing language within a repertoire of degrees of fluency in other languages. This is an important point because there is some evidence that fluent bilingualism and some types of education in another language, such as immersion education developed in Canada, may enhance cognitive flexibility and metalinguistic awareness (the ability to think about and reflect on the nature and functions of language), which are aspects of metacognition; compared to monolinguals, some bilingual children may therefore be better able to analyse their knowledge of language and to control inner language processing (Swain & Lapkin, 1983; Baker, 2001). Concerning EAL pupils, the realization of this possible benefit probably depends upon social and attitudinal factors surrounding their language repertoire and upon their attaining a level of English proficiency for curriculum learning.

Using the term EAL carries an implication that these pupils will need language support and particular help with using English to access the curriculum, at least for a while. There is no implication that they will fall into any particular ability range: on the contrary, all abilities are represented among these pupils (it is worth stressing this point, since limited use of English might, generally mistakenly, be construed as limited cognitive ability). In the UK, EAL pupils now make up around 10% of the school population nationally and the number is rising; numbers are concentrated in large cities (e.g. about 30% in London), and in some particular schools a majority of pupils could be described as having EAL needs (there are similar or higher percentages in

North America and Australia and, in relation to their national languages, in a number of countries in Europe). EAL learners do not, of course, form a homogeneous group. In fact, the diversity seems to be increasing in terms of the number and range of languages spoken; pupils' ethnic, social, cultural and religious backgrounds; their proficiency in English (ranging from *ab initio* to good social use but weaknesses in academic literacy). Any classroom strategies for focused support for the development of EAL to secure access to the curriculum will need to include a strong element of responding to the individual needs of the pupils within this diversity.

Metacognition and EAL learners

One possible difficulty in applying metacognition with EAL learners is the question of which language is used within a learner's repertoire: if we take 'metacognitive awareness' as learners' knowledge of their own mental processes, including awareness of how they understand, learn and remember (Flavell, 1979), then the likelihood is that, mentally and perhaps verbally, this will be carried out in another language in the first instance. This could be translated or re-expressed in English (as part of a legitimate use of other languages in the classroom while learners are learning the requisite areas of English) and at some stage the metalanguage (terminology and language about language) needed to talk about this (Gombert, 1992) becomes itself both a target area and means of further expression in English. We would need to recognize that thinking in English is, for many EAL pupils, a later stage of development that is influenced not only by the level of English proficiency, but regular contexts of use and the uses of other languages in learners' repertoires.

There is a substantial body of linguistic research that examines successful learners' uses of metacognitive strategies as part of a range of language learning strategies (Rubin & Thompson, 1982; Rubin, 1987; O'Malley & Chamot, 1990; Oxford, 1990; McDonough, 1995). While the focus is usually on older and young adults, it is potentially relevant to teaching oral skills to EAL children. Metacognition is used for self-management and thinking about the language learning process, including: prioritizing the aspects of language to be learned; organizing the approach, setting specific goals and using advanced organizers to preview main ideas, concepts of material to be covered; delaying speaking and learning initially through listening comprehension; planning for tasks by describing a task situation and determining the task requirements or checking the language which will be needed; and planning the main ideas and sequence of ideas to be expressed. There is also the crucial metacognitive strategy of evaluation, including first, self-monitoring to evaluate speech, maximize use of what is already known, and identify errors and the effect of speech while also using any external feedback, and second, evaluating task performance and progress, and identifying successful learning experiences—this will include evaluating the strategies used. However, even adult learners may only use a limited range of these essential aspects of language learning, with little self-evaluation. Given the relatively recent prominence of metacognition in classroom practices, and the wide variation in educational practices worldwide which EAL pupils may have experienced, there is no guarantee that these learners may have systematically developed such strategies in another language or in another school system. The likelihood of variation among EAL learners regarding metacognitive strategy use can be further understood by considering that EAL pupils come from many cultures, and research shows that cultural background affects learning strategy choice and use: learners from different cultures may emphasize quite different activities and ways of thinking about learning, with different cultural evaluations of what makes good learning or teaching (Oxford, 1996; Cortazzi & Jin, 2001, 2002b).

All of this points to the need to systematically introduce metacognitive strategies in EAL, both to cater for pupils to whom the whole area is practically unexplored and to enhance strategy use for learners who may be familiar with some strategies but not in English: reflecting upon and talking about metacognitive aspects of learning in English is, after all, itself a way of developing language skills as well as developing approaches to learning.

With children, in principle, an adult would initially introduce and structure classroom activities to develop these metacognitive strategies, and provide a way for learners to coordinate their own learning process with the long-term aim of establishing an internal framework which gradually becomes part of the learners as they accept increased responsibility for using metacognition themselves. However, in practice the direct application of metacognitive strategies to support the language learning of EAL children has been limited. The above research on metacognition in relation to language learning strategies is relatively unfamiliar to many of those working with EAL learners: first, many teachers involved in supporting such learners are not necessarily language specialists since they are mainstream teachers of other curriculum areas; secondly, most research and published examples refer to adults or older school-age learners; and thirdly, the research literature shows that strategies can be highly task dependent, so general guidance needs to be contextualized. In this paper, we concentrate on the context of narrative tasks and development.

Principles for EAL language development

A number of principles can be listed which will inform support strategies for EAL language development in the context of classroom learning (Gravelle, 1996; Cortazzi & Jin, 2002b; DfES, 2002). These principles are informed by classroom applications of second language acquisition research (Ellis 1997; Mitchell & Miles 1998; Cook 2001; Boxer & Cohen, 2004) and are the pedagogic background for the framework suggested here for narrative learning. The principles (see Figure 1) can be thought of in pairs or polarities in tension with each other:

- The recognition that *meaning* is central (in addition to pronunciation or grammatical correctness) and that expressing intended meaning and understanding others' meanings is what drives language development; this is offset by *relevance*, so that pupils learn what is relevant to their curriculum needs, their individuality and interests;

- The need for *repetition*, so that pupils hear many examples and get many opportunities for meaningful practice (rather than a one-off exposure and single chance to get it right); this is balanced by *variation* to avoid boredom and to help learners appreciate similar language in different contexts;
- The need for *simplification* of new language and concepts, so that curriculum topics are accessible; this must be complemented by appropriate *complexity* to avoid superficiality and to ensure EAL pupils are advancing in their learning; similarly, the need for *consolidation*, so that pupils have some security in working with known tasks or language, complemented with a need for *challenge* and cognitive engagement to extend learning;
- The need to offset *being correct* in learning English and subject content to appropriate standards, so adults provide positive feedback and help develop confidence and self-esteem, with *taking risks*, so EAL pupils speak out even if they are unsure of content or form, which is important for extending language and applying learning;
- The need for explicit *models* of the use of language to describe, explain, argue, etc., which demonstrate and exemplify the main idea of classroom tasks; these may be mimicked at some stage in a scaffolding approach but *independent learning* remains a goal as initiative is increasingly transferred from an adult to the learner; similarly, *collaboration* in which an EAL pupil works with an adult or in pairs or groups with peers needs to be balanced with the *individual* work which is necessary for independence and most assessment;
- While *verbal* development is a major goal, in which the skills of listening, speaking, reading and writing are often combined or specifically integrated, *visual* support (in the form of charts, diagrams, drawings or maps) is crucial to illustrate language and concepts and, further, can provide a platform, for language expression and a means to develop key study skills.

A metacognitive implication of these principles is that teachers could explicitly discuss them to help EAL pupils to become more consciously aware of which principles apply to different classroom contexts, so that learners progressively become able to internalize them, discuss their use and apply them productively without external guidance. One way to do this is to make a poster displaying a simplified version of the principles and get learners to refer to it before or after classroom tasks to discuss which principles apply and how they are used; later pupils might make their own posters of selected principles to explain them to peers and tell the story of how they applied them.

Narratives and the development of language and concepts

These principles can be applied to developing stories with EAL pupils using a range of approaches and techniques that are well established in language teaching. Long-standing guidance for working with younger learners includes selecting picture-books or stories from around-the-world collections expressed in language which can be simplified, and which have clear themes that children will enjoy and

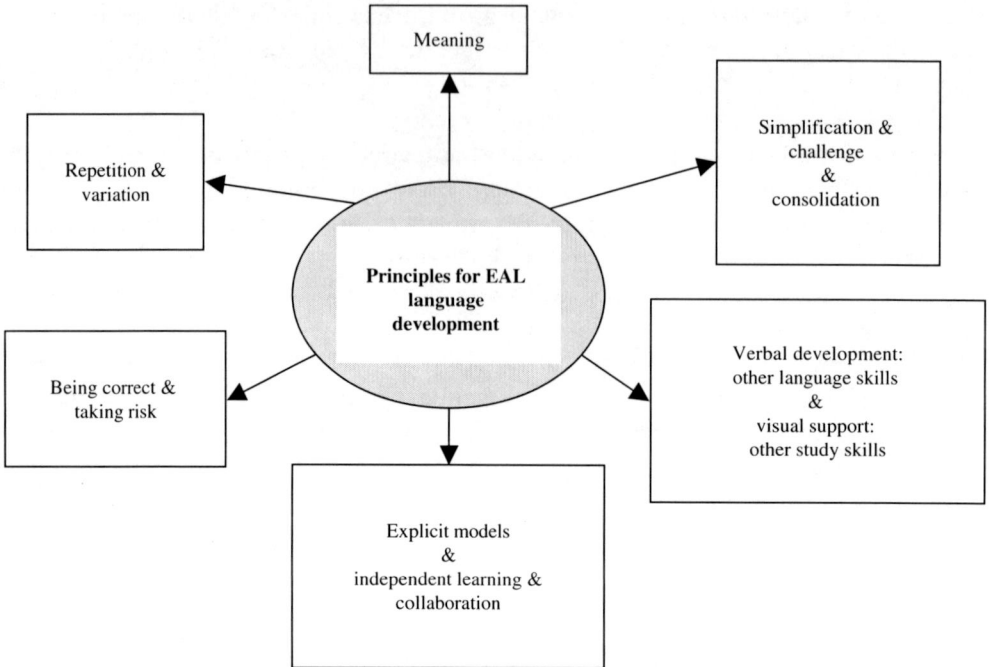

Figure 1.   Principles for EAL language development

can be related to the curriculum (ILEA, 1983; Ellis & Brewster, 1991). To clarify meaning through enactment and repetition (and provide a face-to-face model of telling), there are strong suggestions for adults to tell (rather than read) stories using plenty of gestures, facial expressions, and a degree of dramatization using tone of voice and mime (Sawyer, 1965; Colwell, 1980; Grainger, 1997). This can be practised by clearly visualizing the episodes and verbalizing the envisaged image, if necessary supported by outline drawings or quick sketches. Further ways to enhance comprehension through storytelling, and later to involve learners in follow-up creative activities, include the use of masks, hats, puppets, posters and theme-based displays of stories, and later actions, songs and role plays. Such creative activities provide a format to recycle the language and concepts in a story (with variation and an element of challenge) and make curricular links (Morgan & Rinvolucri, 1983; Garvie, 1990). Further activities may include: identifying and labelling (people, locations, items and props), qualifying and describing attributes (colour, size, shape), examining relations and classifying (comparing, contrasting, sorting into sets and categories), and predicting and sequencing to discuss time and cause and effect (for example, by making a skeleton story outline using brief phrases which can be cut and randomized for sequencing and retelling, with discussion of who, what or which event caused later actions or events). However, in general this range of practical literature does not apply metacognitive principles to EAL, nor does it apply narrative theory or analysis to the classroom.

A practical reason for advocating a narrative stance to learning with regard to EAL learners is that their opportunities for joining in classroom exchanges with those using English as a first language can be quite restricted. Too often in a busy classroom, EAL learners respond to other people's initiatives, predominantly those of the teacher, without having the opportunity to initiate interaction themselves or engage in sustained speech, both of which are crucial for second language development. In a busy classroom, turn-taking opportunities for pupils can be limited. Yet EAL learners generally need additional time to think and plan their contribution. When they do speak, they can experience the constant risk of inadvertent interruption by others since they may not appear ready to talk or may hesitate while thinking. Some find that they are about to speak when someone else does so, and they have to wait. Telling a narrative, however, is a prime speech event which gives a speaker a legitimately long turn to talk and interruptions to stories are rarer. Giving EAL learners this extended opportunity for talking can therefore have major advantages for them, provided they feel some confidence in knowing the content of a story and have sufficient awareness of the likely story structure. The use of keywords and story maps (which we describe later as a part of narrative learning) satisfies these conditions. The approach provides multiple opportunities for re-hearing and retelling, and uses graphic devices which help learners to plan for and reflect on telling a story

Narrative and the development of narrative

Narrative with children has been studied as a key genre in classroom work (mainly in relation to writing; see e.g. Collerson, 1988; Cope & Kalantzis, 1993). This genre is held distinct from other ways of saying things (such as giving instructions, describing, reporting or explaining) because in a narrative the teller recounts events that are generally *remote* in space or time and are retold in a certain order, typically in the *chronological order* in which story events occurred. Stories have a trajectory or *plot structure* with a clear beginning, some crises or turning-points and their resolutions which constitute the body or middle, and a final resolution or ending, in which there is generally strong human interest in the events and *motivations* of story characters and how they solve problems, overcome difficulties or create coherence in their life (Cortazzi, 1993; Linde, 1993). This synthesizing of the meaning of events into story structures (with notions of *causality*, *explanation* and s*ignificance*, and the movement of *time*) has led some scholars to identify narrative thinking as a unique mode of thought which is distinct from the logical classificatory kind of thinking so that 'narrative knowing' is particularly important for children's learning (Bruner, 1986; Polkinghorne, 1988). Not surprisingly, then, stories are held to represent a strongly integrated—and in some ways unique—approach to learning, so that educators have called for a 'narrative curriculum' based around storytelling, especially for the primary stage (Egan, 1988; Lauritzen & Jaeger, 1997). Further, the telling of personal experience and other narratives involves *memory* and *imagination* in the recall of what happened and, at deeper levels, the *evaluation* of what happened (why it is interesting, important or meaningful) and *a point of view*, *voice* or *identity* of the teller (whether the teller directly represented in the story or indirectly represented in the style of telling it). The self-presentation of the teller is evident is the *performance* of oral narratives through gesture, tone of voice, speech style and manner of telling, which is often part of the point of the telling and its *enjoyment* by children (Cortazzi, 1993).

Some of these apparently abstract characteristics can be translated into narrative questions to support EAL learners to generate their own real or imagined story. Using such questions around a simple story line and then reflecting on the characteristics of the questions and why they are important for stories can be one approach to develop narrative metacognition for EAL learners. In the example shown in Figure 2, three simple statements are used as the basis for a plot, elaborating E. M. Forster's minimal definition of plot as 'The king died and then the queen died of grief' (without the last two words, Forster argues, this isn't a plot) (Forster, 1927, p. 82). Here the basic 'and then' is combined with 'so' and 'why?' as learners' answers add to the story ('Everybody was puzzled', 'He was so sad', 'She was jealous', 'Later, she was sorry'. Increasingly more demanding questions are introduced: relating to point of view, evaluation and the telling of the story, and metacognitively orientated questions about task planning, ownership of the story and further questions about remembering and learning. Our experience with this kind of framework is that EAL learners can benefit for the support of using the series of questions (roughly from top to bottom in Figure 2) *cumulatively* to generate, first, a short simple story, then gradually increasing the length and complexity successively prompted by questions. With adult support, EAL learners can remember quite a long oral story because of the repetition involved in the cumulative approach but they have the challenge of adding something new in response to the additional question in each round of telling.

Social aspects of developing narrative and narrative learning

There is substantial research on how children learn to tell stories, often in relation to narrative structures or to examine specific models of narrative (Applebee, 1978; Peterson & McCabe, 1983; McCabe & Peterson, 1991; Bamberg, 1997). This research indicates how oral narratives increase in length and that there is a pathway from age 3 to 9 of recounting single events, then two or more events, which later include a high point and an overall outcome and evaluation. Progressions in development include using connectives (such as 'then', 'so' or 'but') to show chains of chronological events and causation. Later developments may involve embedding events within a larger framework and perhaps understanding and using flash-backs and flash-forwards (which may be familiar from film and TV) and giving clearer accounts of motivation and character. However, much of this research pays insufficient attention to the content and meaning of children's stories and to the cultural settings and situations in which children hear or tell stories. These aspects are relevant to EAL learners because cultural variations may imply that narrative skills may be valued and realized differently in the range of cultures represented by these learners.

Children are socialized into the narrative ways of their culture. Through narrative they are, in turn, socialized into shared knowledge, social experience and cultural

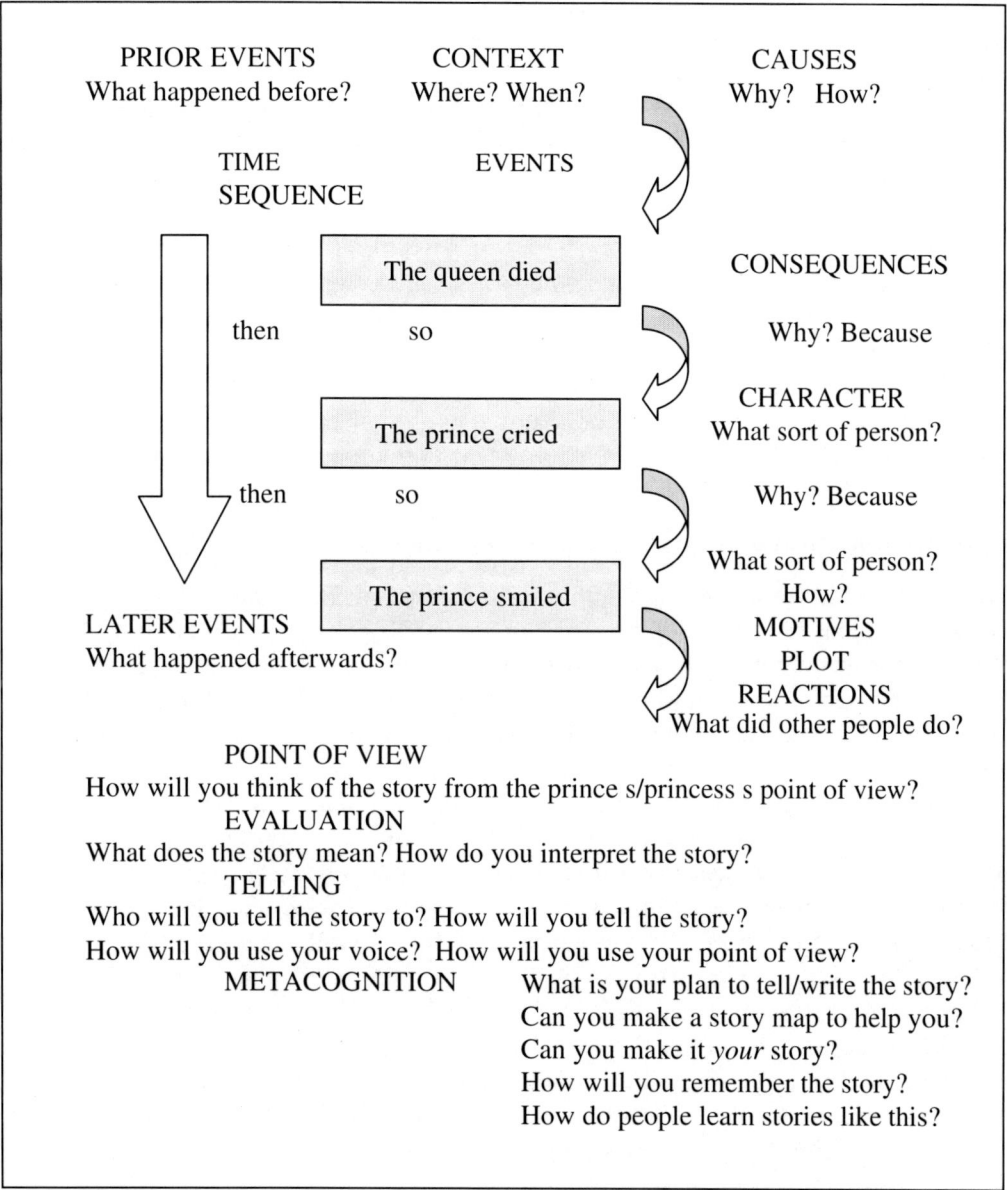

Figure 2.   Using narrative questions to support EAL pupils to generate a story

values. Thus 'narrative learning' may be taken as learning narrative and learning through narrative. However, in different cultural communities children's narrative strategies can vary enormously from the stick-to-the-facts approach of Euro-Americans to the Afro-American oral drama of heightened performance within North America (Heath, 1983), to the oral restraint of succinct strings of experiences of Japanese (Minami, 2002). Stories addressed to children can feature the child as transgressor in Chinese to the child as positive achiever of Euro-Americans—but both can be aimed at socialization through morality (Ochs & Capps, 2001). Structurally, while there is a strong European tradition of cycles of threes (episodes and characters, as in *Goldilocks and the Three Bears* or *The Three Billy Goats Gruff*), other cultures, like Athapaskan, may prefer cycles of twos or fours (Scollon & Scollon, 1981) or, like Navajo, not consider cycles of plot important so much as a way of telling a story, so that it is saturated with repetition (Toelken, 1969). With such cross-cultural variation as a possibility among children, teachers of EAL should surely be open to different storytelling styles that, at first, might have been under-valued. EAL teachers would probably see a need to find out about the ways of storytelling in EAL learners' cultures. They would also need a clear approach to modelling the language of stories in English (so that narrative is a productive vehicle for language development) that allows some choice of the presentation of content and the style of telling (to allow learners to maintain or find their narrative voice and identity in telling in English).

Applications through keywords and story maps

We have found that using visual support and visual means of modelling stories is a crucial complement to developing oral narrative skills, which in turn helps to develop children's metacognitive and written skills. The process of hearing and producing English through visuals could be regarded as an aspect of graphic literacy (Cortazzi *et al.*, 1998) or the use of key visuals that represent content knowledge (Mohan, 1986). Crucially, the content of a chart or map, for instance, can be verbalized in different ways but the act of hearing versions and expressing one's own version while using visual support means that both the content and relevant language are likely to be remembered. Two visual means of conveying story meaning are the use of 'keywords' and 'story maps'. We now relate how these were developed in a Year 3 class (ages 7–8) in an inner-city primary school in the Midlands of the UK, in which nearly all the children were using English as an additional language.

As a first step, children heard a story in English and Gujerati (the first language of most of the class). Then the story was retold in both languages using large pictures; the pictures were not simply illustrations, but were later placed one by one on the board as prompts for the children to retell the story in English. This led to better retellings than simply relying on memory. As the children said, the pictures helped them to organize their knowledge of the story.

As a second step, the teacher worked with the class to choose keywords (nouns and verbs representing stages of the content), write them on cards and use the cards as prompts for another retelling. This had a limited effect, since the written words were not themselves organized visually to support the children's narrative, so the teacher then stuck the words on the board in the story order and drew boxes around them and joined them with arrows to make a story 'map'. The learners then retold the story using the map, and then—crucially—removed the cards and replaced them in sequence into the outlined boxes, while themselves retelling the story step by step. This was done with several stories over a sequence of lessons. Figure 3 shows the

What did the Little Red Hen do? She …

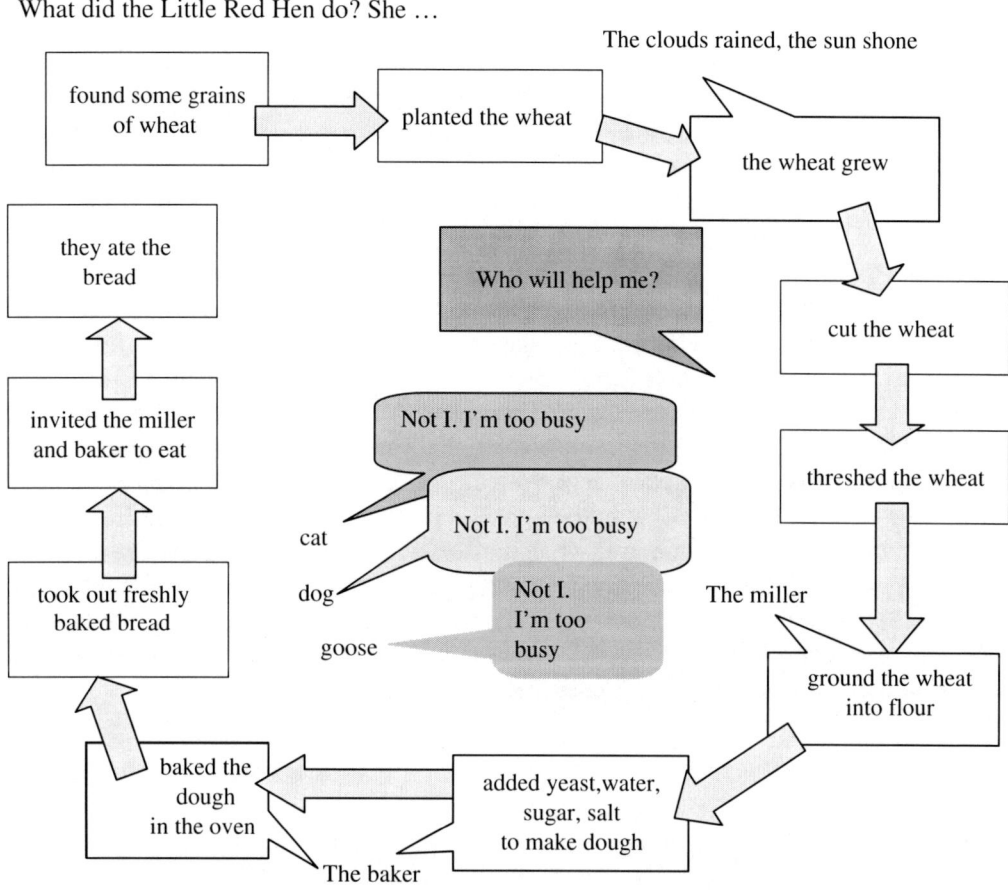

Figure 3.   A possible story map for *The Little Red Hen*

kinds of story maps that were used, in this case the story of *The Little Red Hen* (2005), in which a hen finds some grains of wheat and plants them, then harvests the wheat and, in different stages, gets the wheat ground and made into bread. She asks other farm animals for help but they are too busy, so she works alone, but finally invites the miller and baker, who did help her, to enjoy the bread. The story map provides key verbs and outlines all the steps of the story but a retelling can be expressed as children wish: they have guidance and a modelling from the teacher's version yet they can make their own.

The map in Figure 3 is linear, presented as a circle, but later maps had more complex branches which were shown in the outline and also by colour-coding story episodes or story threads for different characters. Learners used the keywords on the cards and the maps as prompts for retellings; some of these were recorded, so that children in groups could hear their own and others' versions and, later, write them. Many of the activities were done in small groups or pairs, ensuring high social involvement and there were valid reasons for pairs and groups to tell their stories to other pupils. Because the activities and challenges were varied, children engaged productively in multiple retellings of the same story, with noticeable improvements in accuracy, fluency and confidence—particularly important for EAL learners.

Metacognitively, the story maps facilitated the planning of telling the stories. Since the content outline was visually available, children could concentrate on how they would tell the story and how they would express it in English. The children were also encouraged to listen and reflect on how the stories were being told, how they remembered them and what the role of the keywords and story maps were. As children became familiar with the procedure, they chose their own words and composed their own maps in English and Gujarati. Stories were further improved by using other cards with linking words or adverbials ('first', 'next', 'later', 'unfortunately', 'unexpectedly') which the children located on to the map and inserted the expressions into their telling.

As a third step, we had taken photos of the various stages of developing the keywords and story maps successively over a number of stories over several weeks. These photos were now used as metacognitive prompts, so that the children could reflect on what they had done and what they had learned, which they wrote about using the photos as illustrations. The following (uncorrected) extracts from children's written reflections show some elements of narrating learning, bearing in mind that the children were using limited English and were writing about events that had taken place in the classroom several weeks earlier:

> In the photo we are listening to the story of Rama and Sita. It was recorded on the tape recorder by another group of children. We tryed to guess who was speaking. It was fun with Rajal and Jagruti.

> What we were doing in this photograph is we had a pile of cards with writing on them. We were in pairs. We had to ask each other questions about Snow White. When we asked each other questions we had to see if that was in their story.In this photo we war lisnig to the taprickodr [listening to the tape recorder] we war tling a stoe [telling a story].

> In my photo me and Jyoti was looking at the keywords. They are good for rembing [remembering] the story.

> In the photo, I was telling Rajal the story about Hans and Gretal my part was eksiting. I can tell the story with key words and story maps. It was fun with the others both of the stories were good.

> What we did is we did a story of Snow White. Mrs Smith wroite the key words that we gave her. Each person in the class, had some cards. When it was there turn they had to put the card on the board. I had the poisonous comb bit. I learned how to tell stories more better.

The photos and children's explanations were then shared with parents and story-books were made and shared with younger learners. Figure 4 maps this process of using the keywords and story maps. Clearly the same process could be used for developing children's oral versions of information texts.

The narrative process outlined here (see Figure 4) exemplifies the principles for EAL language development, with a strong metacognitive strand. We have trained speech and language therapists in this approach. By developing specific language

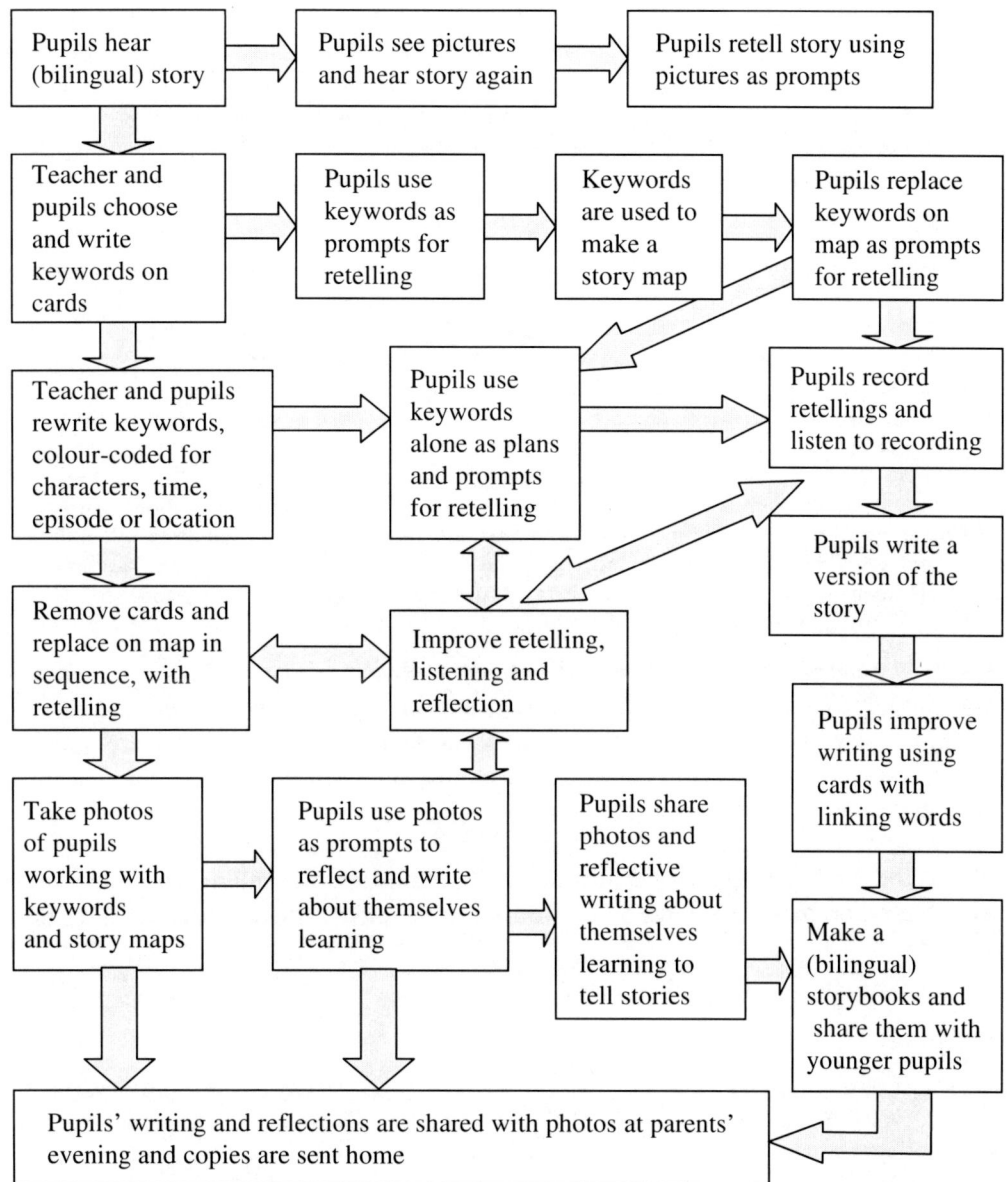

Figure 4. A sequence of classroom activities to develop key words and story maps

activities based on narrative themes within this approach, they report that these activities capture children's imagination, harnessing the intellectual ability of speech and language impaired children. They find that these narrative-based activities help these particular children to develop syntactic structures, to understand and express narrative sequencing story character description and, significantly, to express the evaluative element in narratives.

We would like to move the narrative activity on, so that EAL children use their narrative confidence to tell personal or biographical stories and develop their own voice. Given their status as EAL learners, this seems particularly important as an aspect of strengthening and developing narrative identity. While we do not have available versions from the above classroom, this written account by a 7-year-old Vietnamese girl, given in the 1980s, shows the sort of biographical voice that might be shared, in this case after 18 months in the UK:

> My name's Hoa, my name means flower. I lived in a big house in Vietnam with my mother and my father and Binh and Quan. In Vietnam it was sunny I can play out all day if I like. But one day I can not stay there because the was lot of bombs. So one day my mummy and Daddy packed all the thing that we want we well some clothes for some money when it was dark we when on a cart and a horse pull it we went on the cart and a horse pull it we went on the cart for just one night then we have to walk. When it was morning we saw a river and we went on a little boat. We told the man were we wanted to go and the man row the boat to a beach. We stay on the beach for four weeks and waited for the big boat. We went in the house with five peoples it was not our house. Then we went on the boat. It was very crowded there was 200 peoples. There was one toilet. It was very frightened when O looked down the hole in the toilet because I can see the sea. It was very dirty and wet and it was smelly we have a little bit to eat every day and my Mummy had a little bottle for us to drink. We stay on the boat for two months.

This written narrative is testimony to the child's ability to retell a difficult and dangerous experience (something like this is, sadly, not uncommon among EAL learners of refugee and asylum seeking families). It involves the reader through a narrative voice that has a distinctive tone and testifies to the potential of narrative learning: learning to tell stories better and learning in and through the telling.

We believe that narrative learning has telling points about metacognition, too. To develop these points, the visual approach of supporting the telling with keywords and story maps has helped with children's planning, memory, understanding and reflection.

References

Applebee, A. (1978) *The child's concept of story* (Chicago, Chicago University of Chicago Press).

Baker, C. (2001) *Foundations of bilingual education and bilingualism* (3rd edn) (Clevedon, Multilingual Matters).

Bamberg, M. (Ed.) (1997) *Narrative development: six approaches* (Mahwah, NJ, Lawrence Erlbaum).

Boxer, D. & Cohen, A. (Eds) (2004) *Studying speaking to inform second language learning* (Clevedon, Multilingual Matters).

Bruner, J. (1986) *Actual minds, possible worlds* (London, Harvard University Press).

Collerson, J. (Ed.) (1988) *Writing for life* (Sydney, Primary English Teaching Association).

Colwell, E. (1980) *Storytelling* (London, The Bodley Head).

Cope, B. & Kalantzis, M. (1993) *The powers of literacy: a genre approach to teaching writing* (London, Falmer Press).

Cook, V. (2001) *Second language learning and language teaching* (3rd edn) (London, Edward Arnold).

Cortazzi, M. (1993) *Narrative analysis* (London, Falmer Press).

Cortazzi, M. & Jin, L. (2001) Large classes in China: 'good' teachers and interaction, in: D. A. Watkins & J. B. Biggs (Eds) *Teaching the Chinese learner: psychological and pedagogical perspectives* (Hong Kong, CERC/University of Hong Kong), 115–134.

Cortazzi, M. & Jin, L. (2002a) Cultures of learning: the social construction of educational identities, in: D. C. S. Li (Ed.) *Discourse in search of members, in honor of Ron Scollon* (Lanham, MD, University Press of America), 49–78.

Cortazzi, M. & Jin, L. (2002b) Seven keys: developing writing for EAL pupils, in: M. Williams (Ed.) *Unlocking writing: a guide for teachers* (London, David Fulton), 116–130.

Cortazzi, M., Rafik-Galea, S. & Jin, L. (1998) Seeing through texts: developing discourse-based materials in teacher education, *English Teacher*, 26(1), 39–68.

Department for Education and Skills (DfES) (2002) *Supporting pupils learning English as an additional language* (rev. edn) (London, DfES).

Egan, K. (1988) *Teaching as storytelling* (London, Routledge).

Ellis, G. & Brewster, J. (1991) *The storytelling handbook, a guide for primary teachers of English* (Harmondsworth, Penguin).

Ellis, R. (1997) *SLA research and language teaching* (Oxford, Oxford University Press).

Flavell, J. H. (1979) Metacognition and cognitive monitoring: a new area of cognitive-developmental inquiry, *American Psychologist*, 34, 906–911.

Forster, E. M. (1927) *Aspects of the novel* (London, Edward Arnold).

Garvie, E. (1990) *Story as vehicle: teaching English to young children* (Clevedon, Multilingual Matters).

Gombert, J. E. (1992) *Metalinguistic development* (New York, Harvester Wheatsheaf).

Grainger, T. (1997) *Traditional storytelling in the primary classroom* (Leamington Spa, Scholastic.

Gravelle, M. (1996) *Supporting bilingual learners in schools* (Stoke-on-Trent, Trentham Books).

Heath, S. B. (1983) *Ways with words: language, life and work in communities and classrooms* (Cambridge, Cambridge University Press).

Hen, L. R. (2005) *The Little Red Hen and the grains of wheat* (London, Mantra Lingua).

Inner London Education Authority (ILEA) (1983) *Stories in the multilingual primary classroom, supporting children's learning of English as a second language* (London, ILEA Learning Resources).

Lauritzen, C. & Jaeger, M. (1997) *Integrating learning through story: the narrative curriculum* (New York, Delmar).

Linde, C. (1993) *Life stories, the creation of coherence* (New York, Oxford University Press).

McCabe, A. & Peterson, C. (1991) *Developing narrative structure* (Hillsdale, NJ, Lawrence Erlbaum).

McDonough, S. (1995) *Strategy and skill in learning a foreign language* (London, Edward Arnold).

Minami, M. (2002) *Culture-specific language styles, the development of oral narrative and literacy* (Clevedon, Multilingual Matters).

Mitchell, R. & Miles, F. (1998) *Second language learning theories* (London, Edward Arnold).

Mohan, B. (1986) *Language and content reading* (New York, Addison-Wesley).

Morgan, J. & Rinvolucri, M. (1983) *Once upon a time, using stories in the language classroom* (Cambridge, Cambridge University Press).

Ochs, E. & Capps, L. (2001) *Living narrative, creating lives in everyday storytelling* (Cambridge, MA, Harvard University Press).

O'Malley, J. M. & Chamot, A. U. (1990) *Learning strategies in second language development* (Cambridge, Cambridge University Press).

Oxford, R. (1990) *Language learning strategies—what every teacher should know* (New York, Newbury House).

Oxford, R. (Ed.) (1996) *Language learning strategies around the world: cross-cultural perspectives* (Manoa, University of Hawaii, Second Language Teaching and Curriculum Center).

Peterson, C. & McCabe, A. (1983) *Developmental psycholinguistics: three ways of looking at a child's narrative* (New York, Plenum Press).

Polkinghorne, D. E. (1988) *Narrative knowing and the human sciences* (New York, State University Press of New York).

Rubin, J. (1987) Learner strategies: theoretical assumptions, research history and typology, in: A. Wenden & J. Rubin (Eds) *Learner strategies in language learning* (New York, Prentice-Hall).

Rubin, J. & Thompson, I. (1982) *How to be a more successful language learner* (Boston, MA, Heinle & Heinle).

Sawyer, R. (1965) *The way of the storyteller* (New York, The Viking Press); original work published 1942.

Scollon, R. & Scollon, S. (1981) *Narrative, Literacy, and face in interethnic communication* (Norwood, NJ, Ablex).

Swain. M. & Lapkin, S. (1983) *Evaluating bilingual education: a Canadian case study* (Clevedon, Multilingual Matters).

Toelken, B. (1969) The 'pretty language' of Yellowman: genre, mode and texture in Navajo Coyote narrative, *Genre*, 2(3), 211–235.

Acquisition of hearing, listening and speech skills by and during key stage 1

Helen Robinshaw

We speak what we hear

'We speak *because* we hear, and we speak *what* we hear' (Flexer, 1999, p. 6; emphasis in original). Normally hearing infants are born with the capability of learning to produce the sounds of any spoken language in the world. Within just a few short months they have narrowed down most of their vocalizations to conform to the sounds of the languages they hear around them and that are beginning to hold meaning for their daily lives (Aslin *et al.*, 1983; Jusczyk, 1999; Kimbrough-Oller *et al.*, 1999). Their vocalizations, and later their speech, reflect what they hear, over and over again, on a daily basis. Children whose hearing is impaired do not acquire spoken language without intervention, both technical and educational; they require assistive devices, such as digital signal processing hearing aids (usually worn behind the ear), or cochlear implants (partly surgically implanted), programmed and used to maximum effect in order to stimulate the auditory-neural connections necessary to begin to make speech sounds meaningful (Robinshaw, 1996a, 1996b). A normally hearing infant begins to use single-word speech at approximately 12 months of age, having begun hearing 16 months earlier in the womb. Children with impaired hearing also require at least one year of good listening experience, through hearing aids and/ or cochlear implants, and informed guidance, before they begin to build up a vocabulary of first words. Spoken language is the result of a great deal of listening experience and of auditory-neural development within the brain.

Whether hearing or hearing impaired, the critical period for developing auditory-neural connections across each level of the cortex is the first three years of life, and the process is not thought to be complete until the child reaches about 15 years of age (Chermak & Musiek, 1997). So even the most attentive and normally hearing children in our classrooms do not have fully developed auditory processing or listening skills. Nor do such young children have the life experiences to 'fill in the gaps' when they do miss information. For example, adults who are learning a foreign language, or who are meeting with someone new at a noisy party, may miss some of the information within the conversation; they manage to 'get by', making assumptions based on previous experience, guessing from the context of what they did understand and using well-developed social skills to request clarification. Young children are less likely to have that pool of experience on which to draw, or the social skills to smooth over the break in communication. It is worth remembering that when the class teacher stops to assess the noise levels in a busy classroom, she or he is doing so from a very different perspective than that of the children who are trying to listen with considerably less well-developed auditory processing mechanisms.

The early years are therefore the most important for stimulating auditory-neural development in developing hearing and listening. They are also the most likely time when otherwise 'normally hearing' children go through periods of fluctuating or reduced hearing levels. These changes often go unobserved by parents and teachers, as they may not cause any discomfort to the child. However, even temporary and moderate hearing loss of this nature will impact on a child's acquisition of speech and language skills.

Understanding changes in hearing sensitivity

In order to recognize and manage the effect of these temporary, although sometimes prolonged, changes in hearing sensitivity, the early years teacher must first understand how different hearing levels impinge on the speech signal. The shaded area known as the 'speech banana' on the graph in Figure 1 represents the sounds of speech in relation to broad categories of hearing sensitivity, from normal hearing to profound hearing impairment.

The numbers on the left of the graph in Figure 1 indicate the intensity or loudness of sound, measured in decibels (dB); 10 dB is quiet and 100 dB is loud. The graph does not go beyond 120 dB as the vibration caused by such loud sounds will be felt

**Audiogram
With Levels of Speech and Hearing Sensitivity**

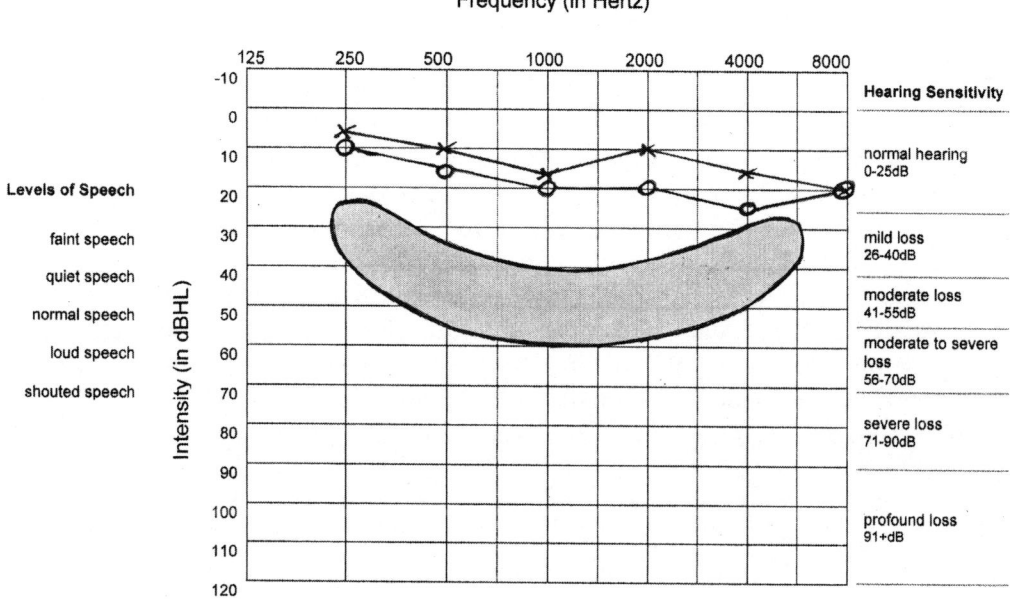

Figure 1.   An audiogram showing levels of speech and hearing sensitivity, and depicting thresholds within the normal range of hearing

by the body even if they are not heard—for example, an aeroplane on take off, a pneumatic drill or a gunshot. People with normal hearing sensitivity may hear sounds as quiet as 0 dB, and certainly sounds as quiet as 20 dB, such as a watch ticking and birds twittering in treetops. The list of speech levels on the left-hand side of the graph give some indication of the loudness of our daily communication at close range, with normal speech levels averaging about 50 dB.

To the right of the graph, the broad categories of hearing sensitivity are indicated. Children with permanent severe or profound hearing impairment are now regularly placed in the inclusive early years classroom. Their success or otherwise owes much to the quality of advice given to the mainstream teacher, diligent maintenance and use of the technology relied upon, and effective home–school liaison. However, the children that are more likely to be taught on a daily basis are children with temporary, fluctuating or even long-term mild to moderate hearing impairment. These temporary, and sometimes repeated losses are typical of children with otitis media (OM). OM is an inflammation of the middle ear, the part of the ear that conducts the sound signal from the visible outer ear to the sensory-neural parts of the inner ear. Otitis media with effusion (OME) is an inflammation of the middle ear where fluid fills the normally air-filled cavity (Hayes & Northern, 1996). When infected, this can cause pain, fever or irritability, otherwise there may be no immediate and obvious signs that a child is suffering a hearing loss.

Frequency of reduced hearing sensitivity in the early years

OM is the most common cause of hearing loss and hearing problems in young children necessitating the most common reason for visits to the doctor in early childhood. Prevalence rates vary according to the methodology and definitions adopted (Davis, 1993; Mauk & Behrens, 1993), but it is likely that some 75% of the children seen by paediatricians have had at least one episode of OME by the age of two years. The incidence may rise to 85% of all school-age children having had at least one episode of OME. By age 3 years, 33% of the population is likely to have had three or more bouts of OME (Flexer, 1999). OME actually alters the structure of the middle ear lining, with recovery occurring more slowly in younger children and with each additional ear infection (Tos *et al.*, 1982). Prevalence rates for otitis media without effusion are far more difficult to establish, given that parents, teachers and even the children themselves may be unaware of its presence. Managing reduced hearing sensitivity as a result of otitis media is therefore a significant feature of early years education.

Implications of reduced hearing sensitivity in the classroom

So what are the implications of conductive loss for children in the classroom? A high percentage of the information delivered to the child from adults and peers in the classroom arrives by speech. Fluctuating hearing loss due to OM presents the child with an intermittent speech signal that is difficult to process. The audiogram in Figure 2 indicates threshold hearing levels (the most quiet sounds detected) typical of a child

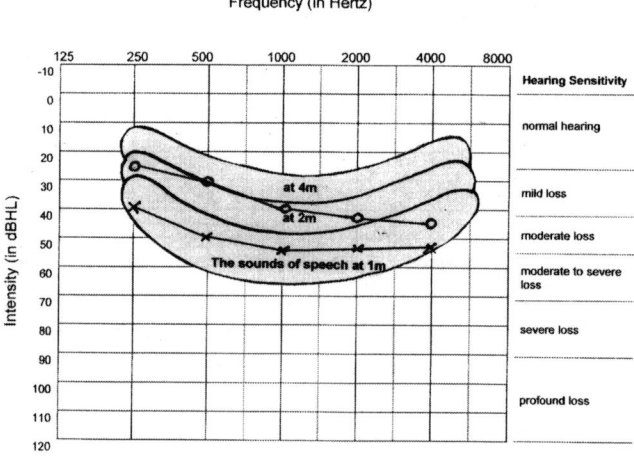

Figure 2.   An audiogram showing a mild to moderate loss in relation to the sounds of speech spoken from a range of distances.

with otitis media or a conductive hearing impairment. These threshold hearing levels are illustrated against a series of '*speech bananas*' that represent the sounds of speech heard at close proximity, a little way from the teacher, and at the back of the class.

The numbers along the base of the graph represent the frequency or pitch of sounds, measured in hertz (Hz). Low-frequency sounds are grouped towards the left of the graph, and high-frequency sounds to the right. It can be thought of as resembling a piano keyboard, ranging from low sounds on the left to high sounds on the right. Middle C on the piano is a mid-pitch tone, with energy at about 1000 Hz.

The 'speech banana' represents the loudness of the sounds of speech when they are produced at, in this example, distances of 1 m, 2 m and 4 m from the child. Some speech sounds, such as the vowels in 'ah', 'aw' and 'oo', are predominantly composed of low frequency energy, with less power in the higher frequencies. Other speech sounds, such as 'sh', 's', 'f' and 't', have most of their energy in the high frequencies and less in the low frequencies. Ideally every child in the classroom needs not only to detect, but also to be able to discriminate differences in speech sounds across the 'speech banana'. The child with normal hearing levels, depicted in Figure 1, can both detect and discriminate between the sounds of speech. The quietest sounds that the child can detect, their 'hearing threshold', are represented by the two lines, where X represents the left ear and O the right ear, and the child can hear any sound that is below these lines. In Figure 1 the whole of the 'speech banana' is well below the child's hearing threshold, so that the child in this example should not experience difficulty in hearing other people's speech or in moderating his/her own speech.

The audiogram in Figure 2 records an example of a child with a mild to moderate hearing impairment such as a child with OM. Again, the two lines represent the quietest sounds that the child can detect, but in this case, the quietest sounds the child can hear, when spoken from just 1 m away, cut through the 'speech banana'. A child with a conductive or middle ear hearing loss will have difficulty in detecting much of the speech signal and struggle to discriminate the phonemes of speech when he or she is very close to the teacher. When just 2 m from the teacher, the child will have difficulty in detecting *any* of the teacher's speech and therefore lack the information to guess the content of the spoken message, even in a very quiet classroom. However, that may be a good-case scenario, for most early years classrooms are a hive of activity, with many occupants at a distance of several feet from the teacher and their movements adding to the overall level of background noise. In practice, children with a mild hearing loss (26–40 dB hearing level) will experience difficulty in detecting faint or distant speech in a busy classroom. They are likely to experience language delays and to read at levels below those of their peers with normal hearing. Children with moderate hearing loss (41–55 dB HL) will understand only loud speech and experience difficulty with group discussions. Their own speech is likely to contain errors, their vocabulary generally limited and presenting deficiencies in language comprehension and usage.

Winskel (in press) critiques recent studies on the effect of OM on children's early language and literacy skills. In her study, a group of children aged between 6 and 8 years, all of whom had an earlier history of repeated episodes of OM, together with a control group, were tested on three different linguistic levels: phonological awareness, semantic knowledge and narration and reading ability. There was a general tendency for children with a history of OM to achieve lower scores on phonological awareness skills of alliteration, rhyme and non-word reading; semantic skills of expressive vocabulary and word definitions; and reading, compared with non-OM children. The role of hearing is therefore critical in developmental and educational processes.

Recognizing fluctuations in hearing sensitivity in the classroom

Children in the early years classrooms are particularly prone to OM. Bouts of OM may last between two weeks and three months, but those children who have it repeatedly may have constant middle ear fluid or negative pressure and therefore reduced hearing levels for much of the school year. Signs that may alert you to the presence of OME include discharge from the outer ear, fever, sickness, disturbed sleep or lack of appetite, irritability or constant pulling or touching of the ear. OM without effusion may, however, be far more difficult to observe. Table 1 lists some suggestions that may aid in classroom observations.

To recap, the acquisition and development of speech, written and reading skills are highly dependent upon hearing and listening. The auditory-neurological foundations for learning to listen are still being developed in the early years. This is also a time when children are more likely to have middle ear infections and reduced hearing sensitivity. A reduction of just a few decibels in hearing levels is enough to impact upon the child's ability to detect and discriminate the sounds of speech. Whether it lasts just a few months or for most of the academic year, the reduction in hearing sensitivity impacts on the child's acquisition of receptive and expressive language skills.

It is, however, not only the children with middle ear problems that are at risk for poor listening and literacy skills in the classroom. Normally hearing children may also be disadvantaged by a poor listening environment. Three factors that influence the quality of the classroom environment for listening are distance, noise and reverberation, therefore teachers also need to have a good grasp of these variables.

Table 1.   Suggested questions to aid observations of reduced hearing sensitivity

Is the child visibly frustrated or anxious?
Does the child respond inconsistently or inappropriately to speech?
Does the child need to visually track conversations?
Does the child tend to turn a particular ear towards a speaker?
Is the child easily distracted and disengaged from classroom activities?
Can the child follow verbal messages without visual clues?
Does the child look to others for confirmation of directions?
Can the child keep up with playground games that are based on verbal arrangements?
Does the child choose to sit near, or turn up the volume control, when using the radio or TV?
How confident is the child at joining in classroom discussions?
Does the child use strategies to request clarification?

Listening to speech in the classroom

Understanding the effects of distance on the ability to hear speech

Sound loses its power or energy as it moves away from its source, so it is an important variable to consider in the classroom. A teacher's speech becomes less audible as it travels further into the classroom. In practice, the signal form the teacher's voice is reduced by 6 dB each time the distance is doubled. For example, teachers typically raise their voice level by about 10 dB to measure 60–65 dB at a distance of 1 m. This means that children sitting at the front of the class hear the teacher at 65 dB, receive approximately 83% of the speech signal and can achieve 95% word recognition (Crandell & Smaldino, 2000; Siebein *et al.*, 2000). Double the distance from the teacher, and children just 2 m away hear the teacher at 59 dB, receive 66% of the speech signal and achieve 71% word recognition. Move to the back of the class and children hear the teacher at 53 dB, receive 55% of the speech signal and achieve just 60% word recognition. Remember that these are children who do not have the maturity of experience to 'fill in the gaps' as adults do. It will not be straightforward for them to guess the 40% of spoken words that are missing.

To consider the same point from a more positive perspective, if one reduces the distance between speaker and child by half the distance, the child will hear the speaker's speech signal 6 dB louder. For example, sit next to the child at just 0.5 m and the child will hear the teacher at 71dB, lean closer to the child and the teacher's voice may be heard at 77 dB. For a child who is known to have a temporary conductive hearing loss, this small piece of knowledge can be the biggest help of all. With appropriate technology, this principal may also be used to maximum effect for the whole of the class, as we consider below.

Understanding the effects of background noise and reverberation on the ability to hear speech

The sound of the speaker's voice also has to compete with the background noise in the classroom. However attentive or disciplined, an early years class brings with it shuffles and sneezes, foot taps and giggles. Add to this heaters and lighting, fans and computers, pupils passing along the corridor or traffic noise outside and the typical classroom noise levels are 60 dB. Since a teacher's comfortable speaking volume is only 60 dB at 1 m, the children have the additional challenge of trying to discriminate the speech signal from the background noise. When teachers raise their voice to project a louder speech signal over the background noise, they in fact reduce the intelligibility of their speech by emphasizing the vowel content at the expense of the consonants. They also increase vocal fatigue and would, in any case, be required to speak at 94 dB (as loud as a motorbike) to achieve the levels of speech required at the back of the room.

Hard walls, high ceilings, glass windows and uncarpeted floors reflect or reverberate environmental and speech sounds, resulting in a further negative impact on speech intelligibility. For the speech signal to remain intelligible, reverberation time should be less than 0.4 seconds, yet the typical classroom averages 0.8 seconds reverberation time. Carpets, curtains, ceiling tiles and soft furnishings or wall displays, all help to reduce reverberation times in the classroom. They are practical suggestions that help, but they do not overcome the competition for attention between the speaker's voice and the effects of distance and general background noise.

Speech- (or signal-) to-noise-ratio (S/N)

The speech-to-noise ratio is the difference between the speaker's voice and the ambient room noise. The greater the S/N, the greater is the speech intelligibility. Children with normal hearing levels generally require an S/N of +6 dB for perception of intelligible speech—in other words, speech needs to be twice as loud as competing sounds. If the average classroom noise is 60 dB and the average teacher speaks at 60–65 dB (measured at 1 m), then the S/N would be between 0 and +5 dB at 1 m from the speaker. As discussed above, this will decline the farther away the speaker is from the listener. In practice, S/Ns range from −7 to +5 dB, that is less than the basic requirement of normally hearing children within the classroom. This begs the question are we really giving our children the maximum opportunity to develop the necessary auditory-neurological foundations for language, reading and learning? In short, the answer is no; however, the technology to help us begin to do so is now widely available and affordable.

Sound field systems

In the same way that sitting close to a child results in a positive S/N of +6 dB, a wireless sound field system can both amplify and bring the teacher's speech to within a short distance of every child within the classroom. The teacher wears a small wireless transmitter with a microphone placed within 6 in (11 cm) of her mouth (microphones can be worn with necklace cords, lapel clips, ear hooks or headbands). The teacher's speech signal is therefore close and clear when it enters the microphone. The speech signal is transmitted across the room by infrared light or radio waves, and therefore bypasses the effects of distance, noise and reverberation. The teacher's voice may also be amplified by a few decibels and reaches the children via a series of speakers that are carefully located around the room, so that wherever a child is seated, he or she is close to the speaker and is therefore close to the speech signal. In effect, the teacher's voice is never more than a few feet from the child. It is not masked by background noise, weakened by distance or distorted by being raised, with the result that even children at the back of the classroom receive a clear speech signal that is +8 dB or better from background noise levels. Installation of sound field systems in early years classrooms is becoming more common as it is the single most effective way of improving the listening environment in the classroom. Table 2 presents some of the other strategies for supporting listening in the classroom.

Table 2.   Strategies for supporting listening in the classroom

Reduce the demands of distance	Use a sound field system
	Move closer to children who may be at risk for reduced hearing
Reducing noise and reverberation	Instal carpets and curtains, acoustic panels and/or floor tiles
	Fit rubber ends to chair and table legs
	Use soft fabrics in wall and table displays
	Turn off unnecessary noise-producing equipment or background music
	Shut windows on noisy streets, or doors on noisy corridors
	Review classroom routines: would a little more structure at certain times support a better listening environment?
Supporting listening in less than ideal acoustic conditions	Keep spoken instructions short and clear
	Move closer to a child, or closer to a needy group of children
	Seat children with limited attention skills away from noise sources
	Alternate heavy listening demands with quiet activities
	Pause frequently to allow for extra processing time and to encourage a response
	Direct the child or class to 'listen closely'
	Rephrase information in several ways
	Use acoustic highlighting—put a slight emphasis on the word or rhythm of the phrase that is new or particularly pertinent
	Write new vocabulary on the board
	Change the task from an open set to a closed set
	Provide a visual clue and then put the stimulus back into hearing
	Repeat or rephrase what other children say in discussions
	Draw attention to changes in topic
	Check for comprehension, ask 'What did you hear?'
	Model clarification strategies for children so they have the skills to say when they have not heard or understood.

Expected listening and speech skills during key stage 1

How children learn to listen

While the first few years of a child's life are most significant in terms of auditory-neural development in the brain, the process of learning to listen continues throughout the early years. It is helpful to think of the development of listening skills as having two dimensions: breadth and depth (Schuyler & Rushmer, 1987). A child not only learns to respond to a wider and wider range of sounds, but he or she also develops increasingly complex levels of response to each sound. This process of learning to listen also occurs over a period of time, so time adds a third dimension to the journey. As the process of learning to listen has been well documented in research with both normally hearing and hearing-impaired infants (Ling, 1976; Northcott, 1978; Pollack, 1985; Estabrooks & Marlowe, 2000), we have reliable indicators as to how much progress children should make given so many months or years of good hearing. The terminology used varies slightly, but the process of learning to listen is typically described in terms of auditory awareness, discrimination, recognition and comprehension.

Auditory awareness means that a child has heard a sound occurring. Infants and young children demonstrate awareness of the presence of sound in a variety of ways. For example, on hearing a knock at the door, they may stop their activity, become quiet or be startled, or they may search for the source of the sound by glancing around. Gradually the child learns to respond to sound, to pay attention to sound and not to respond when there is no sound. *Auditory discrimination* is the next, more complex, level of response; it is the ability to determine whether or not one sound is different from another. A child discriminates between the sounds of speech on the basis of rate, pitch, duration and intensity. As we have seen in the 'speech banana' (above), a child needs to be able to access the whole of the speech range if he or she is to discriminate individual phonemes from one another.

The third level of auditory perceptual development is *auditory recognition*; this is the ability to identify the source of the sound and to attach a spoken message to the object or action it represents. To continue the example, in response to a knock at the door a child may point to the door, thus identifying the source of the sound, or he/she may say 'door', thus labelling the source of the sound. The fourth level, *comprehension*, means that the child has attached meaning to the sounds or words heard. For example, when there is a knock at the door, the child will stop his/her activities to go and open the door, or may say 'hello'. The child understands that there is someone there who needs some attention.

As auditory comprehension of the spoken word (receptive language) is a precursor to speech (expressive language), understanding how children learn to listen is fundamental to our teaching of phonemes in speech, as well as in reading and writing (*we speak what we hear*). How advanced children are in the process of learning to listen to the sounds of speech impacts upon their control and use of phonemes in speech and literacy.

Listening to, and shaping the articulation of, speech sounds

The work of Ling (1976, 1989) has been instrumental in guiding practitioners through the process whereby children listen to and shape the articulation of the sounds of speech. This process follows seven relatively distinct stages, each having both phonetic (articulation) and phonologic (meaningful speech) components. The 'staircase' diagram, in Figure 3, illustrates these broad stages. At the phonetic level, the child is gaining mastery over the basics of talking—listening to speech, articulating speech sounds and auditory feedback skills (i.e. moderating his/her own vocalizations to conform to the sound patterns that he/she hears around them). At the phonologic level, the child is vocalizing and using speech patterns meaningfully, in ways that

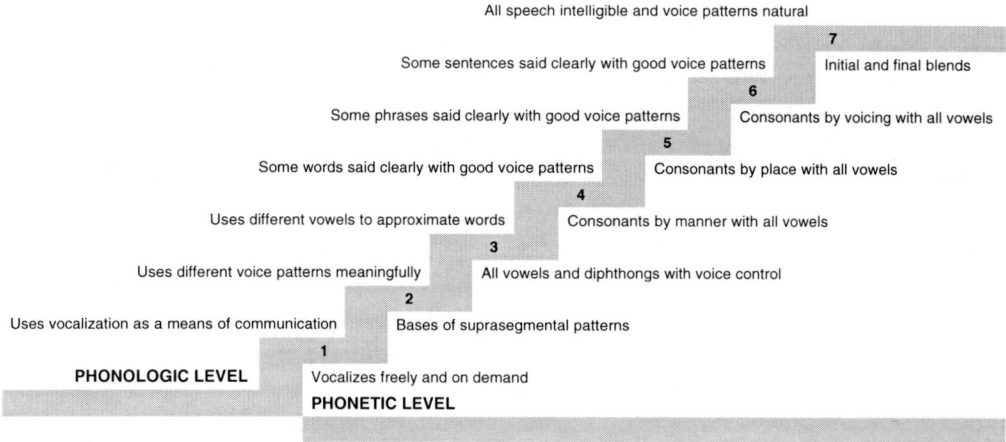

Figure 3.   The seven major stages of speech acquisition, each having both phonetic (motor speech) and phonologic (spoken language) components.
From Ling, D. Speech and the Hearing-Impaired Child: Theory and Practice, AG Bell Assoc. 1976

convey his/her own thoughts and feelings. New phonetic level skills provide children with new voice patterns that can be used to extend their phonologic level skills—their ability to communicate. Similarly, each level of phonetic and phonologic development form the foundation of subsequent speech skill acquisition.

The most basic articulation skill of all is producing an adequate breath stream. When the child can *vocalize freely* and '*on demand*' (with encouragement), the child has enough control to use and vary vocalizations as a means of communication. For example, all babies use loud, demanding cries to tell parents that they need something, and coos and gurgles to indicate when they feel content. This is soon followed by the development of voice control skills—i.e. *the basis of suprasegmental patterns*, or variations in pitch, loudness and duration of sound that help to make communication more meaningful. For example, if you think of a young child beginning to learn nursery rhymes, you may be able to identify the rhyme from the prosodic features of the speech pattern, even though individual words are not distinguishable. As diversity of vocalization comes under control, a range of *vowels and diphthongs* is developed, and these permit the child to make first-word approximations—for example, 'u' with arms stretched indicating 'up', 'Ah oh!' when something has fallen down). The child has to gain control over a wide range of vowels and diphthongs before being in a position to master most of the consonants and blends of speech.

Let us pause in our progress through Ling's stages of speech acquisition, and consider the likely skills of children entering the Foundation stage. Figure 4 illustrates the points at which speech sounds are typically learnt. The beginning of the shaded bar represents the age at which children begin to acquire each speech sound, and the end of the shaded bar represents the age at which most children have mastered the speech sound. For example, while one might reasonably expect a child entering the Foundation stage to have mastered some consonant production and therefore be able to say some phrases clearly and with good voice patterns, there are other consonants that the child will have little experience of producing, and which will impede the intelligibility of their speech. Indeed, full mastery of certain consonants may be unlikely much before the end of key stage 1. If we take a closer look at how consonant production is mastered and the very subtle differences in the dynamics of consonant production, and also recall the impact of classroom acoustics and small variations in hearing levels, then we might have a better insight into how and why some young children find phonemic tasks in the early years trickier than expected.

Stages 4–6 of Ling's model of speech acquisition (Figure 3) focus on consonant production. Ling (1976) details how children use and develop control of different articulators to increase the intelligibility of their speech. Initially, consonants having a different *manner of production* are acquired to release, interrupt and arrest vowels, a stage of development that allows some words to be said clearly. The first column in Table 3 lists the *different manner* or ways in which we use our articulators to make consonants. If we focus on the consonants that we would expect a child to have acquired by entry to the Foundation stage, we will also see that children of this age should have acquired mastery of manner of production. For example, sounds 'p', 'm', 'h' and 'w' are all made through controlling the articulators in a different manner or ways. Plosives, such as 'p' and 'b', are the result of a little burst of energy when two articulators (in this case, the lips) are brought together to restrict the breath stream and then released. Nasals, such as 'm', are made by expelling the breath stream through the nose; fricatives, such as 'h', are made by a turbulent breath stream from vibration of the vocal folds; and the semivowel 'w' is used to interrupt or release vowels.

Once children have mastered control of the different manner of production they have the precursory skills to begin to control the production of consonants made in different *places* of production. For example, the top rows in Table 3 summarize the different places in the mouth where articulators come together to produce different consonants. Plosives are all made by two articulators separating and causing a little explosive burst of air to be released. They can, however, be made by different articulators coming together to cause a restriction in different *places* in the mouth. Plosives 'p' and 'b' are made by bringing the lips together, whereas 't' and 'd' are made by restricting breath when the tip of the tongue touches the alveolar ridge behind the teeth, and 'k' and 'g' are made by lifting the soft palate at the back of the mouth. The difference between each of these pairs of plosives, made in the same manner and place as each other, is simply the difference in timing of the little explosion of air stream— i.e. *voiced/voiceless* distinctions. Mastery of this stage is necessary for some sentences to be said clearly and with good voice patterns. From the chart in Figure 4, we would expect these skills to be well established by entry to key stage 1.

However, if we take a closer look at Figure 4, it is clear that mastery of consonant production continues across key stage 1. If we also map the consonant sounds still to be mastered with the 'speech banana' showing typical classroom noise/distance, then we see how the infant's learning is compounded. The very sounds that a child of this

Table 3. Consonants classified according to manner and place of production and voicing. *Adapted from Ling, D., Speech and the Hearing-Impaired Child: Theory & Practice, A.G. Bell, 1976*

Manner of articulation	Voicing	Place of Articulation						
		Bilabial (Using both lips)	Labiodental (Bottom lip & upper teeth)	Linguadental (Tongue & teeth)	Alveolar (Tongue & jawbone)	Palatal (Tongue & hard palate)	Velar (Back of tongue & soft palate)	Glottal (Using the glottis)
Plosives/stops	Unvoiced	**p** (*pea*)			**t** (*tea*)		**k** (*key*)	
	Voiced	**b** (*bee*)			**d** (*do*)		**g** (*go*)	
Fricatives	Unvoiced	**m** (*whey*)	**f** (*fee*)	θ (*thin*)	**s** (*tea*)	∫ (*she*)		**h** (*hop*)
	Voiced		**v** (*very*)	δ (*that*)	**z** (*zoo*)	**3** (*casual*)		
Nasals	Voiced	**m** (*my*)			**n** (*no*)		η (*ping*)	
Semivowels	Voiced	**w** (*we*)				**j** (*you*)		
Liquids	Voiced				**l** (*look*), **r** (*red*)			
Affricate	Unvoiced					t∫ (*cheap*)		
	Voiced					**d3** (*jeep*)		

Age of Speech Sound Acquisition in Years

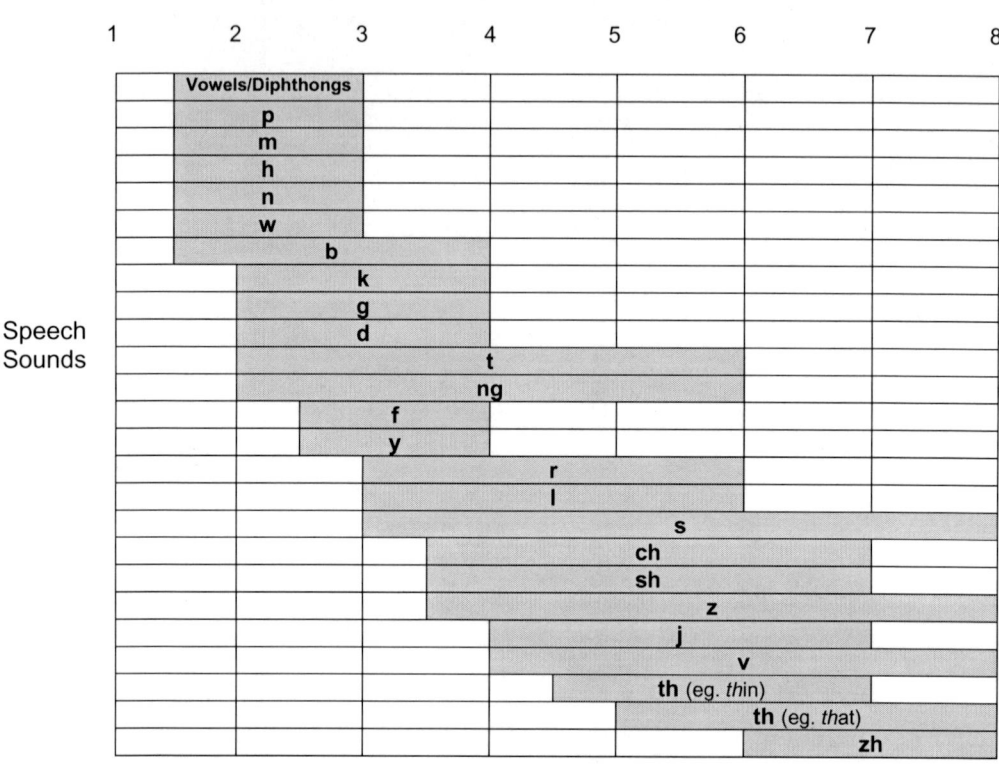

Figure 4.   Age levels at which chidlren with normal hearing typically master consonant production. Adapted from Templin, 1957; Wellman et al., 1931, in Sanders, E., Journal of Speech and Hearing Disorders, 1972 37, 55–63

age is learning to master, learning to articulate, listen to and modify the production of, and use in meaningful speech, are the sounds that he or she is likely to have difficulty hearing in the classroom.

The effectiveness of teaching

> If a child cannot hear speech sounds clearly, or if a child does not have the skills to listen, or if the learning environment does not allow instruction to be heard clearly, any teaching that uses speech as a vehicle for interaction is likely to fall far short of its projected goals. (Flexer, 1999, p. 3)

In monitoring the effectiveness of teaching we are constantly checking whether or not the children in our care have comprehended the intended learning goals. But are we always clear about whether we are assessing the child's progress in receptive language skills or auditory comprehension skills? Early years teachers make the most of action and visual stimuli to support their teaching, but when assessing a child's auditory learning, it is necessary to sit close to, and slightly behind a child, so that the speech-to-noise ratio is at its best and visual cues are kept to a minimum. A teacher who aims to develop the auditory-neural connections taking place in the brain during the early years differentiates between what a child understands with visual clues and what a child understands through listening alone. This does not mean that visual clues are not used in classroom interactions, but that the teacher is aware of the benefits of exposure to the speech pattern on its own, and having used visual clues, will then give the instruction or information again purely verbally and without insisting that the children are looking at her.

Only when teachers fully understand the complexity of skills required to hear and to listen will they really appreciate the dynamics that may cause problems in a child's access to spoken and written language. Think about the following scenarios and then add up the factors in your own classroom, along with the depth of your own knowledge of individual children's hearing sensitivity, and rethink how effective your own projected teaching goals are likely to be.

Is this child hearing?

A boy of 6 is in the class. During the year, he has taken a few days off school due to bad colds or trips to the doctor for earache, but has not been diagnosed as permanently hearing-impaired. Nevertheless, he still has trouble attending to classroom discussions for any length of time; and he wriggles and fidgets. The classroom is large, with a light, airy ceiling and with tall undressed windows. The room borders on to a playground, where the older children in the school have playtimes later than the infants and the lunchtime supervisors trundle the provisions across to the school hall. This child may, or may not, have a fluctuating conductive hearing loss, but he certainly requires the very best from classroom acoustics in order to attend to and hear different phonemes, yet the acoustics of the classroom environment make it virtually impossible for him to access clear speech models and spoken guidance.

Is this child listening?

Here's another little girl, 'bright as a button', but young in the academic year and with such bad asthma that she has missed significant chunks of her Reception year. She drifts listlessly on the perimeter of the class activity, her lack of attention and poor literacy put down to her time off school and her ill-health. No one is worried because she is an intelligent child who grasps concepts quickly and has a lively imagination. It is thought that both her learning and her deteriorating social behaviour will improve with a period of good health. So she continues to sit at a distance from the teacher, by the electric pencil sharpener and other resources frequently accessed by her peers. Her hearing sensitivity levels are within the normal range, but her listening skills and her phonemic recognition are weak. Medical issues and explorations have dominated her early years, resulting in less energy and accessibility to informed knowledge for age-appropriate auditory or educational stimuli. Not only is she a less experienced listener, but her auditory discrimination skills are also constantly undermined by her distance from the speaker and by the competing noise around her. This child requires a focused program to improve her exposure to and experience of listening to the phonemes of speech and in relating this to the backlog of literacy skills she has missed.

Is visual learning supported at the expense of listening?

A young lad with cognitive and language delay sits near the whiteboard as a visiting specialist teacher advised that visual images will be a key method of support for him. Visual images of phonemes are used as props for all the pre-literacy targets within his lively classroom. However, there is very little focus on learning through listening alone, transferring visual learning to auditory skills or facilitating specific developmentally ordered listening skills. Even the highly prized speech trainer uses visual guides to the child's vocal approximations, yet with the same level of supervision, he may well learn to transfer these skills to his auditory learning through a game focused entirely on listening to and discriminating the targeted speech sounds. The latter helps him to develop his own weak auditory feedback loop, in addition to the visual-neural connections of his brain.

Take another example, a girl in key stage 1 who has always spoken in a slightly unusual way. She can initiate and make pertinent contributions to lengthy classroom discussions, with peers across the classroom, but her speech has not become clearer over time. With a little careful listening on the part of the teacher, the speech patterns that are atypical all focus on a range of vowel sounds that would have normally been acquired within a time frame of a couple of months when she was an infant. On enquiry, her mother does remember taking her to the doctor for repeated middle ear problems around that period in infancy. Has she simply not heard these speech sounds and learnt to mimic the lip pattern instead? Referral to a speech and language therapist will clarify if she has the appropriate articulators in place to produce the correct vowel sounds or provide exercise for stimulating more control of the articulators, but in the meantime, a little more focus on learning to hear the differences between what is said and the aspired model may at best suffice, and at worst provide useful evidence. For instance, Ling (1989) details tiny steps in learning to listen to the differences and control the articulation of each speech sound. For the time being, take away the visual cues of the written phoneme or lip pattern and place the child in a position where listening is paramount. Can she imitate the sound, one long-drawn-out sound, then sounds repeated quickly and alternated with a consonant, then alternated with different consonants? It is always worth examining a child's auditory skills first, when concerned about their speech or literacy skills.

Conclusion

Therefore a child's hearing sensitivity and listening ability, and the quality of the learning environment, cannot be ignored or assumed: they must be known and optimized if we are to succeed at our intended teaching goals.

Speech is a fundamentally important instrument for imparting knowledge and for facilitating skill acquisition in the early years classroom. The effectiveness of that spoken word is, however, dependent upon the young child's ability to hear speech, to listen to speech and to process a clear speech signal. A wide range of variables shapes each of these three factors. The early years educator can only begin to manage each of these variables if they first understand the processes by which children learn to listen and speak, and the basics of classroom acoustics. Armed with this knowledge, they are then in a position to use their voice to maximum effect and to foster high levels of auditory comprehension, speech and literacy from each child in their care.

References

Aslin, R. N., Pisoni, D. B. & Jusczyk, R.W. (1983) Auditory development and speech perception in infancy, in: M. M. Haith & J. J. Camas (Eds) *Handbook of child psychology, Vol. 2: Infancy and developmental psychobiology* (New York, Wiley).

Crandell, C. C. & Smaldino, J. J. (2000) Classroom acoustics for children with normal hearing and with hearing impairment, *Language, Speech, and Hearing Services in Schools*, 31, 362–370.

Chermak, G. D. & Musiek, F. E. (1997) *Central auditory processing disorders: new perspectives* (San Diego, CA, Singular).

Davis, A. C. (1993) The prevalence of deafness, in: J. Ballantyne, J. A. M. Martin & M. Martin (Eds) *Deafness* (London, Whurr).

Estabrooks, W. & Marlow, J. (2000) *The baby is listening* (Washington, DC, A. G. Bell).

Flexer, C. (1999) *Facilitating hearing and listening in young children* (San Diego, CA, Singular).

Hayes, D. & Northern, J. L. (1996) *Infants and hearing* (San Diego, CA, Singular).

Jusczyk, P. (1999) How infants begin to extract words from speech, *Trends in Cognitive Sciences*, 3(9), 323–328.

Kimbrough-Oller, D., Eilers, R., Neal, A. & Schwartz, H. (1999) Precursors to speech in infancy: the prediction of speech and language disorders, *Journal of Communication Disorders*, 32, 223–245.

Ling, D. (1976) *Speech and the hearing-impaired child: theory and practice* (Washington, DC, A. G. Bell).

Ling, D. (1989) *Foundations of spoken language for hearing-impaired children* (Washington, DC, A. G. Bell).

Mauk, G. W. & Behrens, T. R. (1993) Historical, political and technological context associated with early identification of hearing loss, *Seminars in Hearing*, 14, 1–17.

Northcott, W. (1978) '*I heard that!' A developmental sequence of listening activities for the young child* (Washington, DC, A. G. Bell).

Pollack, D. (1985) Educational audiology for the limited hearing infant and preschooler (Springfield, IL, Charles C. Thomas).

Robinshaw, H. M. (1996a) The pattern of development from non-communicative behaviour to language by deaf and hearing infants, *British Journal of Audiology*, 30, 177–198.

Robinshaw, H. M. (1996b) Acquisition of speech, pre- and post-cochlear implantation: a longitudinal study of a congenitally deaf infant, *European Journal of Disorders of Communication*, 31, 121–139.

Schuyler, V. & Rushmer, N. (1987) *Parent-infant habituation: a comprehensive approach to working with hearing-impaired infants and toddlers and their families* (Portland, OR, Infant Hearing Resource).

Siebein, G. W., Gold, M. A., Siebein, G. W. & Ermann, M. G. (2000) Ten ways to provide a high-quality acoustical environment in schools, *Language, Speech, and Hearing Services in Schools*, 31, 376–384.

Tos, M., Holm-Jensen, S., Sorensen, C. H. & Morgensen, C. (1982) Spontaneous course and frequency of secretory otitis in 4-year-old children, *Archives of Otolaryngology*, 108, 4–11.

Winskel, H. (in press) The effects of an early history of otitis media on children's language and literacy skill development, *British Journal of Educational Psychology*.

Developing the communicative competence and narrative thinking of four and five year olds in educational settings

Melanie E. Wilde and Rosemary Sage

Introduction

What is meant by communicative competence? Brigman *et al.* (1999) have argued that the competences that contribute to communicative competence, such as being able to listen, attend and follow directions and use cognitive strategies, along with crucial social skills such as working and playing cooperatively with others, as well as forming and maintaining friendships, are essential for school success. Furthermore, they suggest that these capabilities can be taught and integrated systematically into the regular curriculum. It can be suggested that certain other European countries already have these skills at the forefront of the curriculum. Mills *et al.*, cited by Sharp (1998), found in a study looking at the early childhood teaching methods of Hungary, German-speaking Switzerland and Flemish Belgium that these countries share a curricular approach that encourage both the development of motor skills and children's ability to attend by teaching the appropriate use of eye contact, listening and memory skills. Social learning is also developed with a focus on appropriate group behaviour. Importantly, there is a strong emphasis on *spoken* language and numeracy in order to develop children's phonological skills and mathematical understanding of concepts such as size, time, space and quantity.

In England, in recent years, we have faced particular challenges in promoting an understanding of how to foster communicative competence in early years and primary teachers' practice. This can be explained partly due to a lack of awareness among many practitioners of what communicative competence is, and that not only can it be taught but it does not necessarily occur 'naturally'. However, a vital factor has been a change in the pedagogical culture in which children are taught. Children have been exposed to a more formal approach to learning earlier, which has, in practice, emphasised teacher questioning and explanation at the expense of active and interactive learning. Since the mid-1990s, the schooling of children aged under 12 has been subjected to a particularly centralised approach from government in which not only the content of curricula, but the process of how teachers teach literacy and numeracy has been prescribed. They have been obliged to follow specific term-by-term teaching objectives and to provide dedicated time to both literacy and numeracy each day. This more formal approach has been rigorously enforced through the government inspection unit, the Office for Standards in Education (OfStEd), and the resulting 'learning' has been meticulously measured through the use of Standard Assessment Tests (SATs) on all 7 and 11 year olds. The 'achievement' or 'failure' of each school has been published each year in the form of league tables, so creating much pressure to conform and be compliant.

There are two further complications for early years practitioners: firstly, a lack of continuity between recommended curricula; and, secondly, the poor communicative competence of many children on entry to school. The first complication—namely, the hiatus they find between the curriculum guidance issued for three and four year olds (Department for Education and Employment [DfEE], 2000) and the literacy (DfEE, 1998) and numeracy (DfEE, 1999) curricula for children four years and upwards— means teachers of four year olds have had to make a choice between the former's holistic, active and developmental approach, and the latter's target-driven approach dictated by the government's standards agenda. Recent studies suggest that this problem has been resolved by many by allowing the concerns of the literacy and numeracy curricula to take precedence. This suggests that for many children in England the shift between more informal and formal approaches to education in fact begins between the ages of three and four rather than between four and five, which is perhaps earlier than one might expect or desire. It has been noted that teachers of four year olds tend to initiate more of the activities (McInnes, 2002; Sylva *et al.*, 2004) because they feel under pressure to prioritise a more formal approach to literacy and numeracy to appease Year 1 colleagues (Adams *et al.*, 2004). It can be argued that, apart from a decrease in children's opportunities to develop communicative competence, another consequence of a too early adoption of a formal approach to learning is likely to be a negative impact on many children's involvement and engagement (McInnes, 2002), which is likely to lead to an increase in negative behaviour. The second complication that some studies have raised concerns about, namely, children's communicative competence on school entry (Bell, 1991; Boyer, 1992; Lees *et al.*, 2001) compounds the problem. This is because not only is there a pressure to take a more formal approach earlier, but many children are ill-equipped to deal with it. A combination of a lack of opportunity for communication and a lack of communicative competence means it is more difficult for children to make the shift between their informal language to a formal mode in which they are able to use narrative skills to both process large quantities of talk and produce a coherent response and thereby access the curriculum.

In summary, many children come to school with a poor foundation for developing narrative skills and many early years teachers have been able to offer only a limited informal environment conducive for their development. This is further hampered by a limited awareness among practitioners of what communicative competence is and how it can be embedded in the regular curriculum. Therefore, an aim of this research was to investigate how the narrative thinking and ability to communicate of a group of 13 four and five year olds could be developed using an intervention called the Communication Opportunity Group Scheme (COGS).

The intervention

What are the origins of the Communication Opportunity Group Scheme?

The scheme has been developed by Rosemary Sage over a number of years to develop communicative competence and narrative thinking. The scheme emerged as a response to Sage's (1986) conclusion that children who seemed to achieve in some conventional tests, but nonetheless underachieved in literacy, were experiencing diffi-culties for two main reasons. Firstly, they were being asked to perform at a higher level in literacy than they could actually achieve orally. Secondly, they had difficulties in comprehending the gist of a narrative and expressing ideas coherently.

What is the conceptual framework?

In this account of communicative competence, the concepts of narrative thinking and 'message-oriented' communication play key roles. Theorists such as the French philosopher Ricour (Frid *et al.*, 2000) and the psychologist Bruner (1990) view narra-tive as vital to thought. The notion of narrative thinking used pivots on Bruner's view of the role of narrative as the 'organising principle' of our experience, knowledge and transactions within our social worlds. Narrative not only refers to literary text, but includes 'oral narratives which serve to relate personal histories, justifications, plans for the future', as well as the 'living narratives' experienced in family life (Wood, 1998, p. 167). In a social constructivist approach, it can be suggested that narrative thinking and communicative competence are connected because the role of social interaction and cultural practices in shaping human development is stressed (Wood, 1998). Verbal interactions are 'formative', as talking to and with others exposes us to the communicative functions in everyday life. Listening to and telling narratives effectively require the communicator to take account of the listener's perspective and plan a coherent and comprehensible speech sequence (Wood, 1998). Sage (2003) suggests narrative exchanges are particularly helpful for children in terms of reviewing and refining their thinking as verbalising is essential to their mental development.

The notion of 'message-oriented' communication, as 'coined' by Black and Butzkamm, and not to be confused with a term often used in computer science, refers to both 'verbal and non-verbal language used as a means of communication'. Hence, not only words, but gestures, facial expressions' and 'tone of voice' are also significant (Sage 2000a, p.152). It is more clearly understood when contrasted with the notion of 'medium-oriented' communication. The dichotomy between these two levels of communication as explained by Butzkamm (2004) emerged from discourse about teaching methods used in modern language teaching. When communication is 'medium-oriented', the focus of it is solely on the form of language or skill being acquired, which is the only message. Sage (2000a, p. 152) points out that when teaching contexts are geared towards 'skill getting', which tends to involve 'specific exercises and responses', there is also 'an emphasis on the product rather than the process of learning.' In contrast, the focus of 'message-oriented' communication (Butzkamm, 2004) is the actual content of the interactions between individuals, which also provides opportunities for participants to transmit 'real messages' and to satisfy needs that are non-linguistic. Consequently, the opportunity for actual conversation with development in both thinking and relationships becomes more of a possibility. This is in contrast with discourse that is dominated by answering questions that are already known by the teacher.

How is the Communication Opportunity Group Scheme structured to embed narrative thinking and 'message oriented' communication?

The scheme has been designed to enable the narrative development and expression of ideas verbally and non-verbally, over 14 goals. The goals cover a wide range of attainment and can be adapted for children as young as four up to postgraduate level. They are not designed to be applicable to specific ages, but to use the child or adult's zone of 'proximal' (Vygotsky, 1962) or, as Alexander (2000) has suggested, 'potential' development. There are five tasks at each goal level, with four focusing on developing oral language and just one based on writing, which is designed to be at the same narrative level as the verbal task.

Table 1. Progression of ideas embedded in the structure of the COGS framework

Goal	Idea development	Description
1	Record	Produce a range of ideas
2	Recite	Order simple ideas
3	Refer	Compare ideas
4	Replay	Sequence ideas in time
5	Recount	Explain ideas—Why? How?
6	Report	Introduce, discuss describe, evaluate ideas
7	Relate	Setting, events, actions, results, reactions

Source: Sage (2000b).

Table 1 demonstrates narrative thinking development in the first seven goals, which are extended from 8 to 14.

Within sessions, children's or adults' ideas and competences are developed and assessed by facilitating 'message oriented communication' by focusing on four aspects, which are referred to in the scheme as 'clarity', 'content', 'convention' and 'conduct'. These are explained in Table 2.

These notions are also fundamental to the instrument used by the scheme and designed to measure narrative thinking and communicative competence before and after interventions.

How is the scheme taught?

Tasks target specific and core communicative competences. Games are important because they create a relaxed atmosphere and support specific skill development in a circle format that aids interaction. Creativity is valued, and information and opinion gap activities are used to facilitate participants' thinking while allowing them to both contribute ideas and transform them into their own. As such, this mirrors what Frazier (2001) suggests, in a summary of Bruner's ideas—that the gaps in meaning or action during narrative events recruit the listener or reader to fill them.

Table 2. Description of the four aspects of 'message oriented communication'

Aspect	Description
Clarity	Making the message clear with word choices and performance in voice and gesture
Content	Organising the topic of the message according to purpose by making connections within it
Convention	Awareness of protocol, which governs the giving, and receiving of messages in different social contexts as well as in the way words are formed into sentences
Conduct	The image a person presents to others, demonstrated by personal responses in communication exchanges including eye contact and facial expression

A 'tell, show, do and coach approach', which includes systematic sequencing of teaching with review, demonstration, guided practice and corrective, supportive feedback, is used as this has been found to be most effective (Wang *et al.*, 1994). There are five main learning principles (Sage, 2000a):

- interactions are 'message oriented';
- the teacher facilitates 'message oriented' activities, and models communicative competences;
- learning is active;
- activities are learner-centred; and
- empathy and cooperation are encouraged by valuing feelings and mutual support in learning, which encourages self-assessment and peer assessment.

In order to share meanings through talk there is a mixture of group and independent activity, so enacting Vygotsky's (1962) notion that what the child can do in cooperation today he can do alone tomorrow. This is also compatible with a main finding from the Effective Provision of Preschool Education project (Sylva *et al.*, 2004) that the most effective early years settings facilitated opportunities for 'sustained shared thinking' between children and adults as well as between themselves. Furthermore, the researchers found 'sustained shared thinking' happening in practice in association with trained professionals who provided appropriate models and open questioning. The COGS is also compatible with Alexander's (2003) notion of the conditions needed for dialogic teaching. Firstly, the setting is collective, with teacher and pupils addressing learning together. Secondly, it is reciprocal as both listen to each other. Thirdly, it is cumulative, with pupils and teachers building on ideas and chaining them into coherent lines of enquiry. Finally, the atmosphere is supportive and helps all to speak freely, without fear or embarrassment.

How was the scheme adapted for four and five year olds?

In practice, the principles were applied in a number of ways. In general, children were shown how to say things and what was expected of them. They were also facilitated to talk for the majority of the time during a session and were enabled to move around and have fun. An atmosphere conducive with taking risks with ideas was encouraged as activities were open and did not involve 'right' or 'wrong' answers to questions. This encouraged empathy and cooperation as children were encouraged to express what they felt. Effective formative assessment, also highlighted by Sylva *et al.* (2004), was enabled by teachers telling children what they did well, so providing a role model for children to begin the first steps in peer assessment by giving each other positive feedback. At goal 1 level, the 'message oriented' activities were simple and are supported by a myriad of games. To enable children to develop the non-verbal aspect of *clarity* in their interactions they learnt to perform a poem.

Algy met a bear.
The bear met Algy.
The bear was bulgy.
The bulge was Algy!

Although sentence construction is simple, the gist of the narrative has to be inferred—so encouraging children to fill the gap in information in order to successfully understand and communicate the meaning. This provided a meaningful activity with a purpose for the children to practise speaking clearly by making words louder or slower and looking at others to consider whether the audience both heard and thought about what they were saying. The 'activity' designed to develop the idea *content* of children's communication was centred on the learners' own interests and involved constructing a number of sentences about themselves and their families. This final outcome was scaffolded through a number of information and opinion gap games, which supported sentence construction. An example of this included putting objects in a box, which was passed round to music and involved children taking turns to take out an object and say what they liked about it when the music stopped. Furthermore, children were encouraged to bring in their own objects to talk about, which they found very motivating. The activities that focused on *convention*, apart from developing the grammatical convention of developing sentences, within meaningful contexts, with grammatically correct word order, also developed an awareness of such social conventions as asking questions and requesting things politely. The activities that focused on *conduct* involved thinking about the importance of body language, such as using eye contact when communicating and thinking about how the way questions are answered, gives a good or bad impression of the speaker. These are vital skills and are conducive with a further finding of Sylva *et al.* (2004) that effective settings encourage children to rationalise and talk through conflicts.

The study

Research context

The research was a small-scale study that took place in 2001, in the East Midlands, in a co-educational primary school that educated children between the ages of 3 and 11. Many of the children lived on a local authority housing estate where many families had experienced long-term unemployment. There were also a small proportion of children from minority ethnic communities who were either bilingual or in the process of learning English as an additional language.

Sample

The COGS was implemented as part of a Family Numeracy Project, so the 13 children were selected because their parents were prepared to participate in this project. Forty-six per cent of the children were from minority ethnic communities, which was an over-representation when compared with the school's profile.

Why was COGS relevant?

It was important to target the development of narrative thinking and communicative competence in this sample because a report on the school by OfStEd had identified a significant number of three year olds entering the school as having attainment well below norms in language, literacy and social development. The sample was split into two groups, and the youngest group of four year olds had a range of communication challenges that included two children learning English as an additional language and one child each with hyperlexia, dysfluency, dyslalia and mild learning difficulties. In the older group of four and five year olds, three pupils were learning English as an additional language and five lacked confidence to express themselves in class. The oldest child, who was summer born and was in the school year above the children in his group, had not adjusted well to a more formal, educational setting because he 'still wanted to play'.

Research questions and research design

Two questions were posed:

- What progress was made by the children in narrative thinking and communicative competence during the course of the research, using before and after teaching measures?
- To what extent was any progress likely to be due to the COGS?

To pursue the research questions, the aim had been to replicate previous COGS studies (Sage, 2000c). Quantitative data were to be collected in a strong quasi-scientific design, which employed pre and post teaching measures and also included a control group, plus qualitative evidence from the children, staff and parents. In the event, this was not possible and a weak quasi-scientific design without controls was used with tests before and after teaching. However, qualitative data were strengthened by non-participant observation of the children in their classes after the project had finished. An action research approach was also taken, as a primary objective was to improve participant abilities. Planning, teaching and researching the COGS simultaneously was a benefit as it enabled the researcher to have first-hand insights into the process. Plans were co-constructed between the lead teacher and the researcher, then reflected on and evaluated after each session before deciding on the next steps.

How was the scheme organised?

The children, as already mentioned, were split into two separate teaching groups and participated in the COGS intervention for half an hour twice a week. The two Sage Assessment of Language and Thinking (SALT) tests (Sage, 2000b), which consist of children answering a range of questions in an interview situation and a story re-telling task, were used to establish narrative thinking and communication levels. Although these levels were diverse, goal 1 was appropriate to pursue with both the younger four year olds and the older four and five year olds, but the activities were differentiated according to need. The researcher and course leader, who were both COGS trained, team taught, planned and facilitated sessions with a ratio of 2:5 (younger group) and of 1:4 (older group) adults to children.

How was narrative thinking and communicative competence measured?

The instruments used to measure the level of children's narrative thinking before and after the intervention were the two aforementioned SALT tests. In the interview test, children answer a range of questions and their responses are recorded verbatim and assessed according to the following criteria:

- Content—ideas contained in what is said.
- Convention—grammar of what is said.
- Clarity of speech.
- Conduct in terms of body language.

Judgement about the clarity and conduct aspects of the test is necessarily more subjective, as it involves the assessor making certain judgements during the administration of the task and is based on unretainable evidence. In the narrative retell test, children retell a story, which is again recorded verbatim and analysed according to the number of:

- Correct propositions expressed.
- Propositions in correct order.
- Correct propositions with correct syntax.
- Correct propositions with intact information.

Results from the tests

In response to the first research question, the results of an analysis of these test results, using a one-tailed *t*-test, indicate that the overall levels of the group's improvement in narrative thinking and communicative competence was statistically significant among the sample as a whole. As can be seen in Table 3, the score increase varies from test to test. In the interview test when 'content' and 'convention' scores are combined and compared with 'clarity' and 'conduct', there is greater progress in the former. Furthermore, when a *t*-test is applied to these tests separately, progress in 'content' and 'convention' remains statistically significant, but progress in 'clarity' and 'conduct' does not. This may be due to how the instrument was applied as the assessor was relatively inexperienced, especially as qualitative data indicated perceptible improvements in both the clarity of children's speech and their conduct during interactions. The large increase in achievement on the retell test can be explained because a few did not respond at all on the pre-intervention test, which changed considerably on the post-intervention test.

Table 3.   Group 1 and group 2 SALT scores before and after the COGS intervention

Test		Test mean totals	Raw score increase	% increase
Total scores SALT narrative retell	Before	6.625		
	After	14.625	8	120.7
Total scores SALT interview	Before	54		
	After	68.25	14.25	26.3
Content and convention scores only from SALT interview	Before	20		
	After	30.2	10.2	51
Clarity and conduct scores only from SALT interview	Before	34.66		
	After	38.1	3.44	10

Observation method

Due to lack of control groups, the claim that these successful results are solely due to participation in the COGS is limited. Other factors to consider are the possible beneficial effects on children's competences of participating in extra small-group numeracy lessons, parent involvement in numeracy lessons, extra attention at home and also engagement in their ordinary educational settings. As part of the research also involved observing children in these settings, discussion will centre on making a case for why the children's apparent progress in narrative thinking and communicative competence was more likely to have developed as a result of participating in the COGS rather than in their usual learning environments. With this in mind, one of the aims of observing children in their classes was to get a sense of any key differences between the approach to learning children experienced during the COGS and their experience during everyday lessons, which might suggest that the development of narrative thinking and communicative competence was more likely in one context than the other. The key learning principles and teaching foci embedded in the COGS were extrapolated and then looked for during the classroom observations. The project children were observed in their three settings over a period of four school days, which although limited in time is still perhaps more time than an OfStEd inspector would spend. The evidence collected from this protocol is presented in Table 4.

Findings from observation

Compared with the COGS, the other settings showed little evidence of providing children with opportunities for the 'sustained shared thinking' seen as so important by Sylva *et al.* (2004). In all settings there was a lack of systematic focus on 'message orientated communication'. In the setting for the youngest four year olds, a number of opportunities for structured play and adult led activities were observed. However, structured play extended by adult intervention, which is a hallmark of excellent

Table 4. Comparing learning opportunities promoted in the COGS sessions with similar examples observed in ordinary lessons

Aspect of 'message orientated communication'	Setting			
	COGS group	Class of five year olds and oldest four year olds (autumn born)	Class of four year olds (spring born)	Class of youngest four year olds (summer born)
Clarity				
• Coached in voice techniques	Part of teaching objectives	Incidental	Incidental	Incidental
• Speak and present in front of peers	Embedded in activities for all children	Done by a few children during the literacy plenary	Done by a few children during the literacy plenary	Done by a number of children during large circle time
Content				
• Verbalise and develop a number of ideas	Embedded in activities for all children	Very rarely observed in whole class situations. Done by one child during a practical maths session. More opportunities for small groups of children working with classroom assistant	Very rarely observed in whole class situations. Done by whole class during an assembly	Children's ideas elicited more during the nursery teacher's small group time, and when children could work individually with an adult
• Think laterally and creatively	Embedded in activities for all children	Observed once during a practical mathematics session	Observed during an assembly	Observed during structured play
Convention				
• Activities grounded in children's interests	Embedded in activities for all children	Children's own interests incidental	Children's own interests incidental	Structured play and circle time tended to be embedded in children's own interests
• Structured activities that encourage children to actively listen to and interact with peers	Embedded in activities for all children	Part of the plenary encouraged children to listen to peers, but did not involve interaction	Part of the plenary and assembly encouraged children to listen to peers, but did not involve interaction	Structured play enabled children to interact with each other but due to the high number of children to adults these interactions were rarely structured

Table 4.   (Continued)

Aspect of 'message orientated communication'	Setting			
	COGS group	Class of five year olds and oldest four year olds (autumn born)	Class of four year olds (spring born)	Class of youngest four year olds (summer born)
• Ask questions of their peers and the teacher	Some activities were structured to scaffold children's questioning	No questions, except procedural ones were observed	No questions, except procedural ones were observed	No questions, except procedural ones were observed
• Evaluate their peers' performances and ideas	Sensitively elicited by the teacher	Not observed	Not observed	Not observed
Conduct				
• Made aware of the importance of eye contact, facial expression and gesture	Embedded in the purpose of some of the activities	Incidental	Incidental	Incidental
• Encouraged to make their message interesting to the listener	Embedded in the purpose of some of the activities	Not observed	Not observed	Not observed
• Answer questions from their teacher	Questions open, all children to answer	Question tended to be closed and only some children answered during the whole class part of the lesson	Question tended to be closed and only some children answered during the whole class part of the lesson	Some children answered their teacher during small group time.
• Answer questions from their peers	Activities scaffolded children to answer questions from their peers	Observed during informal choosing time.	Observed during independent, small group work	Children interacted informally, during play activities, but were not observed to formulate or answer each other's questions

practice (Sylva *et al.*, 2004), was not observed—nor was the facilitation of small group work. In the foundation stage 2 setting and, to an even greater extent, in the setting for the oldest four year olds, 'sustained shared thinking' was not observed. This, it can be argued, was due to the overly formal nature of the teaching, which provided few opportunities for the more informal interactions between children and between children and adults, which children need to build both their confidence and skills. The strength of the COGS as an intervention for these children can be seen as a 'half-way house' between the informality of home and overly formal modes of communication. Importantly, COGS provided them with many opportunities to co-construct their understanding of what is happening and what is being learnt with both peers and teachers, and it can therefore be argued that it was this context that was more likely to be instrumental in the development of narrative thinking and communicative competence. Therefore, a further finding in the study was that the progress that was made by the children was more likely to be due to the conditions provided by the scheme than the children's everyday educational settings.

Final reflection

The pivotal argument that has been explored is that for narrative thinking and communicative competence to develop effectively, certain conditions need to be created. There is evidence to suggest that both teachers and pupils need more knowledge and skills in narrative thinking and communicative competence to enhance the teaching and learning process. This provides a strong rationale for a less formal, prescriptive approach to the curriculum in England for five to seven year olds, especially as this appears to skew how teachers feel how four year olds should be taught in preparation for the next stage in their schooling. Therefore, a key question is to consider how the learning principles and teaching foci in the COGS can make the transition between being a useful intervention to being embedded in ordinary lessons. This is feasible because although the scheme took place in small groups in this study, there is evidence of its success in larger classes (Sage *et al.*, 2004) using the narrative framework to differentiate activities for groups of children, which could contribute to enabling a better balance between child initiated and adult initiated activities (Sylva *et al.*, 2004). This possibility is perhaps only likely if a gentler shift between informal and formal learning can be achieved. However, there are concerns about the transition between the teaching of four year olds and that of five year olds being voiced; for example, a recent study by Sanders *et al.* (2005) suggests that more play-based activities should be extended to five year olds in the first year of compulsory schooling.

This—along with other signs that the suggestion that practitioners should take a more creative approach to the curriculum, espoused in the government document *Excellence and enjoyment: a strategy for primary schools* (DfEE, 2003), is starting to filter into schools—perhaps signifies that the pendulum is now swinging in England against excessive formality in the schooling of children in their early years. This in turn raises the question of whether primary teachers are able to take on the role of managing a more interactive classroom practice. Therefore, with a changing philosophy, a new approach to educating teachers is also needed.

References

Adams, S., Alexander, E., Drummond, M. J. & Moyles, J. (2004) *Inside the foundation stage: recreating the reception year* (London, ATL).

Alexander, R. (2000) *Culture and pedagogy: international comparisons in primary education* (Oxford, Blackwell).

Alexander, R. (2003) Talk in teaching and learning: international perspectives. *New Perspectives on Spoken English: discussion papers* (London, QCA).

Bell, N. (1991) *Visualising and verbalizing* (rev. edn) (Paso Robles, CA, Academy of Reading Publications).

Boyer, E. L. (1992) *Read to learn: a mandate for the nation* (Princeton, NJ, The Carnegie Foundation for the Advancement of Teaching).

Brigman, G., Lane, D. & Switzer, D. (1999) Teaching children school success skills, *The Journal of Educational Research,* 92(6), 323–329.

Bruner, J. S. (1990) *Acts of meaning* (Cambridge, MA, Harvard University Press).

Butzkamm, W. (2004) Medium-oriented and message oriented communication, in: M. Byram (Ed.) *Routledge encylopedia of language teaching and learning* (London. Routledge).

Department for Education and Employment (1998) *Framework for teaching: national literacy strategy* (London, QCA).

Department for Education and Employment (1999) *Framework for teaching mathematics from reception to year 6* (London, QCA).

Department for Education and Employment (2000) *Curriculum guidance for the foundation stage* (London, QCA).

Department for Education and Skills (2003) *Excellence and enjoyment: a strategy for primary schools* (London, QCA).

Frazier, I. (2001) Narrative modes of thinking applied to piano pedagogy, *Piano Pedagogy Forum,* 4(2). Available online at: www.music.sc.edu/ea/keyboard/PPF/4.2/4.2.PPFpp.html (accessed 29 July 2005).

Frid, I. Ohlen, J. & Bergbom, I. (2000) On the use of narratives in nursing research, *Journal of Advanced Nursing,* 32(3), 695–703. Available online at: www.ingentaconnect.com/content/bsc/jan/2000/00000032/00000003/art01530 (accessed 29 July 2005).

Lees, J., Smithies, G. & Chambers, C (2001) Let's talk: a community-based language promotion project for Sure Start, paper presented at the *RCSLT National Conference: Sharing Communication,* Birmingham, April.

McInnes, K. (2002) What are the educational experiences of 4-year olds! A comparative study of 4 year olds in nursery and reception, *Early Years,* 22(2), 119–127.

Sage, R. (1986) *A question of language disorder.* (Sheffield, MRC Trent).

Sage, R. (2000a). *Class talk: effective classroom communication* (Stafford, Network Educational Press).

Sage, R. (2000b) *COGS: Communication Opportunity Group Scheme* (Leicester, University of Leicester).

Sage, R. (2000c) *'Successful students'. A project to teach communication skills and support learning* (Leicester, University of Leicester).

Sage, R (2003) *Lend us your ears: listen and learn* (Stafford, Network Educational Press).

Sage, R., Rogers, J. & Cwenar, S. (2004) *The Dialogue, Innovation, Achievement and Learning (DIAL) project. Research in England and Japan* (report 1) (Leicester, University of Leicester).

Sanders, D., White, G., Burge, B., Sharp, C., Eames, A., McEune, R. & Grayson, H. (2005) A study of the transition from the foundation stage to key stage 1. *DfES Research Report SSU/2005/FR/013* (London, DfES).

Sharp, C. (1998) *Age of starting school and the early years curriculum: a select annotated bibliography* (NFER) Available online at: www.nfer.ac.uk/nfer/index.cfm?B9AB5F57-955C-35B3-1EC7-9940B40286F0 (accessed 29 July 2005).

Sylva, K., Melhuish, E., Sammons, P., Siraj-Blatchford, I. & Taggart, B. (2004) *Effective provision of pre-school education (EPPE) project: final report* (London, DfES). Available online at: http://www.dfes.gov.uk/research/data/uploadfiles/SSU_SF_2004_01.pdf (accessed 29 July 2005).

Vygotsky, L. S. (1962) *Thought and language* (Cambridge, MA, MIT Press).

Wang, M. C., Haertel, G. D. & Walberg, H. J. (1994) What helps students learn?, *Educational Leadership*, 51(4), 74–79.

Wood, D. (1998) *How children think and learn* (Oxford, Blackwell).

Oracy: social facets of language learning

Olivia N. Saracho and Bernard Spodek

> By the time they come to school, all normal children can show skill as thinkers and language users to a degree which must compel our respect ... (Margaret Donaldson, 1978, p. 127)

In recent years, there has been an increased concern for language development and language learning on the part of researchers and educators. This concern is related to the cultural context in which language is learned and developed, as well as to the relationship of language development to cognitive development. The concern has been manifest in different ways in different countries.

The UK has focused its educational concerns on the development of communicative expression in relation to intellectual abilities. This has led to the integration of speaking and listening skills, referred to as *oracy* in the National Curriculum. The concept of oracy involves both the discourse activities and a variety of speech events. The importance of talk and narrative in the children's self-expression is included in the concept of oracy and is important in promoting children's learning and intellectual development (Hewitt & Inghilleri, 1993). Wilkinson (1970) described oracy as the *verbalization of experience*. He defined it as:

'Verbalization' is what other people write and what other people say. And we as readers read what they write and we as listeners listen to what they are speaking. This definition seems to include something essential, expressed fairly simply. It seems to me that one cannot subtract any more words from it. (p. 71)

Wilkinson (1970) argued that, as part of a verbalization experience, oracy is integrated with listening, writing, literacy and other subject areas. The verbalization of experiences can occur in different areas which each require specific language. For example, as children engage in group discussions of a story they may discuss the plot and characters. They may then write about it. Then, they share what they have written with the group. Children may also discuss poems, share them and read them to each other. Children will use different types of language with each situation. Wilkinson (1970) also points out that people change the way they talk to each other based on the situation, often without being aware of this change. For example, one speaks to an employer one way and to a spouse in a different way. He believed that the spoken language should be used in more group situations, so that it becomes a living language. Wilkins also extended his concept of oracy to include literacy.

In the USA, although the researchers are interested in oral discourse, they do not label it oracy. Researchers in the USA have conducted studies in the classroom to include oral group work, discussion, and other forms of classroom talk. With young children, oral language takes place mainly in a social context. Children use language as a tool for socializing. The purpose of this paper is to review studies on the children's oral language development within a social context.

Language development

Children first construct their representations of the sounds of language based on the speech they hear (Hoff, 2005). Infants hear a variety of sounds and sights and perceive tactical sensations from adults who care for them. First, children perceive these to be 'a buzzing, blooming confusion', but they gradually acquire form and definition (Handel, 2005). Children learn language, and make the relationship between sounds and words, and from words to utterances, to larger discursive constructions (Baquedano-López, 2003). The sounds they hear have meanings attached to them. These sounds—the speech they hear—become incorporated into their own language.

Children will differ in the language they create based on the nature of the speech they hear. For example, children who hear English spoken around them acquire English as their language, while children who hear another language will acquire that language (Hoff, 2005). Studies indicate that children who are exposed to a variety of languages develop phonological systems of those languages (Hoff, 2005). As children learn the language of their communities, they establish and test hypotheses about language rules and process whatever linguistic feedback they receive. Children learn the symbolic systems of the reality in their world that is shared by members of their cultural group. They develop the ability to use important symbols as they become part of the cultural group's social life.

Each cultural group integrates a set of categories within its language to structure meaning in relation to its social world. For example, Eskimos have several terms for snow, with each definition referring to a specific kind of the snow. Our society merely distinguishes between 'snow' and 'other forms of precipitation'. Thus, Eskimo children learn to think of snow in a more complicated mode than do children in our society (Handel, 2005).

Regardless of their cultural group, children use their language to express, convey, mediate and manage actions, emotions and knowledge. Their language is inextricably connected to their local, social, emotional and cognitive experiences (Baquedano-López, 2003), which requires them to use thinking skills. Naudé *et al.* (2003b) recommend the use of both print and non-print experiences to develop the children's thinking skills. In the language experiences, children can be presented with literacy objects that can develop the preschooler children's vocabulary, comprehension, speech sound awareness and listening skills.

Often, children learn language through incidental learning situations that may not be seen as didactic yet provides learning opportunities. Saracho and Spodek (1993) support the importance of incidental learning and recommend that children be provided with multiple opportunities to experience language to understand the function and power of language in different contexts. They state, 'It requires learning not only linguistic features and knowledge of the language, but simultaneously learning the social knowledge needed to participate effectively in the new discourse community' (p. 6).

During their socialization process, children develop knowledge of their own language, including both vocabulary and a set of rules to generate sentences that are appropriate in their social situation. At an early age, children establish these rules and use them to create sentences that they have never heard, sometimes over-generalizing the rules. For example, young children may say, 'I throwed the ball', a sentence that they never have heard. Somehow they have learned the rule about adding '-ed' to a verb to make it past tense, even if they are applying the rule incorrectly in this situation (Handel, 2005). The young children's acquisition of language extends their abilities to regenerate roles and relationships even to use available tools and technologies that develop appropriate written accounts (Chomsky, 1965). According to Genishi (1988):

> In or out of the classroom, language gives our thoughts substance, as we talk to ourselves, language helps us plan, understand what happens to us, and form our ideas. Language is part of the individual's uniquely human ways of knowing, feeling, and being. As we use language with others, it shapes our identities and social lives. The way our own language sounds to listeners leads them to make judgments about where we are from, what our occupation is, how friendly or clever we are. (p. 78)

It is important that children construct meaning in their language learning. When children engage in conversations and interact with their peers, they are required to pay attention and respond to others, which is similar to the learning process. According to McKeown and Beck (2005), children will succeed in that learning when they experience more than mere exposure to information. They need to process incoming information, join all the parts of information, and integrate the new information with their prior knowledge. Specifically, Hart and Risley's (1995, 1999, 2003) longitudinal study illustrates the learning process about language learning.

In their first study, Hart and Risley (1995) studied children learning to talk, recording the children's exposure to and involvement in language beginning with their first words. They found that the children's exposure to the number of words made a significant difference in their language development at age 3 years and was significant at age 9 in their literacy development. When Hart and Risley (1999) examined their data with greater depth, they found significance when the children were exposed to the language, as well as when they engaged in dialogue through the conversational interaction of listening to and responding to each other. In addition, reciprocal conversational interactions between parents and children influenced the children's verbal and cognitive competence. They inferred that, in conversations, children were required to provide a response with an utterance that made it possible for the conversation to continue. When children engage in conversations, they are motivated to respond and practice appropriate responses to a specific situation.

Hart and Risley (1999) observed that children who successfully began speaking were able to make themselves understood and communicate their needs and wants, and so forth. The children learned to interpret what others said, respond to others and take turns talking during the conversation. The concept of transforming turn-taking into conversation is essential to the children's learning. According to Hart and Risley (2003), language experiences in the early years should include knowledge or skill, as well as a complete general approach to experience that is developmentally appropriate. For example, cognitive experiences are sequential. Infants develop language habits when they search, become aware and integrate new and more complex experiences, when they use their schemas to categorize and think about their experiences. The adults' one-to-one interactions with infants have pervasive language effects. As children become independent and are able to speak for themselves, they are able to notice and select opportunities for language experiences.

According to Bus *et al.* (2007), language experiences need to promote oral communication with discussions that include a complex vocabulary and grammar. Children need to come into contact with language situations where they learn about subordinate clauses, quotes that are literally spoken between two characters, passive constructions, unknown expressions and unfamiliar idioms. McKeown and Beck (2005) add that children need more than language exposure. They need to learn how to respond by explaining, elaborating and relating their ideas in a dialogue. This is an important factor to help children to make sense of decontextualized language. Understanding decontextualized language is the primary source for learning (McKeown & Beck, 2005). Children can best make sense of decontextualized learning in a natural context such as during social play.

Language-related play

Children can learn language best in natural settings, such as during their socio-dramatic play. When children play, they acquire a better understanding of (1) themselves and others, (2) their knowledge of the physical world and (3) how to communicate with peers and adults. Play promotes the children's language development as they interact with others, label, organize a sequence of play events, negotiate and engage in 'pretend talk', which is a form of 'non-immediate talk' that fosters discourse. Toohey (2000) 'considered how social relations among learners, or among learners and those who judge their performances, might affect judgments of cognition, social adjustment or learning styles' (p.7). The results indicated that learning English was influenced by the child's social relations. During play, children become aware of different points of view (e.g. their own and others), which helps them to learn to communicate with peers and adults. They also become more knowledgeable of their physical world as they assume a variety of roles and transform objects to convey their ideas and feelings about their social world. For example, children may act out a restaurant experience by pretending to order from a menu. They plan play procedures through discussions and explicitly negotiating rules, relationships and roles (e.g. you be the baby and I'll be the mother).

Children learn about their social world through both their eyes and speech (Vygotsky, 1978). Katz (2001) described the children's language development during play. She observed that in a play context children interacted with each other and with significant others, participated in labeling, organized a series of play events in sequence, and negotiated procedures through conversation. The teachers' support of sociodramatic play fosters children's language development (McGee, 2003). This is supported by a study of three and four year olds during spontaneous play with a telephone (Guillen, 2002). Children selected appropriate speech genres and discourses as well as stimulated their use of technological literacies. This is the focus of the children's learning in relation to their activities, actions and discourses of their social reality (Baquedano-López, 2003).

In play children use 'pretend talk'. According to DeZutter (2007), at the beginning, the path for a play episode is unpredictable as children participate in ongoing explicit and implicit negotiations for joint meaningful play. This engagement is a critical part of play's benefit for literacy development. DeZutter (2007) shares a play episode that she adapted from Sawyer (1997). In the block area three preschool children (Muhammed, Corinna, Artie) are playing with toy jungle animals and the following dialogue occurs (The numbers in parentheses indicate the children's turn in the conversation):

(1) Corinna:		Guess what? At the museum, someone is, uh, robbing us! And they wanta take us to jail!
(2) Muhammed:		That very bad. How do you know a hippo is robbing you?
(3) Artie:		Uh, you saw them?
(4) Corinna:		Yes, I saw him last night, he was robbing my owner. And I can't get him [*inaudible*] my favourite food, mashed, mashed bugs.
(5) Artie:		[*inaudible*] to get out of here. The [*inaudible*] took it out. And I can get out, BOOM. I blasted open the door.
(6) Corinna:		Artie, you killed, you, uh, got killed, alright?
(7) Artie:		And, we found him, OK? He wasn't dead, he just in jail.
(8) Corinna:		OK.

(9) Artie:	[*inaudible*] where were you?
(10) Corinna:	I'm in jail.
(11) Artie:	OK! Boom. And here's the bad guys coming in [*inaudible*]
(12) Corinna:	I wanna thank you
(13) Artie:	Let's pretend when you turned around, the bad guys were [*inaudible*] in back of you, OK?
(14) Corinna:	I love you for saving me!
	(adapted by DeZutter, 2007, from Sawyer, 1997, pp. 160–161)

In this episode, children needed to select from different options. For example, in the second turn, Muhammed could have added more information about going to jail to elaborate on Corinna's jail idea. He could also have introduced a new thought about the museum.

These options would allow the play episode to continue on its course. On the other hand, if Muhammed had started talking about birthday parties, monster trucks, or other unrelated topics, the conversation may have deteriorated. Muhammed's conversation needed to conform to the topic that he and his friends were developing in their play world (Griffin, 1984; Curran, 1999; DeZutter, 2007). Also after Muhammed contributed to the conversation, his friends had several choices to make, including accepting his idea of a hippo to be the robber (which is what they did), modifying it, ignoring it or definitely rejecting it (Verba, 1993; Sawyer, 1997; DeZutter, 2007). His friends' responses determined his contribution to the play situation, just as his response to Corinna determined the way her contribution in the first turn influenced the sequence of their play. Naturally, Muhammed's friends also had the same limitations in introducing *non sequiturs*, if they expected to sustain the continuity of play. Their reactions to his hippo idea were also restricted to the previous events. Muhammed and his friends engaged in a proposal and response process when they negotiated in the development of their play world. Negotiation is a fundamental part of the children's play experience; it occurs spontaneously. The children may be acting out a familiar story, which is improvised without a developed script. They may assume roles in a familiar story such as from a popular television program, they have the freedom to deviate and embellish the plot (Corsaro, 1992; Sawyer, 1997).

When children plan their play event, they also negotiate what they will play, how they will play, what roles they will play, what available materials in the block area will represent the door and the jail. Children improvise in their play world, which becomes a shared meaning-making activity. They collaborate in acting out a story that is meaningful to them, while simultaneously they use their play experience to make sense of the real world (Corsaro, 1985; Paley, 2004; Löhfdahl, 2005). Children generate action plans, which become blueprints on how to relate to and sequence actions and events. Popular action plans include family situations as well as plans to treat, cure and guard against threats (Garvey, 1990). This process helps children learn how to be part of a literate community, which is a social group whose members join in their meaning making of their experiences when they share different forms of representation (DeZutter, 2007).

Children enjoy participating in pretend play where they interpret experiences symbolically. Pretend play is an important activity; because it allows children to act out their plans, assume different roles, and modify objects to communicate their ideas and feelings about their social world (Garvey, 1990). When children act out roles, they assume these identities in their play. Their roles may be functional, family orientated or stereotypes of characters. *Functional roles* are those that are essential for a particular theme; for example, an automobile trip requires passengers and a driver. *Family-oriented roles* may include a mother, father and baby. *Stereotyped character roles* relate to the children's larger culture, which may include a nurse, storybook or TV fictional characters like He-Man. These roles are more predictable and limited than those roles related to direct experiences like family life (Garvey, 1990).

When adults, including teachers, support socio-dramatic play, they are able to enhance language development (McGee, 2003). Tabors *et al.* (2001) believe that children acquire some level of meaning of a new word with just a single exposure to it. They tested this belief and observed the frequency children use 'rare words' during toy play, mealtime and storybook reading. They found that children learned new words in all three contexts. Children generated meaning from the new words by depending on (a) the *physical context* to refer to an action or object; (b) their *prior knowledge* to refer to an interpretation of new vocabulary; (c) the *social context* to refer to social norms; and (d) the verbal explanation for *semantic support*. The children's exposure to different new or rare words positively related to later measures of language knowledge.

Contemporary studies provide support that children gain meaning within their socio-cultural context in which they acquire language, including their interactions with family members and their peers. Dickinson and Tabors (2001) showed that the language between mothers and children during play influenced their later literacy. During play with mothers, children may used utterances that are not related to the setting of the discourse. Children also engaged in pretend talk with parents. Katz (2001) found considerable variations across parent–child dyads in relation to the amount of pretend and non-pretend talk. The results showed that there was more pretend talk with four year olds than with three year olds, while pretend talk again decreased with five year olds. Katz (2001) concluded that, 'A skill with the extended discourse of pretend talk in the preschool years is related to the language and literacy skills that are important for kindergarten' (p. 71).

Older children can develop their language through family conversations. Children learn language. They acquire language when they listen or engage in the family's conversations. They may also engage in narratives when telling stories, exploratory talk and vocabulary development, which ultimately contributes to the children's language development.

Children can also engage in language learning when they accompany their parents on their daily errands such as visits to the supermarket, the post office or the bank. For example, at the supermarket, children attach meaning to print when they identify products by their labels. Although parents do not provide instruction on these outings, children still learn about the world around them. They learn about the functions of a bank or a post office, as well as the reasons for buying stamps, having a savings account, and making cash deposits or withdrawals. When parents take children on excursions away from the neighbourhood (such as to the zoo, museum or park), children learn about their extended world (Naudé *et al.*, 2003b). They also become aware of the print that is around them such as the street signs, food labels, newspapers, headlines, printing on books and billboards and how this print is used to communicate information (Saracho, 2004). Children will transfer the routines and discourse patterns that they practise at home into the preschool (Gregory, 2001).

The community is another socio-cultural context. Children are reliable interpreters of their experiences. The children can capture fragments of their community's everyday events. Children can be taken on neighbourhood walks, which can be used as a springboard for discussion (John, 2003). In the study by Mitchell and Reid-Walsh (2003), children assumed the role of a photographer to gain an understanding of culture. Then they discussed the photographs where children revealed an insight into what they perceived to be important enough to photograph and, equally important, their edited versions of their conscious or subconscious observations. Two of the children, who photographed their bedrooms, discussed their possessions and their use of space, including where they slept, played and spent other social times.

Roles of teachers

Classroom teachers depend on the children's knowledge to extend and enrich their language. Teachers' language instruction has been transformed over the past decade. Earlier teachers used a behaviouristic and sub-skills orientation, but they have moved away from this approach. Dudley-Marling and Searle (1991) have described the type of talk that is most effective in early childhood classrooms; they recommend using 'talk around the edges' instead of the stilted, formal, question-and-answer drill, which is an important component of the published literacy curricula. Still conversation is, for most children, the most effective way for children to practice and refine their language skills. The continuous verbal give-and-take of the ongoing school day provides many opportunities for speaking, listening, reading and writing. These become the basis for social interactions and cognitive processes.

Preschool children need to be provided with a variety of receptive and expressive language experiences that include children's literature, poetry, storytelling, puppetry, and creative dramatics (Saracho & Spodek, 1998; Naudé *et al.*, 2003a). Williams and Rask (2003) identified factors that promoted children's literacy; they showed that it was important for children to hear the sounds in words to develop phonemic awareness. Using games and nursery rhymes contributes to their early reading success. Repetition of nursery rhymes, jingles and poems helps children learn the sounds of their language and develop phonemic awareness where they hear the individual phonemes in words (Fisher & Williams, 2000). Williams and Rask (2003) also concluded that there was a relationship between the children's imaginative play and facets of school literacy.

Spoken and written language experiences emphasize written communication skills, which help children to see the relationship between the spoken word and the written word. Children should be given opportunities to receive and express ideas, impressions and feelings in speaking and writing (Saracho, 2004). They need to participate in activities that encourage them to learn written communication skills, where actual formal reading and writing skills unfold later. Thus, the emphasis in the preschool years should be on oral language experiences, which is a prerequisite that will help children learn and understand the relationship between the spoken and the written language. They will learn to interpret ideas and impressions through reading; to listen and respond through speaking; and to convey their ideas, impressions and feelings through writing.

Conclusion

A language program should include a focus on both receptive (listening and reading) and expressive (speaking and writing) activities. Preschool and kindergarten programs need to include a variety of language activities (e.g. social play, children's literature, poetry, storytelling, puppetry, creative dramatics). These language activities are related to one another and to other areas of the curriculum. Children observe the world around them, using all of their senses. They should be encouraged to generate and express ideas, using language and other means of communication. They should also test these ideas, listening to the ideas generated by others, and gong back to their experiences to see if the meanings they generate hold up. They then should have the opportunity to record these ideas, using art or with the opportunity to dictate their ideas to teachers for them to record the children's thoughts.

Over a period of time, such experiences will help children to recognize the relationship between the spoken and written language through both listening and reading, as well as through sharing their own ideas, impressions and feelings with others through speaking and writing. Children can be provided with multiple experiences to promote their listening, speaking, reading and writing skills and also helping them appreciate the beauty and purpose of language. A high-quality language program needs to include such activities as children's literature, choral speaking, puppetry, creative dramatics, discussions and other language development activities, in which children describe sensory experiences and interpret pictures. Children in the primary grades begin to acquire more complex oral and written language skills (e.g. handwriting, spelling, grammar, compositions, writing and other forms of communication).

References

Baquedano-López, P. (2003) Language, literacy and community, in: N. Hall, J. Larson & J. Marsh (Eds) *Handbook of early childhood literacy* (Thousand Oaks, CA, Sage), 66–74.

Bus, A. G., de Jong, M. T. & Van Ijzendoorn, M. H. (2007) Language, literacy, and social experiences in early childhood: progress, problems, and interventions, in: O. N. Saracho & B. Spodek (Eds) *Contemporary perspectives on social learning* (Charlotte, NC, Information Age Publishing Inc.).

Chomsky, N. (1965) *Aspects of a theory of syntax* (Cambridge, MA, MIT Press).

Corsaro, W. A. (1985) *Friendship and peer culture in the early years* (Norwood, NJ, Ablex).

Corsaro, W. A. (1992) Interpretive reproduction in children's peer cultures, *Social Psychological Quarterly*, 55, 160–177.

Curran, J. M. (1999) Constraints of pretend play: explicit and implicit rules, *Journal of Research in Childhood Education*, 14(1), 47–55.

DeZutter, S. L. (2007) Play as group improvisation: a social semiotic, multimodal perspective on play and literacy, in: O. N. Saracho & B. Spodek (Eds) *Contemporary perspectives on social learning* (Charlotte, NC, Information Age Publishing Inc.).

Dickinson, D. K. & Tabors, P. O. (2001) *Beginning literacy with language: young children learning at home and school* (Baltimore, MD, Paul H. Brookes).

Donaldson, M. (1978) *Children's minds* (London, Fontana).

Dudley-Marling, C. & Searle, D. (1991) *When students have time to talk: creating contexts for learning language* (Portsmouth, NH, Heinemann).

Fisher, R. & Williams, M. (2000) *Unlocking literacy* (London, David Fulton).

Garvey, C. (1990) *Play* (Cambridge, MA, Harvard University Press).

Genishi, C. (1988) *Young children's oral language development* (Urbana, IL, ERIC Clearing-house on Elementary and Early Childhood Education. ERIC Document Service No. ED 30136).

Gregory, E. (2001) Sisters and brothers as language and literacy teachers: synergy between siblings playing and working together, *Journal of Early Childhood Literacy*, 1, 301–322.

Griffin, H. (1984) The coordination of meaning in the creation of a shared make-believe reality, in: I. Bretherton (Ed.) *Symbolic play* (Orlando, FL, Academic Press), 73–100.

Guillen, J. (2002) Moves in the territory of literacy? The telephone discourse of three- and four-year-olds, *Journal of Early Childhood Literacy*, 2(1), 21–43.

Handel, G. (2005) Socialization and the social self, in: G. Handel (Ed.) *Childhood socialization* (New Brunswick, Aldine Transaction), 11–19.

Hart, B. & Risley, T. R. (1995) *Meaningful differences in the everyday experience of young American children* (Baltimore, MD, Paul H. Brookes).

Hart, B. & Risley, T. R. (1999) *The social world of children learning to talk* (Baltimore, MD, Paul H. Brookes).

Hart, B. & Risley, T. R. (2003) The early catastrophe: the 30 million word gap by age 3, *American Educator*, 27(1), 4–9.

Hewitt, E. & Inghilleri, M. (1993) Oracy in the classroom: policy, pedagogy and oral group work, *Anthropology and Education Quarterly*, 24(4), 308–317.

Hoff, E. (2005) Environmental supports for language acquisition, in: D. K. Dickinson & S. Neuman (Eds) *Handbook of early literacy research*, Vol. 2 (New York, Guilford Press), 163–172.

John, M. (2003) *Children's rights and power: charging up for a new century* (London, Jessica Kingsley).

Katz, J. (2001) Playing at home: the talk of pretend play, in: D. Dickinson & P. Tabors (Eds) *Beginning literacy with language* (Baltimore, MD, Paul H. Brookes), 53–74.

Löhfdahl, A. (2005) 'The funeral': a study of children's shared meaning-making and its developmental significance, *Early Years*, 25(1), 5–16.

McGee, L. (2003). *Designing early literacy programs: strategies for at-risk preschool and kindergarten children* (New York, Guilford Press).

McKeown, M. G. & Beck, I. L. (2005) Encouraging young children's language interactions with stories, in: D. K. Dickinson & S. Neuman (Eds) *Handbook of early literacy research*, Vol. 2 (New York, Guilford Press), 281–294.

Mitchell, C. & Reid-Walsh, J. (2003) *Researching children's popular culture: the cultural spaces of childhood* (New York, Routledge).

Naudé, H., Pretorius, E. & Vaneyar, S. (2003a) Teacher professionalism—an innovative programme for teaching mathematics to foundation level learners with limited language proficiency, *Early Child Development and Care*, 173(2–3), 293–315.

Naudé, H., Pretorius, E. & Viljoen, J. (2003b) The impact of impoverished language development on preschoolers' readiness-to-learn during the foundation phase, *Early Child Development and Care*, 173(2–3), 271–291.

Paley, V. G. (2004) *A child's work: the importance of play and fantasy* (Chicago, University of Chicago Press).

Saracho, O. N. (2004) Supporting literacy-related play: roles for teachers of young children, *Early Childhood Education Journal*, 31(3), 203–208.

Saracho, O. N. & Spodek, B. (1993) Language and literacy in early childhood education, in: B. Spodek & O. N. Saracho (Eds) *Yearbook of early childhood education: early childhood language and literacy*, Vol. 4 (New York, Teachers College Press), v–xiii.

Saracho, O. N. & Spodek, B. (1998) A play foundation for family literacy, *International Journal of Educational Research*, 29, 41–50.

Sawyer, R. K. (1997) *Pretend play as improvisation: conversation in the preschool classroom* (Hillsdale, NJ, Lawrence Erlbaum).

Tabors, P., Beals, D. & Weizman, Z. (2001) 'You know what oxygen is?': learning new words at home, in: P. Tabors (Ed.) *Beginning literacy with language* (Baltimore, MD, Paul H. Brookes).

Toohey, K. (2000) *Learning English at school: identity, social relations and classroom practice* (Clevedon, Multilingual Matters).

Verba, M. (1993) Cooperative formats in pretend play among young children, *Cognition and Instruction Discourse and Shared Reasoning*, 11(3–4), 265–280.

Vygotsky, L. S. (1978) *Mind in society: the development of higher psychological processes* (Cambridge, MA, Harvard University Press); original work published 1930.

Wilkinson, A. (1970) The concept of oracy, *English Journal*, 59(1), 71–77.

Williams, M. & Rask, H. (2003) Literacy through play: how families with able children support their literacy development, *Early Child Development and Care*, 173(5), 527–533.

The prosaics of figurative language in preschool: some observations and suggestions for research

Niklas Pramling and Ingrid Pramling Samuelsson

Introduction

When making observations or experiences for which we as yet lack a language, we tend to use the language we have, in terms of which we will try to come to grips with the new and unfamiliar. One strategy people use in such situations is to use metaphors as vehicles of thinking and communication. A working definition of metaphorical or figurative speech is that it is a way of using language in which something is spoken about in terms of something else that it cannot literally be (cf. Lakoff & Johnson, 1980; Pramling, 2006). For example, 'thinking' may be spoken about in terms of 'constructing' knowledge or 'DNA' may be explained as a 'text'. In speaking metaphorically, the learner uses knowledge from one domain as a resource in making sense of or communicating about something else that typically is more abstract, complex or unfamiliar.

This further means that while a metaphor states that one thing 'is' another, the utterance needs to be interpreted as saying that it may be useful to speak about the one *as if it were* the other. This as-if character of metaphor also points to how we play with language. In the words of Johan Huizinga in his classic book *Homo ludens* (1955, p. 4):

> In the making of speech and language the spirit is continually 'sparking' between matter and mind, as it were, playing with this wondrous nominative faculty. Behind every abstract expression there lie the boldest of metaphors, and every metaphor is a play upon words. Thus in giving expression to life man creates a second, poetic world alongside the world of nature.

If this is the case, metaphor should be pervasive in the practices of preschool, with its traditional emphasis on play as a mode of activity.

However, as Mercer (2000, p. 79) argues, 'metaphors are such a normal and pervasive feature of our use of language that we often do not realize we are using them'. This, in our view, points to the importance in analyses of figurative language to attend to what Cameron (2003) refers to as 'the prosaics of metaphor', that is its mundane use (see below). Also, Mercer (2000, p. 79) makes the point that what historically can be shown as metaphorical meanings of words are often used by people 'with little sense of metaphorical use' (see also Bowdle & Gentner, 2005). This last point, in our view, suggests the need in analyses of metaphorical use of language to consider the analyst's as well as the participant's perspective. We will return to these issues.

In the perspective taken in this paper, 'metaphor' is understood in a wide sense, including 'similes' and 'analogies'. We will use 'figurative language' and 'non-literal language' as synonymous to metaphoric language, as this is common practice in the research literature.

If and when children understand and use figurative language are highly contested and debated issues (for overviews see Winner, 1988; Gibbs, 1994; cf. Knowles & Moon, 2006; and for critical comments on this research see Cameron, 1996). However, we shall not go here into this debate. Instead, we will by way of a few examples of everyday conversation in the preschool setting attempt to: (a) exemplify some of the ways in which language is used in a figurative way in the discourse of preschool; (b) discuss which opportunities for learning these communicative exchanges *could* offer children, that is what experiences of these kinds of uses of language imply for the communicative and cognitive development of children; and (c) point to some further questions which, in our view, merit empirical research in the preschool setting.

'The ability to understand and use metaphor', Knowles and Moon (2006, p. 62) writes, 'is sometimes referred to as figurative (or metaphoric) competence' (emphasis omitted). Most studies of children and metaphor have investigated children no younger than three years and most studies focus on children from school age and onwards: 'Generally, children seem to have acquired figurative competence somewhere between the ages of ten and twelve, and to have begun to acquire it by the age of five or six' (2006, p. 63); 'However, even very young children are capable of accessing imaginary worlds—they follow stories, and understand what it means to pretend and play' (p. 63). That is, even young children are able to go beyond the existing, actual, to the possible, fictional, in acting 'as if' (see also Säljö, 2005): 'It has been argued that this ability to deal with the unreal is an early form of figurative competence' (Knowles & Moon, 2006, p. 63). In connecting to this issue, a critical question posed in this paper is: how does the everyday language use in preschool—the prosaics of preschool discourse—provide opportunities for children to develop this figurative ability? Mastering figurative aspects of language use is in our view an important aspect of what is sometimes referred to as 'oracy' (e.g. Haworth, 2001), that is 'the development of oral language' in the child (Kirkland & Patterson, 2005, p. 394).

We will analyse and discuss two brief examples of verbal data from preschool conversations between children and their teacher. In line with the theoretical point of departure in the need to study metaphor in terms of prosaics, as will be argued below, we will analyse two apparently trifling and insignificant episodes of verbal exchange. The point with this strategy is that it is in the everyday 'little' or ordinary situations and speech that metaphors work and that we use and learn how to use language and what we mean with ways of speaking—what people to a large extent master without necessarily knowing that they do so (i.e. without being able to verbalize it as such, to lift it to a reflective level, as it were).

Some theoretical and methodological considerations in the study of figurative language

Here we present a perspective on metaphor as an everyday feature of our ways of speaking. After that, a sociocultural framework for the study of learning and development will be briefly presented, followed by a few analytical guidelines for the study of figurative language.

The prosaics of metaphor

Following Cameron (2003), we argue for the need for research on children and non-literal language in terms of 'a prosaics of metaphor': 'Prosaics', explains Cameron (2003, p. 6), 'is concerned with the ordinary rather than with the special artistic use of language'. 'The prosaic', she further argues:

> is the site of linguistic creativity. Creative acts take place in ordinary events working with
> the raw material of the everyday, not just in the special exceptional events that are labelled
> 'creative' (2003, p. 7)

Ordinary language use is, in Cameron's view, 'rich' and 'complex' and should be studied. It is against this background of the ordinary use of language that Cameron introduces metaphor into the equation: 'If we are to see how metaphor contributes to that complexity and power, we must take a prosaic approach to metaphor in discourse, exploring metaphor in its "most ordinary" guises, as well as in its more poetic forms' (p. 7).

What could a prosaics of figurative language mean in the preschool setting? How and when might this kind of language use occur? And what may the 'cognitive and communicative socialization' (see below) of partaking in such communicative patterns imply for children's development? These questions warrant more extensive and systematic studies than what we will report here. In this paper, we will only tentatively point to how the concept of 'the prosaics of figurative language' can be considered relevant to the educational practices with, and development of, even young children in preschool.

A sociocultural framework

We take a sociocultural perspective on learning and development (Säljö, 2000, 2005; Vygotsky, 1978, 1986), according to which 'the development of the individual' is viewed 'as an answer to the communicative challenges she or he is exposed to' (Mauritzson & Säljö, 2003; our translation). This perspective, in our case, implies posing questions such as the following:

- What kinds of use of language in a figurative way appear in the discourse of preschool?
- What do experiences of these kinds of language use imply for the 'communicative and cognitive socialization' of children (cf. Mauritzson & Säljö, 2003)?

Learning can be understood as the appropriation of tools (including, but not exclusive to, the tools of language). In Säljö's (2000, p. 73; our translation) words, 'one of the foundational principles for describing learning in a sociocultural perspective' is 'the ability to see something new as an example of, or as a variant of, something already familiar. And we develop this ability through learning to master intellectual tools'. Metaphor, we argue, is a tool (and a feature of our language) in terms of which we are able to do this. Discursive or intellectual tools have cognitive as well as communicative functions for people.

With Vygotsky's (1986) metaphor, these tools have an 'inside' and an 'outside', that is they are tools for social communication as well as for individual cognition. In a famous passage, Vygotsky (1978, p. 57) considers the development of psychological functioning as taking place on two 'levels':

> Every function in the child's cultural development appears twice: first, on the social level, and later, on the individual level; first, *between* people (*interpsychological*), and then *inside* the child (*intrapsychological*). This applies equally to voluntary attention, to logical memory, and to the formation of concepts.

The idea is that, through participating in social practices and communication with others, the child will eventually come to 'take over' the tools and become able to use them by herself, a process referred to in sociocultural theory as 'appropriation' (Wertsch, 2002; Säljö, 2005). Hence, communicative patterns to which the child is exposed will become the mould of her subsequent individual development. We will here focus on one aspect of these tools, their figurativeness or metaphoric. Appropriating such tools is not just a cognitive act, it is also a communicative one, that is a social act, in the sense that it requires the child to be sensitive to what s/he needs to make clear in her/his speech in order to be understood by someone else (Pramling, 2006).

Analysing figurative language use

A metaphor states that something is what it cannot literally be (Cameron, 2003). For this reason, analysing metaphorical language means identifying and clarifying such cases of 'discrepancy' or 'incongruence' (Fichtner, 1999) between the terms in which something is referred to and what is being referred to. In addition, when analysing figurative language, what Goatly (1997) calls 'metaphorical markers' need to be attended to. Some examples of such markers would be: 'as if', 'kind of', 'similar to' and 'as it were'. These kinds of terms signal that an utterance is not meant to be understood 'literally', but rather figuratively as a way of speaking. We will refer to these kinds of markers as 'meta-communicative markers' (Pramling, 2006); these markers should be attended to by the analyst, since they signal how an utterance is intended to be 'taken'. How speakers intend their own utterances to be understood by others (and how these utterances are communicated as being understood by the speakers themselves) is visible, we argue, in the employment of the various kinds of 'markers' that speakers use in discourse to signal a non-literal use of language.

Figurative features of language use in everyday conversation in preschool

This presentation reports some preliminary observations and ideas about the uses of 'non-literal' modes of speaking in preschool. When explaining something, or trying to come to terms with something unclear or unfamiliar, children as well as adults tend to reduce it back to something more familiar or well known. The new is spoken about as if it were like something else that one knows, yet different. The use of metaphor in making sense is, in a general sense, well known (e.g. Lakoff & Johnson, 1980). However, there is still little empirical work on how metaphors are used in learning, especially in the preschool setting.

Two brief empirical examples will be presented, analysed and discussed. The empirical data consists of video observations (here transcribed) of children and teachers in Swedish preschools. The first example is from a recurrent form of practice in preschools, the 'circle time'. The teacher and the children sit in a circle on the floor facing each other.

Excerpt 1

Teacher: Now I was thinking that you will ... lay yourselves on the floor. [*The children lie down on the floor and close their eyes.*] I would like that you think about that tree that we went to look at. And all the branches. And what was it that laid under the tree?

Children: Leaves.

Teacher: One closes one's eyes and thinks, then one can almost see it, just as a TV inside the head. You can pretend that you are that tree. [*The children get up, and stretch their arms in the air.*]

Child: It falls off.

Teacher: What is it that falls off?

Child: The leaves.

The teacher 'anchors' what she wants the children to imagine, to think about, by referring to a concrete experience they share, in the form of an actual tree that they had previously looked at. She departs from something known and concrete through which the children can 'go on' imagining. However, what is of most interest in this excerpt for the present purpose is two things. First are the communicative markers that the teacher uses.

She says that 'one can almost see it, just as a TV inside the head'. The first critical term here is 'almost'; she explains in an as-if manner (it is almost like something else, but not quite). Notice also how this is done by analogy: 'just as [if there were] a TV inside the head', so it is to imagine. The words 'just as' are of further interest; these kinds of expression tend to be used in communication as signalling that something is not intended literally, but rather metaphorically (cf. terms such as 'kind of', 'quite', 'practically', 'like', 'as if', or even 'literally': Goatly, 1997). To learn to mark out, or to qualify, one's own communication in such manner is an important competence to appropriate. It is a way of making the intended meaning clearer to one's communicative partner. We often, as in this case, speak in a more 'indirect' way—that is, in terms of something else. To do so makes more sense, for it reconnects what is being referred to with some presumably (more) familiar knowledge and/or experience of a person.

In passing, it may additionally be noted that the historically predominant way of reasoning about our minds and intellectual activities (such as, in this case, 'imagining'), in at least the Western intellectual tradition, is employed; that is, to see the (activities of the) mind in terms of artefacts, and more specifically, technologies. Consider as but one illustration of this principle the metaphor of 'mind as computer', as used in cognitive psychology since the 1960s. Thus, the children are, however indirectly, introduced to a form by which we make sense of ourselves in our culture. This includes learning the cultural forms in which we speak of what, in some sense, escapes us and/or our language, for example, how we speak about ourselves as human beings not directly, but indirectly, through our own creations and artefacts. Historically, as in the empirical example above, the tools of our creation have been the tools of our imagination and self-understanding (Draaisma, 2000). This is something that a teacher could make children aware of in working metacognitively (Pramling, 1996), that is in making children aware of their own sense-making activities. In language, we cannot simply point to what we refer to (e.g. our selves), but we need to constitute what we speak about as a certain kind, in some terms rather than others, to speak about it. In this sense, our way of speaking is 'indirect' or 'figurative'.

The second point to be noted, in the empirical excerpt above, is the suggestion by the teacher to the children that: 'You can pretend that you are that tree.' To anthropomorphize phenomena—to speak of non-human entities as if they were human—may be a fundamental form of metaphor to master, and one that children appropriate early in life. Developmental psychologist Paul Harris (2000, p. 30) has observed that from about 2 years of age children tend to engage in a new form of play, where they 'start to act on the world and to talk about it as if they were experiencing it from the point of view of the invented person or creature'. This is a prevalent form of making sense of the world that even adults tend to fall back on when confronted with something unclear or (partly) unknown, or trying to explain something difficult (see e.g. Ochs *et al.*, 1996; Corts, 2006). In fact, 'pretending' (as in play) can be perceived as analogous to a figurative use of language, in acting and speaking as if something were what it cannot literally be. This 'as-if' character is important (see e.g. Egan, 1997; Säljö, 2005) in learning to go beyond what is, in some sense, 'given,' to the possible. Speaking 'as-if', hence points to a creative aspect of cognition. 'As-if' modes of speaking, of course, are not new in research on children's play; however, in relation to learning it appears to be rather a neglected issue.

In the second example, once again taken from an exchange between the teacher and the children, the following took place:

Excerpt 2

[*Together they sing about an elephant that makes different sounds. A child starts to talk about the elephant 'farting in there'. The children laugh, and some children start to wave with their hands as if wanting to get the 'smell' away from the nose.*]
Child: It smells skunk.
Teacher: How peculiar, an elephant smelling skunk!

Figuratively speaking, an elephant may be like a skunk in this manner. To play with language in this way may be an early example of the teacher trying not only to joke with the children, but also make it possible for them to begin to 'see' language as a medium. Though obviously not intended and/or made explicit in these terms, the teacher can—from the analyst's viewpoint—be seen as beginning to make visible for the children how language can be used figuratively in making sense of experiences and phenomena. How peculiar that we say this, speak of something in terms of something else, as if it were so.

However, with time figurative expressions tend to become conventionalized or institutionalized, and hence cease to be perceived as figurative by speakers (Pramling, 2006). This means that for an experienced speaker it may be difficult to see the figurativeness of one's own language; it is simply 'how we say'. For a 'new speaker', such as a child (or a second language learner), the figurativeness of common expressions tends to 'stand out' and appear somewhat 'odd'. In our experience of preschool children, they tend to find these kinds of wordplay great fun and readily engage in participating in such activities (cf. Kirkland & Patterson, 2005). To be able to perceive 'peculiarities' of our language use (such as this example) and to start to make up these kinds of expressions, could pave the way for children to start exploring the potentialities of language as a dynamic and creative set of tools.

Discussion

The two empirical examples analysed in this paper are certainly nothing extraordinary to the discourse of preschool. These ways of speaking are mundane and may therefore not be something teachers pay attention to. This is precisely why we propose considering figurative language as 'prosaics' (Cameron, 2003) in the study of preschool discourse. Such an analytical stance allows researchers and teachers to see how figurative language is a highly common feature of ordinary, everyday conversation also with young children in preschool. So what may the implications of this feature of language be for children's learning, hence also why should researchers and teachers be mindful of this figurativeness? This is something we will try to discuss in the following.

In a general sense, this paper points to preschool as an arena for what Mauritzson and Säljö (2003) refer to as the 'communicative and cognitive socialization' of children. This socialization includes learning different meta-abilities, such as being able to distinguish the representation from what is being referred to, making clear how one speaks and how one's utterances are intended to be understood (Pramling, 2006).

Figurative language is frequent in discourse in learning practices (see e.g. Littlemore, 2001; Cameron, 2002; Corts, 2006), including, but certainly not exclusive to, preschool. Such use of language may have important implications for children's learning, if made explicit and aware. For example, Egan (1997) has proposed that playing with language (as in jokes) may foster metalinguistic awareness. In his view, a 'joke can be a fertile means of building awareness of language and of developing increasingly sophisticated language use' (Egan, 1997, p. 211). And metaphor may be perceived as 'the play of language' (Huizinga, 1955) between what is and is not the case.

Situations of wordplay like the second brief example above may provide children with some early experiences of language as a means for making sense, and not just to 'seeing through' language, as it were. To learn to be aware of language, not just to use it 'invisibly', is an ability that has been argued to be of pivotal importance to the forms of institutional schooling that the children will later come to attend. To be able to distinguish the representational system (verbal language, gestures, pictures, etc.) from what it is being used to conceive of is a critical knowledge to be learned in the children's later schooling.

These examples, from an analytical viewpoint, may be seen as providing early encounters for children to learn to see how we make sense of experiences in terms of something else, and how language provides a means for reasoning imaginatively. Whether children actually attend to this, and are made aware of it, is another question. In fact, there is an indication in the first example, above, of the children focusing attention on other aspects of the situation. This is not unexpected. However, communicative experiences like the two brief illustrations here may, in a longer perspective, be of importance for children's learning. To empirically study how 'as if' is used in educational practices already in preschool, and on through the school system, could prove to be of some pedagogical interest.

A critical question for any teacher in preschool is: what kind of knowing do I want to develop in children? If reconnecting to our examples, we may ask: what could a teacher make children aware of in these cases? In addition to what we have already pointed to, we will give one example. A common feature in preschool is organizing learning activities in terms of encompassing themes, an example of such a theme could be 'human beings'. If we take this example and reconnect it to example 1, above, where 'imagining' was spoken about as being like a 'TV inside the head', the teacher could use this as a 'stepping-stone', asking children how a human being is like a TV, and vice versa, and what else is like a human being but unlike a TV, etc. Such a strategy enables children to be aware of what it is *like* to be human, but also how some aspects are 'merely human' and not something that we share with other 'things'. As analysts, we find questions such as the following requiring systematic empirical study in the preschool setting: do teachers (and if so, to what extent and how) make these (or other) kinds of relations and distinctions in their talk with children; and if they do, how do children respond to this (what abilities do they develop)?

We do not suggest that (all) children actually learn all these things, only that the communicative milieu of preschool (as here but briefly exemplified) provides the opportunities for learning, among a large number of communicative abilities, also these figurative aspects of language use. In order for children to actually learn these, the teacher would probably have to make these aspects explicit for the children, that is engage children in meta-dialogues (see Pramling, 1990, 1996 for such successful work in preschool, though not, as we have done here, focused on figurative aspects of language use). Hence, these learning opportunities exist from the analyst's viewpoint; in order to exist also from the child's viewpoint, teachers would probably need to make these aspects more explicit than they do in the two excerpts here. The distinction between the analyst's and the participant's perspective is an important one. Perhaps the concept *teaching opportunity* could be used to analytically account for what the analyst can identify in a conversation, and the concept *learning opportunity* be reserved for what is explicitly made available for learners to 'discover' in teachers' talk? Research questions emerging from this discussion include whether teachers make use of the 'discursive space' (Haworth, 2001) that is 'opened up' by figurative language in relation to its referent, and how learners respond to the learning opportunities they encounter. Do teachers (and if so, how?) turn 'teaching opportunities' into 'learning opportunities' for children?

Making explicit for children a figurative use of language holds promise of providing opportunities for children already in preschool of learning: (a) how to use the language they have in new ways in new situations (i.e. becoming creative language users); and (b) distinguishing a way of speaking from what it refers to, which is a very important communicative and cognitive ability that becomes accentuated when learning about more abstract forms of knowledge not directly accessible to our senses as, for example, with scientific knowledge that children encounter in their further schooling. This 'indirectness' of figurative language, in Fichtner's (1999, p. 322) view, 'can provide a link to the acquisition of theoretical concepts', since such 'concepts are never directly related to an object', but have their meaning by way of other concepts. Mastering the figurativeness of some use of language may be a preliminary knowledge for such subsequent understanding.

In this paper, we have attempted to point to: (a) an important aspect of language use in preschool, that is how language is used figuratively; (b) the opportunities for learning these verbal exchanges can provide for children; and (c) what, in addition, would probably be required for such learning to take place (more effectively).

Our preliminary illustration and discussion of the mundane nature of figurative language—of the 'prosaics' of metaphor (Cameron, 2003)—calls for more extensive and systematic study of the repertoire of, occasions of and ways of using figurative language in communication between children and between children and teachers in preschool. Other analyses worth pursuing, in this context, would include the *in situ* development of this figurative ability and its implications for children's development and learning, and the learning opportunities provided young children in preschool practices.

Acknowledgement

The research reported here was financed by the Swedish Research Council.

References

Bowdle, B. F. & Gentner, D. (2005) The career of metaphor, *Psychological Review*, 112(1), 193–216.
Cameron, L. (1996) Discourse context and the development of metaphor in children, *Current Issues in Language and Society*, 3(1), 49–64.
Cameron, L. (2002) Metaphors in the learning of science: a discourse focus, *British Educational Research Journal*, 28(5), 673–688.
Cameron, L. (2003) *Metaphor in educational discourse* (London, Continuum).
Corts, D. P. (2006) Factors characterizing bursts of figurative language and gestures in college lectures, *Discourse Studies*, 8(2), 211–233.
Draaisma, D. (2000) *Metaphors of memory: a history of ideas about the mind* (Trans. P. Vincent) (Cambridge, Cambridge University Press).
Egan, K. (1997) *The educated mind: how cognitive tools shape our understanding* (Chicago, University of Chicago Press).
Fichtner, B. (1999) Metaphor and learning activity, in: Y. Engeström, R. Miettinen & R.-L. Punamäki (Eds) *Perspectives on activity theory* (New York, Cambridge University Press), 314–324.
Gibbs, R. W., Jr (1994) *The poetics of mind: figurative thought, language, and understanding* (New York, Cambridge University Press).
Goatly, A. (1997) *The language of metaphors* (London, Routledge).
Harris, P. L. (2000) *The work of the imagination* (Oxford, Blackwell).
Haworth, A. (2001) The re-positioning of oracy: a millennium project? *Cambridge Journal of Education*, 31(1), 11–23.
Huizinga, J. (1955) *Homo ludens: a study of the play-element in culture* (Boston, MA, Beacon); original work published 1944.
Kirkland, L. D. & Patterson, J. (2005) Developing oral language in primary classrooms, *Early Childhood Education Journal*, 32(6), 391–395.
Knowles, M. & Moon, R. (2006) *Introducing metaphor* (London, Routledge).
Lakoff, G. & Johnson, M. (1980) *Metaphors we live by* (Chicago, University of Chicago Press).
Littlemore, J. (2001) The use of metaphor in university lectures and the problems that it causes for overseas students, *Teaching in Higher Education*, 6(3), 333–349.
Mauritzson, U. & Säljö, R. (2003) Ja vill va Simba å du ä Nala: Barns kommunikation och koordination av perspektiv i lek, in: E. Johansson & I. Pramling Samuelsson (Eds) *Förskolan: barns första skola* [*Preschool: children's first school*] (Lund, Studentlitteratur), 159–196.

Mercer, N. (2000) *Words and minds: how we use language to think together* (London, Routledge).

Ochs, E., Gonzales, P. & Jacoby, S. (1996) 'When I come down I'm in the domain state': grammar and graphic representation in the interpretive activity of physicists, in: E. Ochs, E. A. Schegloff & S. A. Thompson (Eds) *Interaction and grammar* (Cambridge, Cambridge University Press), 328–369.

Pramling, I. (1990) *Learning to learn: a study of Swedish preschool children* (Trans. G. Thylander) (New York, Springer).

Pramling, I. (1996) Understanding and empowering the child as a learner, in: D. R. Olson & N. Torrance (Eds) *The handbook of education and human development: new models of learning, teaching and schooling* (Oxford, Blackwell), 656–592.

Pramling, N. (2006) *Minding metaphors: using figurative language in learning to represent* (Göteborg Studies in Educational Sciences No. 238) (Göteborg, University of Göteborg).

Säljö, R. (2000) *Lärande i praktiken: ett sociokulturellt perspektiv* [*Learning in practice: a sociocultural perspective*] (Stockholm, Prisma).

Säljö, R. (2005) *Lärande och kulturella redskap: om lärprocesser och det kollektiva minnet* [*Learning and cultural tools: on processes of learning and collective memory*]. (Stockholm, Norstedts Akademiska).

Vygotsky, L. S. (1978) *Mind in society: the development of higher psychological processes* (Eds M. Cole *et al.*) (Cambridge, MA, Harvard University Press).

Vygotsky, L. S. (1986) *Thought and language* (Trans. A. Kozulin) (Cambridge, MA, MIT Press); original work published 1934.

Wertsch, J. V. (2002) *Voices of collective remembering* (New York, Cambridge University Press).

Winner, E. (1988) *The point of words: children's understanding of metaphor and irony* (Cambridge, MA, Harvard University Press).

Language development in the years before school: a comparison of developmental assets in home and child care settings

Daniel J. Weigel, Jennifer L. Lowman and Sally S. Martin

Researchers have long been interested in understanding the language development of children. We now have evidence that the preschool years are a time when language abilities are emerging, and language acquisition for children is dependent on participatory, social interaction with significant others (Hart & Risley, 1995; Dickinson & Tabors, 2001). Variation in language development (also referred to as the development of oracy) is a function of both the quantity and quality of exposure to sounds in a meaningful context. Positive outcomes depend on adults and peers exposing children to a variety of sounds and discourse. Current research shows that some children have a receptive vocabulary as early as 9 months of age and they start producing words around 12 months (Fenson *et al.*, 1994). However, Fenson *et al.* (1994) revealed a great amount of variation in vocabulary comprehension and production—more than was expected with respect to existing research—and the gap between the highest and lowest performing children increased with age. Fenson and colleagues suggest that increasing variability for both receptive and expressive vocabulary indicates that maturation becomes less of a constraint as children age, while factors external to children become more influential.

In this paper, we argue that two key external sources of variation in children's listening (receptive language), speaking (expressive language) and communicative interactions with others are the home and child care environment. We first present some theoretical assumptions to help guide our study of language development that occurs before formal schooling. We then briefly review the literature on various factors in the home and child care settings that have been shown to foster children's language development. We supplement this review by presenting some selective results from our own work. Lastly, we examine the implications of the research for ensuring the optimal language development of children.

Theoretical assumptions

Our work on language and literacy development has been guided by a developmental assets approach. Rather than the more common deficit-based approach, researchers and professionals who work with children and youth have turned their attention to strength-based models of child and youth development. Under the broad rubric of positive youth development, such models pursue new ways to conceptualize, measure and promote optimal outcomes for children and youth (Catalano *et al.*, 2002; Sesma *et al.*, 2005). There is a specific focus on intentional and meaningful relationships with children. In addition, facilitating positive youth development is viewed as a common-place occurrence; that is, the entire community, not just professionals and agencies, has a responsibility to provide a positive, enriching environment and experiences (Sesma *et al.*, 2005).

The concept of strengths or assets lies at the heart of the developmental asset framework. Developmental assets are defined as a set of interrelated experiences, relationships, skills and values that enhance child outcomes (Benson *et al.*, 1998; Scales & Leffert, 1999). They are categorized as either internal, referring to attributes and qualities within the child, or external, encompassing the various ecologies interacting with the child (e.g. home and child care). In terms of language development, such assets might include the richness of conversations in the home or child care setting, adults valuing their roles in enhancing language development, and an abundance of early language and literacy activities in the child's environment.

Furthermore, the developmental assets approach views children from Bronfenbrenner's ecological perspective (Bronfenbrenner & Morris, 1998), recognizing that children influence and are influenced by families, schools and communities. The home and child care environments are two prominent settings in the lives of young US children. The home context includes interactions between the child, his/her parents and siblings, or other adults that are present in the home or family unit. The child care or preschool setting includes interactions between the child, his/her peers and preschool teachers, and other adults that are present in that setting.

There are several assumptions underlying the developmental asset framework. A fundamental assumption is that the more positive experiences and assets children have, the greater the chance that they will thrive. A second assumption is that assets have a direct and positive effect on all children, regardless of their risk status. In other words, these assets will be a boost for all children, rich and poor, young and old. We also recognize that many assets are bi-polar. For example, having a parent with a higher level of education can be considered a positive or protective factor, whereas having a parent with relatively little education may function as a risk factor for preschool children. It also is assumed that developmental assets are interconnected, so that having or acquiring one asset is expected to contribute to and reinforce the attainment of other developmental assets (Sesma *et al.*, 2005). In addition, recent research provides evidence that there is a link between assets measured at one point in time and child outcomes measured a year or two later (e.g. Scales & Roehlkepartain, 2003). This concept is especially important when applied to early learning and language acquisition, thought by many to form the building-blocks for later school and life success (Pullen & Justice, 2003; Van der Ven & Mannes, 2005).

Using the developmental assets framework and its emphasis on ecological systems, in this paper we focus on two important external contexts in children's early years: the home and child care settings. We examine the contributions of each, as well as their combined influence on preschool children's language skills. We seek to understand the positive factors, processes and belief-systems that contribute to children's early language development. We examine the effect of parental and child care characteristics on children's language development both concurrently and long term. Our discussion is organized around several questions: (1) What strengths and assets in the home setting influence young children's language development? (2) What strengths and assets in the child care setting influence young children's language development? (3) In what ways do the assets in the home and child care settings combine to impact children's language development? (4) What does a developmental assets approach offer to our understanding of the development of young children's language skills and in the enrichment of those skills?

What strengths and assets in the home setting influence young children's language development?

Figure 1 presents a graphic model identifying the key assets in the home and child care settings that have been shown to optimize children's language development. As seen in the figure, the research of others as well as our own research, has identified specific assets in the home setting, which we have grouped into family demographic features, parent conversational style, language activities in the home, and parental beliefs about language development.

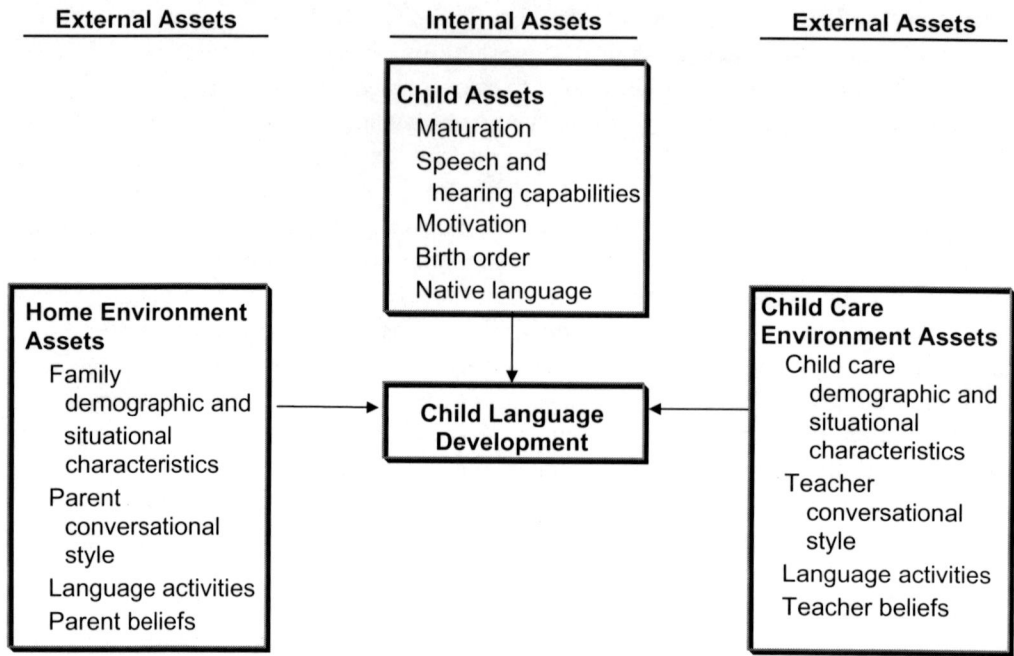

Figure 1.   Key assets in the home and child care settings that have been shown to optimize children's language development

Family demographic and situational characteristics

A number of demographic and situational characteristics of the home setting have been shown to foster young children's language development. The mother's education, for example, appears to be a consistent indicator of child language development. The higher mother's level of education the higher preschool children's receptive and expressive language skills (Burchinal *et al.*, 2002; NICHD ECCRN, 2004). Also, Rowe *et al.* (1999) found that parental education influences the expression of genetic potential for learning vocabulary. Children whose parents had higher levels of education were more likely to reach their verbal potential than were children whose parents had lower levels of education. Children also tend to make greater language gains when their parents have more advanced language skills and model those skills through conversations and taking pleasure in reading (Weigel *et al.*, 2005).

The number of children in the household can also impact opportunities for language practice. More children appear to reduce the opportunity for language-stimulating parent–child conversations. Although mothers tend to speak equally with each of their children, the addition of each new child causes parents to reallocate their total amount of talk among all the children (Hart & Risley, 1995). Likewise, mothers are less likely to use questions and engage in conversations in families with more than one child (Jones & Adamson, 1987). However, Gibbs *et al.* (1987) found that the presence of additional children increases the occurrence of sibling communication, with further spaced siblings interacting more than closer spaced siblings.

Socioeconomic status (SES) also can be an asset in language development. For example, mothers in poverty tend to use more directive language (Snow *et al.*, 1982; Hoff-Ginsberg, 1991). Directive language is less complex and characterized by the use of few words. Hoff-Ginsberg (1991) found that as the rate of directives increased, the rate of supportive language decreased. Higher SES mothers tend to see their children as a conversational partner and, subsequently, structure the conversation in a way that elicits a participatory response from their child. Lower SES parents tend to use language to direct their children's behavior (Nelson, 1981; Hoff-Ginsberg, 1991); perhaps as a consequence, they tend to use more negative imperatives, such as 'stop' and 'don't' (Hart & Risley, 1995). Hart and Risley (1995) also observed that professional parents gave more affirmative feedback more often. Further, they found a positive relation between the overall amount of talk in a household and a child's language skills, and mid and high SES parents simply talked more to their children. Time for talk, especially non-goal-directed conversational talk, has been implicated as a primary difference between families in poverty and other families (Snow *et al.*, 1982). Thus, many social demographic characteristics of the home can operate as assets to young children's language development.

Parent conversational style

Beyond demographic features of the home, parent–child conversational style appears to be another important asset in increasing children's language skills. Conversational talk can take many forms and functions; it can be descriptive, informative, explanatory, directive or narrative. Several aspects of parent–child conversations have been recognized as connected to greater language skills in young children. From observations in the homes of low-income families, DeTemple (2001) found two different types of parent–child talk: the here and now (immediate talk) and generalized or abstract knowledge or personal experience (non-immediate talk). Through immediate talk, the parent actively draws the child's attention to objects and descriptive features of the object. During shared book reading, for instance, parents who employ immediate talk tend to prompt their children to name characters, colours or count the number of objects. In contrast, non-immediate talk is a conversational style through which parents encourage their children to make generalizations and inferences from the present to past experience or knowledge. For example, in addition to labelling objects in a book, parents will remind the child of a relevant personal experience related to the object. DeTemple's (2001) found that the *proportion* of immediate to non-immediate talk was more indicative of the child's language and literacy skills than was the overall amount or type of talk. A higher percentage of immediate talk was negatively associated with measures of toddler language, emergent literacy and performance in kindergarten. A greater frequency and proportion of non-immediate talk, however, was positively associated with measures of expressive and receptive vocabulary, use of superordinates, story comprehension and emergent literacy as measured at 3, 4 and 5 years of age. Through non-immediate talk a parent supports and challenges a child to construct a relevant frame of reference from the child's own experience.

Non-immediate talk is a form of extended discourse. Other forms of extended discourse include narrative talk and explanatory talk (Beals, 2001). Exposure to narrative storytelling, for example, helps a child learn to construct an event narrative, past or present, and to identify a theme in a story. Describing, defining and drawing connections between concepts, especially cause and effect relationships, characterizes explanatory talk. Also, extended discourse is characterized by longer, more precise and complex utterances. Maternal mean length utterance (MLU) and the grammatical complexity of a mother's speech are positively associated with vocabulary growth (Rollins *et al.*, 1996; Hoff, 2003). In addition to the fact that more words are used in a longer utterance, longer utterances tend to have more word types, provide a richer context from which to infer meaning and tend to be more grammatically complex and varied (Hart & Risley, 1995; Rollins *et al.*, 1996; Hoff, 2003). Metalinguistic comments also support a child's use of language. Metalinguistic utterances are questions or comments that elicit replies from the child such as topic continuing replies and affirmative feedback. In Jones and Adamson's (1987) study, metalinguistic comments were the only type of comment positively related to vocabulary size. In general, exposure to different narrative and exploratory styles is beneficial for language skills at 4 and 5 years, specifically emergent literacy, vocabulary growth, description of word definitions and listening comprehension (Beals, 2001).

In addition to the content of talk and the length of the utterance, a supportive conversational style is also important for language development. A supportive style helps a child attend to and make connections between utterances and objects or activities (Hoff-Ginsberg, 1991). A supportive style not only encourages a child to use language, but also provides a child the opportunity to use language. For instance, mothers who pause to talk or ask questions of their children during book reading have children who also tend to interrupt and ask more questions (DeTemple, 2001). Providing space for the child to talk is an important supportive element of conversation.

Language activities

In addition to parental conversational style, the frequency of opportunities to engage in specific language activities also is an asset to language development. In our own work (Bennett *et al.*, 2002), for example, we found that preschool-age children's language outcomes were improved when their parents engaged them in language activities, such as singing songs, reciting rhymes, telling stories, drawing pictures, and playing games. Likewise, parents in Baker *et al.*'s (1995) study reported that their children enjoyed singing songs, chanting nursery rhymes and playing other rhyming games. Such parent–child activities added to children's language and literacy outcome scores. As Snow *et al.* (1998) argued such activities help children develop oral language and promote emerging literacy skills.

Perhaps the most goal-oriented parent–child activity is shared book reading. Exposure to print and book handling is associated with emergent literacy and receptive vocabulary (DeTemple, 2001). Snow and Ferguson (1977) note that book reading, in comparison to speech, utilizes a wider variety of vocabulary and complex grammatical structure. Further, books provide an opportunity for the introduction of novel information and rare words (Whitehurst & Lonigan, 1998; Tabors *et al.*, 2001a, 2001b). Rare word exposure has positive influences on a child's receptive vocabulary growth and emergent literacy (Tabors *et al.*, 2001a, 2001b). The impact of shared reading on oral language skills is somewhat mixed. In a meta-analysis, book reading frequency was positively related to a child's acquisition of only the written language register (Bus *et al.*, 1995). In contrast, story-book exposure accounted for a statistically significant amount of unique variance in kindergartners' and 1st-graders' oral language skills (Senechal *et al.*, 1998).

In our own work, we have collected data that has examined the links between the home and child care environments with preschool-aged children's language and literacy development (Bennett *et al.*, 2002; Weigel *et al.*, 2005, 2006). We assessed the language skills of 85 children's using the *Preschool language scales 3* (PLS-3) when children were 3–4 years old and again one year later. The PLS-3 assesses receptive language (how well children understand verbal language) and expressive language (how well children express their thoughts verbally). The children were primarily Caucasian and lived in middle-income homes. We also gathered data from their parents and child care teachers as to their own language and literacy behaviours, beliefs, activities in the home or school and demographic information. We found that children's language skills are strengthened when parents engage them in enriching activities, such as shared book reading. Children more readily gain language and early literacy skills when parents encourage their children to help read the story, let children ask questions, ask questions of the children during reading, and relate the story to children's lives.

Parent beliefs

In our work, we also have looked at parents' beliefs about language development and their role in that development. In accordance with shared book reading activities, we have found that the parents of children with greater language skills believe in the power of sharing books with their children and think that stories help build children's imaginations. These parents also believe that their children gain lessons and morals from stories and can learn new things and important life skills from books. In addition, we have found that children's language skills (receptive and expressive) are greater when their parents value their roles in their children's learning. For instance, children tend to have greater receptive and expressive language skills when parents believe that they play an important role in their children's learning and when parents feel they are effective in fulfilling that role. Such parents tend to feel good about their children's current language skills and have high expectations for their children's success in school. Such beliefs may create expectations and stimulate behaviours supportive of children's language development. In fact, we have found that the more supportive parents' beliefs about children's language development, the more likely they are to provide language activities and opportunities for language use for children in the home (Weigel *et al.*, 2006).

In summary, it appears that a number of assets in the home setting help foster children's listening and speaking abilities. In other words, research has shown that these assets provide a context for the optimal development of children's language skills. Moreover, this research, including our own, has shown that these language-related developmental assets have a lasting impact on children's language development.

What assets in the child care environment influence young children's language development?

Just as homes provide assets for children's language development, so too do child care settings. Although not as frequently studied as the home, the child care assets can be organized similarly to those presented above for the home setting. Figure 1 shows some of the types of positive assets in the child care setting that parallel those found in the home.

Child care demographic and situational characteristics

Although several studies have documented the overall long-term contributions of high-quality child care on children's academic success (e.g. Currie, 2001; Gorey, 2001; Caputo, 2004), a number of studies have looked at specific features in the child care setting and their relationships to children's language development. For instance, Burchinal *et al.* (1996) have found that children have greater expressive language scores when their teachers had higher levels of education. Similarly, children tend to make better language gains when they are with more experienced teachers who have stronger language skills and regularly model those skills (Weigel *et al.*, 2005). Burchinal *et al.* (1996) also examined the ratio of teachers to children in infant care classrooms and found that those infants who scored better on their receptive language and communication indicators at 12 months had classrooms with lower teacher–child ratios. The authors speculated that fewer infants per adult should give teachers more opportunities to interact with infants, and infants, in turn, should have more opportunities to interact with their teachers and practice their communication skills. In the longitudinal NICHD project (2006), language skills were more advanced in children who spent more hours in child care at 24 and 36 months. Time spent in child care appears to provide the opportunity for children to interact with other adults and peers.

Teacher conversational style

The type and quality of teacher–child interaction in the preschool classroom also appears to influence children's language skills. The NICHD (2000) project observed language stimulation by child care teachers, defined as how often teachers asked questions of the child, responded to the child's vocalizations and talked positively to children. They found that the amount of language stimulation observed at 15 months in the classroom was significantly associated with children's vocabulary production and verbal comprehension at 24 months and expressive language and verbal comprehension at 36 months. Those authors contend that the more child care environments are characterized by caregiver–child interactions that are both supportive and verbally stimulating, the better children perform. Conversely, the less verbally stimulating and supportive the care experience, the more poorly children perform. In addition, Burchinal *et al.* (1996) found that children tended to have higher receptive and communicative scores when centres had more frequent and more positive teacher–child interactions.

Dickinson and Tabors (2001) reported on a series of studies they and their colleagues have conducted that examined the types of teacher–child interaction during mealtimes and free play. They found that the more rare words (i.e. words that preschool age would not commonly be expected to know) used by teachers, the greater children's receptive vocabulary and narrative production. In other words, children seem to gain receptive and expressive language skills when teachers use words that stretch children's vocabularies. Furthermore, the researchers found that the use of rare words by the children while talking to their teachers in the classroom also related to children's receptive vocabulary and narrative production. Dickinson and Tabors also report on teachers' conversational styles during free play. Children had stronger language skills in classrooms where teachers had a lower rate of teacher talk to child talk and spoke to children in ways that extended children's comments. Thus, it appears that children gain language skills when teachers do not dominate conversations with children; rather, they indicate interest, ask questions designed to encourage children to clarify themselves, and comment on children's efforts. These conversational skills are similar to those presented earlier on parents' conversational skills that have been associated with increased language development.

Language activities

Research has shown that child care teachers can provide ample language activities and experiences in the classroom, such as shared book reading, reading and writing centres, singing songs and telling stories, listening games, group games, dramatic play and, more recently, technology-assisted games (Lapp *et al.*, 2000). Such activities provide preschool-aged children opportunities to hear speech, explore sounds, gain vocabulary and practise their ever-growing language skills (Lapp *et al.*, 2000).

One of the most frequently studied language activities in the preschool classroom is shared book reading. The more teachers actively engage children in shared book reading, the higher children's vocabulary and story comprehension (Dickinson & Smith, 1994). Also, children gain expressive vocabulary when they use skills such as expanding upon the story, providing feedback to children's inquiries and following the interests of the child (Lonigan & Whitehurst, 1998). In our own work, we also have found that children's language skills are greater when teachers actively engage them in language activities in the classroom, especially shared book reading (Weigel *et al.*, 2005). Specifically, children make the best gains in language skills when teachers tell stories, actively engage children in reading experiences (i.e. sounding excited when reading books, having children help to tell story, wanting children to ask questions, asking children questions and relating stories to children's lives), as well as simply spending more time in shared book reading, buying books for the classroom and taking the children to the library. This active engagement of children in discussion of stories appears to be especially important for children's expressive language skills, providing opportunities for young children to use those skills.

Teacher beliefs

Just like parents, we have found that children make gains in their language skills when teachers value their roles in children's learning (Weigel *et al.*, 2005). For instance, we have found that the children with teachers who believe in the power of sharing books with the children (e.g. reading helps children be better talkers and listeners, stories help build children's imagination, children learn lessons and morals from stories, reading helps them learn new things and important life skills) have greater language skills than children whose teachers do not hold this belief. Likewise, children tend to have greater receptive and expressive language skills when teachers believe that they play an important role in children's learning, and when teachers feel they are effective in fulfilling that role. In fact, in our data we have found that the more supportive teachers' beliefs about children's language development, the more likely they were to provide language activities for children in the classroom.

In summary, it appears that critical assets in the child care setting can enhance the language skills of children before they start formal schooling. These findings parallel those found regarding the home setting. For example, structural features in the classroom, teacher conversational styles, language activities in the classroom and teacher's beliefs have all been found to be associated with children's gains in receptive and expressive language. A question remains, however, as to how these home and child care assets combine to bolster children's speaking and listening abilities.

In what ways do the assets in the home and child care settings combine to impact children's language development?

A fundamental assumption of a developmental asset framework is that the developmental assets in the home and child care settings are interconnected and children's language skills thrive when both environments foster children's development. Some research has supported this claim. Dickinson and McCabe (2001), for instance, report on a series of studies in which they examined the combined language richness of the home and child care settings on children's vocabulary development. They found that the more rich the conversations in both settings (e.g. varied vocabulary used during mealtimes and free play times, engagement of children in intellectually challenging conversations and informative conversations during book reading), the stronger preschool children's vocabulary skills.

With our own data, we also have sought to determine the combined impact of the home and child care environments on children's language skills (see Weigel *et al.*, 2005 for more detail). When we combined assets in the home and child care settings in regression analyses, we found that homes and child care programs contribute significantly to children's receptive and expressive language development. As can be seen in Figure 2, we found that home assets account for 27% of the variance in children's receptive and expressive language scores. In addition, the child care assets accounted for 11% of the variance in children's receptive language and 15% in children's expressive language scores. Even more telling, these assets continue to explain significant amounts of variance in children's receptive and language scores after one year. Overall, these assets combine to explain between 38% and 46% of the variance in children's language scores. These findings reinforce the importance of both the home and child care setting in helping to advance the language skills of preschool children. Furthermore, they show that there is a link between home and child care assets measured at one point in time and child language outcomes measured a year later, demonstrating that language-related developmental assets have a long-term impact on children's language development.

We also wanted to examine whether home and child care assets act independently or interactively. When we included interaction terms between home and child care assets into the regression analyses, we found that the interaction terms were not significant. Therefore, it appears that the developmental assets of both the home and child care settings are important in promoting children's language development; the influences of these two settings, however, appear to act independently. Strong assets in both settings are needed to ensure optimal language development by children before they begin formal schooling.

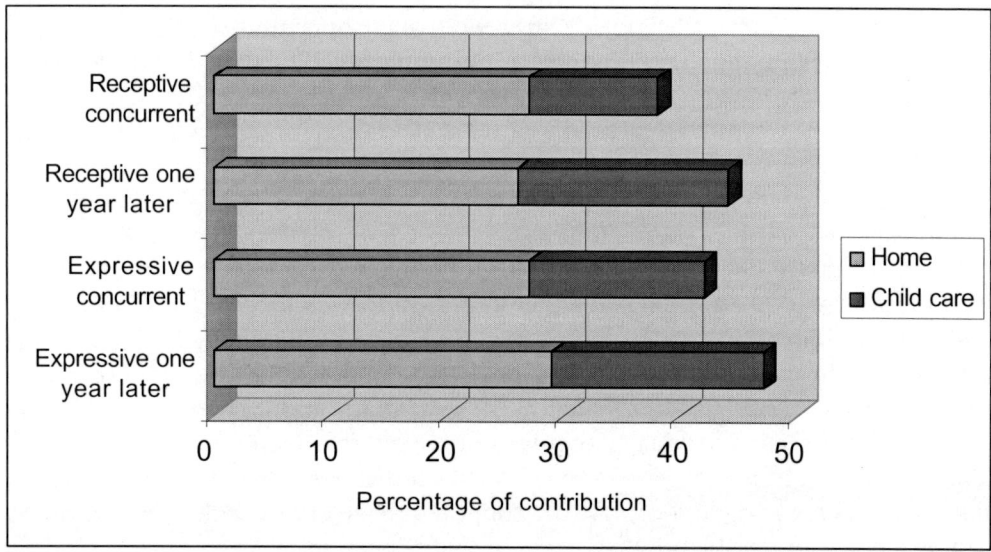

Figure 2.   Relative contributions of home and child care assets to preschool-aged children's receptive and expressive language skills

What does a developmental assets approach offer to our understanding of young children's language skills?

In this paper, we have identified several specific attributes in the home and child care settings that promote language development before children enter formal education. Even within this short time span, the literature suggests that early language development is predictive of later language and literacy skills. Further, there may be a snowball effect in which children with numerous assets early on make greater gains than their less fortunate peers over time, thereby widening the gap between children with rich and poor language environments (Fenson *et al.*, 1994). In bringing together studies that examined the home and child care setting alone, as well as research that examined both, we found evidence of the contributions of those environments to preschool children's language development. Furthermore, these contributions seem to have long-term impacts. At this point, we want to turn to the final question posed above: what does a developmental assets approach offer to our understanding of the development of young children's language skills and in the enrichment of those skills?

One benefit is that the developmental assets approach focuses on a strengths-based approach to children's language development. A fundamental assumption of this approach is that the more positive experiences and assets children have, the greater the chance that they will thrive (Sesma *et al.*, 2005). Such assets should be a benefit for all children no matter what their risk status. The asset approach does not downplay risks, such as poverty, disability or second-language acquisition, but rather, it focuses on factors that can help all children thrive no matter what their level of risk. Such assets include supportive demographic and situational characteristics of the home and child care settings, the quality of conversations adults have with children, the variety and amount of language experiences and opportunities afforded to children, and beliefs among central adults in the importance of their role in fostering young children's language development. Rather than focusing on deficits, an asset approach looks at ways to enhance the optimal development of all children (Sesma *et al.*, 2005).

Another benefit of the developmental assets approach is the emphasis it puts on contexts and settings that influence young children's language development. Children's language development does not occur in a vacuum. Rather, it takes place in a powerful environment that can either help or hinder children's gains in speaking and listening abilities. Although in this paper we have intentionally focused on the home and child care contexts, we do not want to downplay the importance of internal factors within children, such as normal maturation, speech and hearing capabilities and second language acquisition, or external factors, such as poverty, public policy or cultural values. However, for sheer manageability, this paper focused primarily on home and child care, two settings that have critical influences on young children's development before they begin formal education.

Perhaps one of the most important benefits of the developmental assets approach is that many of the assets reviewed here are amenable to change. Through education and training, parents and caregivers may be able to learn skills that are known to improve children's language development. For instance, a number of training programs have been designed to teach parents and care givers specific book-sharing skills associated with positive children's outcomes. Whitehurst and colleagues (Whitehurst *et al.*, 1988; Arnold *et al.*, 1994; Lonigan & Whitehurst, 1998), for example, have shown that their dialogic reading program can produce substantial changes in preschool children's language skills. Rather than the typical shared-reading style in which the adult reads and the child listens, in the dialogic reading approach the adult assumes the role of an active listener, asking questions, adding information and prompting children to increase the sophistication of their descriptions of the material in the picture-book. The authors found that both parents and child care teachers can produce significant changes in the development of oral language using these book-sharing tactics.

We have developed a similar program focusing on book-sharing skills (Weigel *et al.*, 2001). The program includes six family sessions during which parents: (1) discuss and learn basic book-sharing techniques, including previewing a book, using expression as they read, pointing to pictures and labelling, reviewing and retelling, having children predict and linking the book to life; (2) watch a video that models the book-sharing techniques; (3) practise reading with each other, then share the book with the children; (4) learn about activities that extend the learning from parent–child workshops into family homes; and (5) receive a book and materials to complete the extender activities at home. We have found that the program is effective in increasing parents' book-sharing skills and increasing children's vocabulary and print awareness.

Another focus of training could be directed at parent and child care teacher conversation skills. As noted earlier in this paper, adults' styles of communicating with children can go a long way to fostering children's speaking and listening skills. Parents and child care teachers could be trained in the types of conversational skills that are associated with positive language development in children (Hoff-Ginsberg, 1991; DeTemple, 2001). Such training sessions should include practice on the use of non-immediate styles, such as describing, defining, drawing connections between concepts, and cause-and-effect relationships. Further, the use of more metalinguistic comments could be emphasized. Parents and child care teachers could be trained on how to use language that indicates interest, ask questions that encourage children to clarify themselves, make topic-continuing replies, provide affirmative conversational feedback and comment on children's efforts.

Conclusion

Much language development takes place in the preschool years—the years before children begin formal schooling. It is during this time that the foundation for children's listening, speaking and communication skills with others is set. In this paper, we have presented a different way of viewing young children's language development. The developmental assets approach places the focus on strengths both internal and external to young children, and stresses new ways to conceptualize, measure and promote optimal outcomes for children. We have seen evidence of the additive nature of developmental assets and resources that impact children's language development, especially at home and in child care. These findings suggest that the greater the number of positive developmental factors that a child is exposed to before formal schooling, the more likely he or she will experience optimal language and literacy outcomes and thrive.

The developmental asset approach represents a shift away from relying solely on prevention and intervention efforts to the enhancement of assets within homes, child care settings and communities in the service of optimal language development for children at all levels of risk. This discussion of home and child care assets in no way is meant to replace or supplant targeted programmatic efforts—one of the implications of the asset model is that strong and effective programs are a necessary component of a developmentally responsive community, and that programs are eminently complementary to positive child development approaches (Sesma *et al.*, 2005). In the coming years we need to better understand how the network of assets support children's development, and how we can more effectively enable children from all backgrounds to become successful speakers, listeners and communicators.

References

Arnold, D. H., Lonigan, C. J., Whitehurst, G. J. & Epstein, J. N. (1994) Accelerating language development through picture book reading: replication and extension to a videotape training format, *Journal of Educational Psychology*, 86, 235–243.

Baker, L., Serpell, R. & Sonnenschein, S. (1995) Opportunities for literacy and learning in the homes of urban preschoolers, in: L. M. Morrow (Ed.) *Family literacy: connections in schools and communities* (Newark, DE, International Reading Association), 236–252.

Beals, D. E. (2001) Eating and reading: links between family conversation with preschoolers and later language and literacy, in: D. K. Dickinson & P. O. Tabors (Eds) *Beginning literacy with language* (Baltimore, MD, Paul H. Brookes), 75–92.

Bennett, K. K., Weigel, D. J. & Martin, S. S. (2002) Children's acquisition of early literacy skills: examining family contributions, *Early Childhood Research Quarterly*, 17, 295–317.

Benson, P. L., Leffert, N., Scales, P. C. & Blyth, D. A. (1998) Beyond the 'village' rhetoric: creating healthy communities for children and adolescents, *Applied Developmental Science*, 2, 138–159.

Bronfenbrenner, U. & Morris, P. A. (1998) The ecology of developmental processes, in: R. M. Lerner (Ed.) *Handbook of child psychology, Vol. 1: Theoretical models of human development* (5th edn) (New York, Wiley), 993–1028.

Burchinal, M. R., Roberts, J. E., Nabors, L. A. & Bryant, D. M. (1996) Quality of center child care and infant cognitive and language development, *Child Development*, 67, 606–620.

Burchinal, B. R., Peisner-Feinberg, E., Pianta, R. & Howes, C. (2002) Development of academic skills from preschool through second grade: family and classroom predictors of developmental trajectories, *Journal of School Psychology*, 40, 415–436.

Bus, A., van Ijzendoorn, M. H. & Pellegrini, A. D. (1995) Joint book reading makes for success in learning to read: a meta-analysis on intergenerational transmission of literacy, *Review of Educational Research*, 65, 1–21.

Caputo, R. K. (2004) The impact of intergenerational Head Start participation on success measures among adolescent children, *Journal of Family and Economic Issues*, 25, 199–223.

Catalano, R. F., Hawkins, J. D., Berglund, M. L., Pollard, J. A. & Arthur, M. W. (2002) Prevention science and positive youth development: competitive or cooperative frameworks? *Journal of Adolescent Health*, 31, 230–239.

Currie, J. (2001) Early childhood education programs, *Journal of Economic Perspectives*, 15, 213–238.

DeTemple, J. M. (2001) Parents and children reading books together, in: D. K. Dickinson & P. O. Tabors (Eds) *Beginning literacy with language* (Baltimore, MD, Paul H. Brookes), 31–52.

Dickinson, D. K. & McCabe, A. (2001) Bringing it all together: the multiple origins, skills, and environmental support of early literacy, *Learning Disabilities Research and Practice*, 16, 182–202.

Dickinson, D. & Smith, M. (1994) Long-term effects of preschool teachers' book readings on low-income children's vocabulary and story comprehension, *Reading Research Quarterly*, 29, 105–122.

Dickinson, D. K. & Tabors, P. O. (Eds) (2001) *Beginning literacy with language* (Baltimore, MD, Paul H. Brookes).

Fenson, L., Dale, P., Reznick, J. S., Bates, E., Thal, D. & Pethick, S. (1994) Variability in early communicative development, *Monographs for the Society for Research in Child Development*, 59(5), Serial No. 242.

Gibbs, E. D., Teti, D. M. & Bond, L. A. (1987) Infant–sibling communication: relationship to birth-order spacing and cognitive and linguistic development, *Infant Behavior and Development*, 10, 307–323.

Gorey, K. M. (2001) Early childhood education: a meta-analytic affirmation of the short- and long-term benefits of educational opportunity, *School Psychology Quarterly*, 16, 9–30.

Hart, B. & Risley, T. R. (1995) *Meaningful differences in the everyday experience of young American children* (Baltimore, MD, Paul H. Brookes).

Hoff, E. (2003) The specificity of environmental influence: socioeconomic status affects early vocabulary development via maternal speech, *Child Development*, 74, 1368–1378.

Hoff-Ginsberg, E. (1991) Mother–child conversation in different social classes and communicative settings, *Child Development*, 62, 782–796.

Jones, C. P. & Adamson, L. B. (1987) Language use in mother–child and mother–child–sibling interactions, *Child Development*, 58, 356–366.

Lapp, D., Flood, J. & Roser, N. (2000) Still standing: timeless strategies for teaching the language arts, in: D. S. Strickland & L. M. Morrow (Eds) *Beginning reading and writing* (New York, Teachers College Press), 183–193.

Lonigan, C. J. & Whitehurst, G. J. (1998) Relative efficacy of parent and teacher involvement in a shared-reading intervention for preschool children from low-income backgrounds, *Early Childhood Research Quarterly*, 13, 263–290.

Nelson, K. (1981) Individual differences in language development: implications for development and language, *Developmental Psychology*, 17, 170–187.

NICHD Early Child Care Research Network (2000) The relation of child care to cognitive and language development, *Child Development*, 71, 958–978.

NICHD Early Child Care Research Network (2004) Type of child care and children's development at 54 months, *Early Childhood Research Quarterly*, 19, 203–230.

NICHD Early Child Care Research Network (2006) Child-care effect sizes for the NICHD study of early child care and youth development, *American Psychologist*, 61(2), 99–116.

Pullen, P. C. & Justice, L. M. (2003) Enhancing phonological awareness, print awareness, and oral language skills in preschool children, *Intervention in School and Clinic*, 39, 87–98.

Rollins, P. R., Snow, C. E. & Willett, J. B. (1996) Predictors of MLU: semantic and morphological development, *First Language*, 47, 243–259.

Rowe, D. C., Jacobson, K. C. & Van den Oord, E. J. C. G. (1999) Genetic and environmental influences on vocabulary IQ: parental education level as moderator, *Child Development*, 70, 1151–1162.

Scales, P. C. & Leffert, N. (1999) *Developmental assets: a synthesis of the scientific research on adolescent development* (Minneapolis, MN, Search Institute).

Scales, P. C. & Roehlkepartain, E. C. (2003) Boosting student achievement: new research on the power of developmental assets, *Search Institute Insights and Evidence, 1*. Available online at: http://www.search-institute.org/research/Insights/IE-10-03-Achievement.pdf (accessed 29 October 2006).

Senechal, M., LeFevre, J., Thomas, E. M. & Daley, K. E. (1998) Differential effects of home literacy experiences on the development of oral and written language, *Reading Research Quarterly*, 33, 96–116.

Sesma, A., Mannes, M. & Scales, P. C. (2005) Positive adaptation, resilience, and the developmental asset framework, in: S. Goldstein & R. B. Brooks (Eds) *Handbook of resilience in children* (New York, Kluwer Academic Publishers/Plenum), 281–296.

Snow, C. E., Burns, M. S. & Griffin, P. (Eds) (1998) *Preventing reading difficulties in young children: Committee on the Prevention of Reading Difficulties in Young Children, National Research Council*. Available online at: http://www.nap.edu/readingroom/books/prdyc/ (accessed 6 May 2006).

Snow, C. E., Dubber, D. & de Blauw, A. (1982) Routines in mother–child interaction, in: L. Feagans & D. C. Farran (Eds) *The language of children reared in poverty* (New York, Academic Press), 53–77.

Snow, C. E. & Ferguson, C. (1977) *Talking to children* (Cambridge, Cambridge University Press).

Tabors, P. O., Beals, D. E. & Weizman, Z. O. (2001a) 'You know what oxygen is?' Learning new words at home, in: D. K. Dickinson & P. O. Tabors (Eds) *Beginning literacy with language* (Baltimore, MD, Paul H. Brookes), 93–110.

Tabors, P. O., Roach, K. A. & Snow, C. E. (2001b) Home language and literacy environment, in: D. K. Dickinson & P. O. Tabors (Eds) *Beginning literacy with language* (Baltimore, MD, Paul H. Brookes), 111–138.

Van der Ven, K. & Mannes, M. (2005) *The Early Childhood Developmental Assets Framework (ECDAF): a practical and ecological approach to promoting positive development*. Available online at: http://www.search-institute.org/research/ECDAF.html (accessed 29 October 2006).

Weigel, D., Behal, P. & Martin, S. (2001) The family storyteller: a collaborative family literacy program, *Journal of Extension*, 39(4). Available online at: http://www.joe.org/joe/2001august/iw2.html (accessed 2 September 2001).

Weigel, D. J., Martin, S. S. & Bennett, K. K. (2005) Ecological influences of the home and child-care center on preschool-age children's literacy development, *Reading Research Quarterly*, 40, 204–233.

Weigel, D. J., Martin, S. S. & Bennett, K. K. (2006) Contributions of the home literacy environment to preschool-aged children's emerging literacy and language skills, *Early Child Development and Care*, 176(3–4), 357–378.

Whitehurst, G. J., Falco, F., Lonigan, C. J., Fischel, J. E., DeBaryshe, B. D., Valdez-Menchaca, M. C. & Caulfield, M. (1988) Accelerating language development through picture-book reading, *Developmental Psychology*, 24, 552–558.

Whitehurst, G. J. & Lonigan, C. J. (1998) Child development and emergent literacy, *Child Development*, 69, 848–872.

From folktales to algorithms: developing the teacher's role as principal storyteller in the classroom

A. K. Daniel

Introduction

With the advent of the *Primary framework for literacy and mathematics* (http://www.standards.dfes.gov.uk/priaryframeworks/) the opportunities for children to engage in storytelling and study of narrative have received a muc-needed boost in the primary schools of England and Wales. However, unless teachers feel that they themselves are equipped to be classroom storytellers, then the activity of classroom storytelling delivered by an adult will remain the preserve of the professional teller of tales instead of its being regarded as a general teaching method, rich in potential for assisting children to become effective learners.

In this paper, I approach the role of teacher as storyteller and outline what I believe are five fundamental aspects of classroom storytelling, both in the telling of tales specifically and more general teaching:

- The use of the unmediated text.
- The employment of narrative storytelling and narrative teaching.
- The informed selection of suitable material.
- The place of the teacher as principle storyteller in the classroom.
- Absence and completion—engagement and story.

The unmediated text: reading or telling?

Storytelling is a very different activity to *story reading*. In the wider world there is a perception that stories are to be read. 'So, you read stories to the children, do you?' is a frequently asked question when I give my profession as 'storyteller'. Perhaps this is excusable in (what passes for) a literate society as the occasions when we stop and listen to a story that we think of as a story are few, but we will sit happily with friends as they regale us with holiday mishaps and pay money to listen to the stand-up comedian who has created a whole act from one simple narrative idea (such as buying a pair of shoes). This is storytelling, even though it may not be thought of as such: it is the telling of story unmediated by a written text and, as such, it is a fundamental human activity. Booker (2004) writes:

> At any given moment, all over the world, hundreds of millions of people will be engaged in what is one of the most familiar of all forms of human activity. In one way or another they will have their attention focussed on one of those strange sequences of mental images which we call a story.

> We spend a phenomenal amount of our lives following stories: telling them; listening to them; reading them; watching them being acted out on the television screen or in films or on stage. They are far and away one of the most important features of our everyday existence. (Booker, 2004, p. 2)

Although I work in the oral tradition, I would never deny the power of reading a book with a group of students: both reading and telling of tales have their place; however, I would suggest that for many professionals the storybook can provide a source of protection as much as a source of stories. The tale told by the storyteller is unmediated[1]: there is no defined text to provide the teller with the words they are going to use; telling as opposed to reading a story leaves the teacher more dependent on their own resources and thus more vulnerable before their pupils.

While I cannot imagine that any teacher working in the primary years has not, or will not, read stories to their class(es), to put the book down and tell the story is quite another thing. No one is going to suggest that reading a book with children is undesirable, let alone wrong, but it is not storytelling. As there is a wealth of material extolling the virtues of using the printed text in the classroom, I will take the opportunity to identify some of the less positive aspects:

- The reader of the text becomes the voice of the author; they are not the speaker of their own story. As creative as the teacher may be in his/her vocal production and use of pace and rhythm, it cannot alter the fact that this is a tale expressed in the words of a third party.

- The writer of the printed text has aimed their work at a general readership of a particular age (and perhaps a specific demographic), it was not written for a particular group of pupils. Although words might be changed or phrasing adapted, the printed text leads both reader and hearer down a fixed path that allows little adaptation to a specific group of students.
- The book creates a physical barrier between the speaker and the hearers. Even rested across the knees, the paper and cardboard come between the teacher and the pupils.
- The pictures that form part of most books at this level represent the imaginative response of the illustrator to the narrative that will not coincide with the response of the children. A picture, in effect, says: 'We are not talking of your imagined wolf, but the wolf in this picture.'

The *told* story, however, has a flexibility and immediacy:

- The teacher can adapt the language to the needs of children—this frees the teacher from finding published texts at a specific linguistic level, the story itself becoming the primary concern, not the author's mode of expression.
- The children's responses to the story can be incorporated into the telling. The storyteller's command of the underlying structure of a tale enables them to use predictive questioning where students' answers are able to shape details without imperilling the integrity of the narrative.
- The absence of a physical object permits freedom of expression for the teller and removes a barrier between them and their hearers.
- It is frequently said that 'the best pictures are on radio', and it so with the told tale, with the storyteller taking their hearers on an imaginary journey individual to each one as they create characters, settings and encounters in their own minds. This *imaging* (in which mental images are manipulated and associations between them are made (Rosenberg, 1987)) is the first step in the visualization process key to understanding any narrative schema (Schreiber, 2005); it may be stimulated with questioning from within the storytelling not just at its conclusion (it is often the case that teachers question children about aspects of a story at the end of the tale, reluctant to interrupt the flow, but targeted questioning throughout the storytelling allows the pupils to be fellow creators of the imagined world (see 'Absence and completion', below).

None of the above could possibly justify the exclusion of reading to children as an activity, but it does suggest that the story unmediated by a written text also has a place in the classroom.

Narrative storytelling and narrative teaching

To use the phrase 'narrative storytelling' may seem tautologous, but I have used these words in combination to emphasize the necessary link between storytelling and that which I believe characterizes effective teaching: an understanding of how narrative frames our understanding of the world in which we function. Bruner (1990) and others suggest that narrative is the principal means by which we organize our experiences of the world. For Riceour, 'time becomes human to the extent that it is articulated through a narrative mode, and narrative attains its full meaning when it becomes a condition of temporal existence' (Riceour, 1984, p. 52).

As, it could be argued that storytelling represents the principal exemplar of (crafted) narrative communication, the distance between the skills needed by the competent storyteller and those required for teaching within a narrative framework should not be great. Toolan (2001) gives a series of defining characteristics of narrative:

1. A degree of artificial fabrication or constructedness not usually apparent in spontaneous conversation.
2. A degree of prefabrication; in other words, narratives often seem to have bits we have seen or heard, or think we have heard, before.
3. Narratives typically seem to have a 'trajectory'; they usually go somewhere, and are expected to go somewhere, with some sort of development and even a resolution or conclusion provided.
4. Narratives have to have a teller, and that teller, no matter how backgrounded or 'invisible', is always important.
5. Narratives are richly exploitative where that design feature of language called *displacement* (the ability of human language to be used to refer to things or events that are removed, in space or time, from either speaker or addressee) is present.
6. Narratives involve the recall of happenings that may be not merely spatially, but, more crucially, temporally remote from the teller and his audience.

My assertion is that, as storytellers, teachers need to have a grasp of how to construct clear narrative, and as teachers, *per se*, they should exploit their abilities as storytellers in giving their teaching a clear narrative form. Through the narrative structuring of teaching we can provide students with a framework that not only contextualizes elements of a programme of learning, but also provides a tool for metacognitive reflection.

There are many models of narrative structure to which one may refer but they are dominated by linear processes (dealing with the surface level of the story as a series of linked episodes). While it is necessary to be able to sequence events in order to create a coherent narrative (initiating event, episodes and resolution), the connections between these elements need to be understood in order to make sense of the events themselves; citing the analysis of the Watergate trial by Edwards and Potter, Lyle (2000) asserts that 'human beings make sense of the world by interpreting actions, inferring motives, and ascribing values to acts'.

In my own work, I have taken to using a simple rendering of the actantial analysis of the French semiotician A. J. Greimas. This process analyses the relationships between the underlying elements of a story, and although the task of revealing the metalanguage of a narrative may appear a complex one at first, at the level at which we are working the task becomes simple and enables storytelling to be coherent and memorable.

Sitting on the shoulders of Vladimir Propp, and his classification of Russian folktales, Greimas leads us to consider not so much individual character types (such as king, step-mother or child), but to the *functions* that the characters serve in the story. Greimas identified six functions within narrative (Greimas & Cortes, 1982):

1. *Subject*: the character around whom the narrative turns.
2. *Object*: what the subject wants to achieve or acquire.
3. *Sender*: the person(s) or force(s) that moves the Subject to seek the Object.
4. *Receiver*: the person(s) that benefits from the Subject's successful quest for the Object.[2]
5. *Helper*: the person(s) or force(s) that aid the Subject in their quest for the Object
6. *Opponent*: the person(s) or force(s) that opposes the Subject's completion of their quest for the Object

These form binary pairs: subject and object; sender and receiver; and helper and opponent. These may be arranged in diagrammatic form:

$$\text{Sender} \rightarrow \text{Object} \leftarrow \text{Receiver}$$
$$\uparrow$$
$$\text{Helper} \leftarrow \text{Subject} \leftarrow \text{Opponent}$$

While a work of literature may generate a complex diagram with more than one Subject, a series of Opponents and layers of Objects, it is possible to reduce the global narrative of folktales (and other stories that best serve oral conveying in the classroom) to a simple schematic diagram of binary pairs. Taking the example of 'Little Red Riding Hood' (as told by the Brothers Grimm):

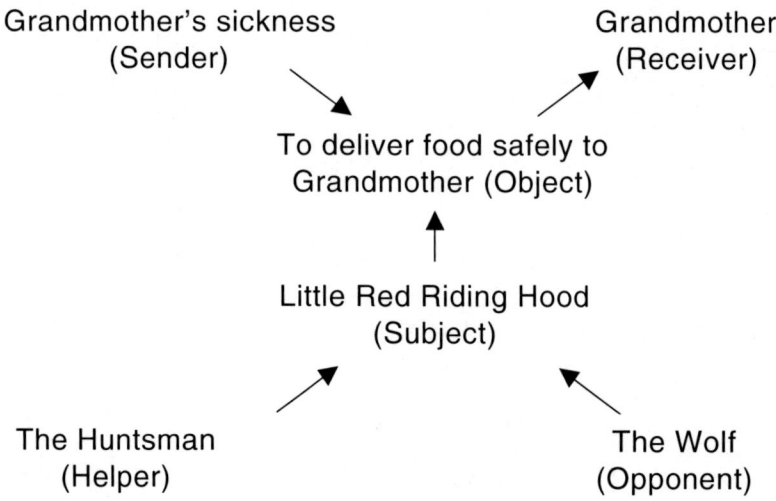

If we consider, then, the two suppositions of this section:

1. that as humans we understand ourselves and our world in narrative terms;
2. that narrative can be reduced to six functions: subject, object, sender, receiver, helper and opponent

then there is an implication for teaching in general where we should be construct-ing narratives in which these functions are clearly differentiated and, further, assisting our students to monitor their own learning by the same method. Related to storytelling specifically, the teacher should be creating narratives whose coherent internal structures support the child's quest to become an effective and compre-hending listener, skills that will, in turn, inform enable them to create their own narratives.

The methodology can be illustrated by taking the example of the Norman Conquest. In order to understand the story, we may wish to consider the two oppos-ing leaders, William and Harold, by identifying the functions that operate within the historical narratives of their respective leaderships:

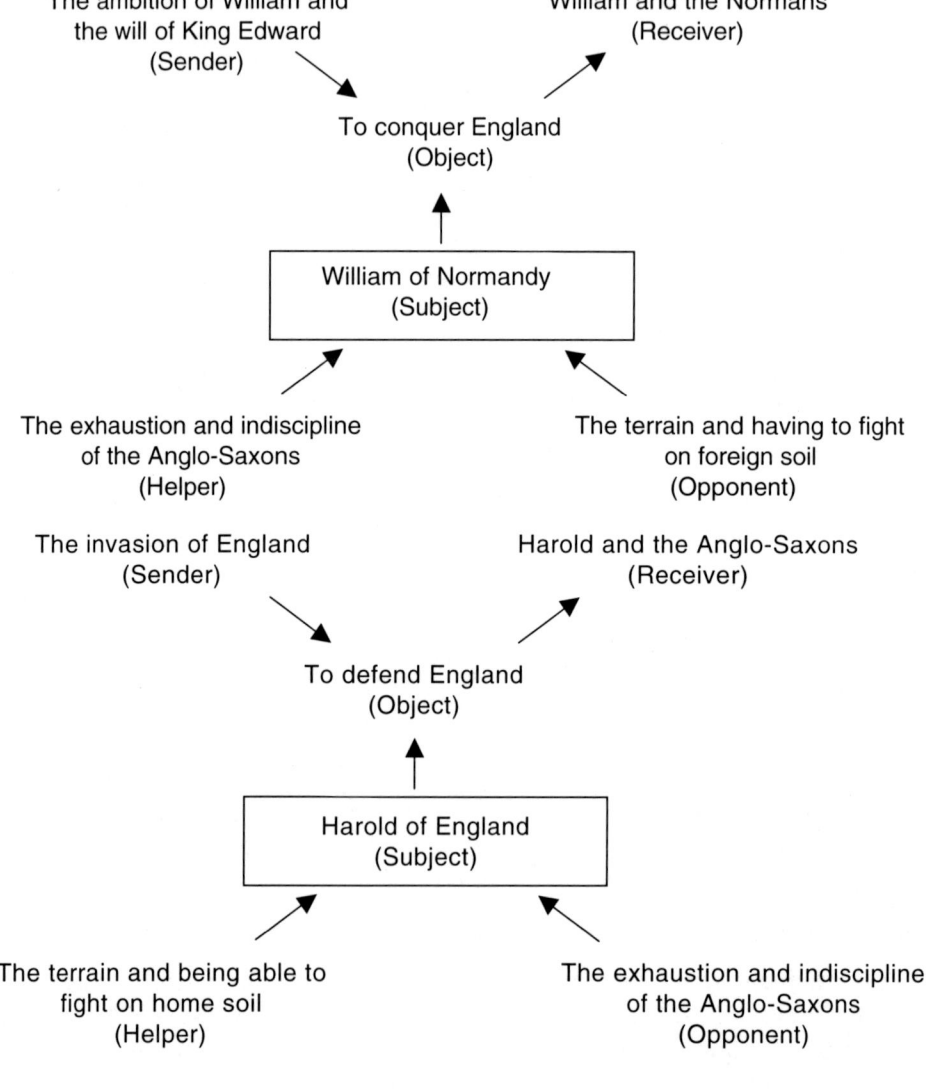

I am not suggesting that the above schemas provide a sufficient study of the Conquest, nor that students should be taught to make schematic diagrams of actantial function at key stage 2, but in trying to make sense of the story this analysis allows the teacher to identify the key functions that create a coherent narrative from the history. Remove one of these functions and the narrative is incomplete and fails to make sense. Hence by concentrating on narrative teaching, we are simply connecting with the way in which we naturally deal with information.

Although I have yet to adapt the diagrammatic form of the schema to student use, I have used a series of prompt questions which establish the functions as a means of supporting children in their construction of narratives (printed as postcards they can also be paired (subject/object, sender/receiver, helper/opponent, by the students):

- who is the story about? (subject)
- what do they want to do? (object)
- why do they want to do this? (sender)
- who or what will benefit if they succeed? (receiver)
- who or what is trying to help them? (helper)
- who or what is working against them? (opponent)

The questions also frame the way in which I explore stories with students, reinforcing their value as a model for the children as they consider existing stories and develop their own narratives.

How, then, can this schematic approach be applied to domains beyond those which naturally lend themselves to the use of recounting (such as history)? Although the direct teaching of multiplication (as opposed to recalling how a problem was solved) lacks the temporal or spatial displacement already identified as a characteristic of narrative, it is still possible to identify the six functions of the actantial analysis:

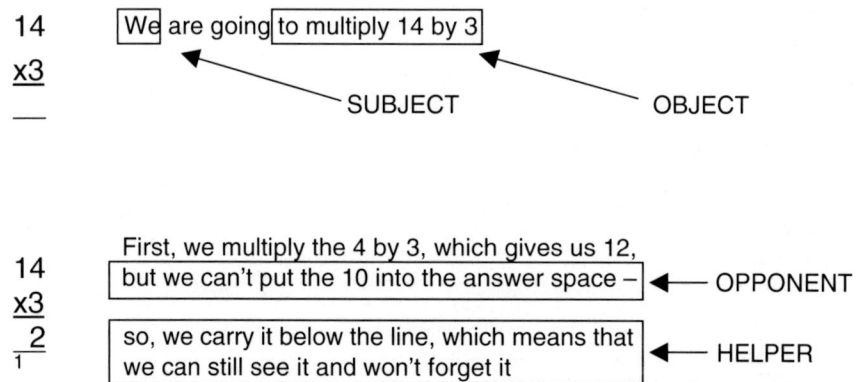

The *sender*, in this case, is contextually understood to be the teacher who initiates the activity, but the *receiver* is still to be identified. A simple introduction that explains that this revisit to multiplication is to remind everyone of the methodology before we go onto more complex problems would imply that 'we' are the *receivers* of the benefit of the activity—in reality, the 'we' which suggests an inclusive beneficiary will be understood by the students to refer to themselves alone in improving their command of multiplication (however, the teacher also clearly benefits from their students' competence).

Narrative and memorization

Returning to classroom storytelling, the representation of a coherent narrative is key, not only for the comprehension of the children, but also for the memorization of the story by the teacher.

Many writers on the craft of storytelling have suggested methods for memorizing stories that have included the creation of mental storyboards in which images can be linked together, the drawing of a 'spider diagram' showing the relationships between the major characters and linking them with events or writing a three-line précis of the tale. While I have often used simple flowcharts in order to remember strongly sequential narratives (such as creation myths), I have found that the actantial analysis, outlined above, is the most effective method of setting a story in my head that it has internal coherence when I tell it. Instead of trying to remember a list of events, I simply have to remember the motivating and opposing forces that come to play on the protagonist as s/he pursues their quest.

In order to memorize a traditional tale, so that you can make it your own and tell it, I would suggest the following:

1.   Make a schematic diagram, as outlined above.
2.   If the story is strongly sequential make a flowchart:

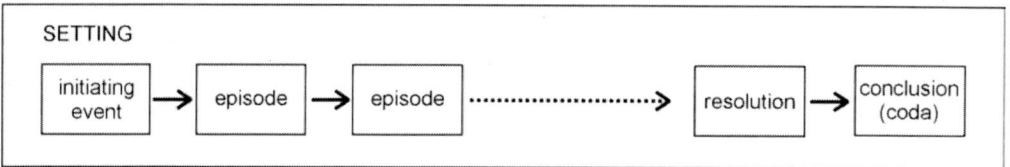

3.   Or identify the turning points of the narrative:

> Little Red Riding Hood skipped through the woods;
> The Wolf met her;
> The Wolf ate Grandmother, etc. Each of which can be visualized as a storyboard tied to the action the characters undertake:

> Little Red Riding Hood <u>skipped</u> through the woods
> The Wolf <u>met</u> her
> The Wolf <u>ate</u> Grandmother, etc.

The basic rule is to use whatever method works for you, with one proviso: do not learn a story word-for-word. Not only does this restrict the flexibility in the telling, it makes errors easier to make and harder to recover from. As the actantial method does not, by necessity, use phrasing drawn from a written text, and depends on a more imaginative approach, it therefore allows a freer flow of ideas.

Above all, busy teachers need to find ways in which to memorize stories that suit their personality as well as the available time. Once the story is learned, it becomes incorporated into the teller's personal repertoire and can be told and retold and retold, again and again, remembering that the story needs to change with every telling as the hearers change, and as each group of children is unique, so is each storytelling event.

As pupils develop their own storytelling abilities, the teacher also needs to be aware of different strategies for remembering tales that can be employed by their pupils. Memorization is far from an isolated cognitive activity (Wood, 1998) and there needs to be a recognition that effective memorization is not bound to one particular methodology, as much for the child-storyteller as for the teacher-storyteller. This implies that children need opportunities to experiment with different methods of memorizing that draw on a variety of stimuli (spatial, iconic, verbal and symbolic[3]) in order to discover those strategies most useful to them; these can vary from simple visual cues (the 'story hand', suggested by Grainger *et al.*, 2004), which enable an elaborative process in which a simple icon (a chair) becomes associated with Goldilocks trying out the Bear's individually, suited furniture, to more complex verbal stimuli, such as the flow-chart suggested above.

Selecting a story

I would love to be able to say that I learned this or that story sitting at the feet of an old woman as she unfolded the traditions of her people to her gathered family, but sadly, I am dependent on my collection of storybooks (picked up on my travels, but rarely found at the feet of the elderly). Of course, stories can be drawn from all manner of sources, and so here we look at the way in which teachers, as busy professionals, can identify stories suitable for classroom use. Zipes (2004, p. 35) writes:

> The best storytellers are thieves and forgers. They steal their tales from everywhere—books, television, films, radio, the Internet, and even other living human beings. Sometimes they steal tales from their own experience that they revise, adorn, and dress in such a way that those who might have witnessed the real incidents would never be able to recognise them. Storytellers appropriate their stolen goods, make them their property, and re-present them as if the goods were their won material, which, in many ways, they are because storytellers always forge the tales they steal anew.

In my own work, I regularly tell the story of 'The Dog Gellert', relating how I heard it as a child while I stood weeping next to the hound's grave in North Wales. Sadly, 'The Dog Gellert' is actually a literary tale masquerading as a legend, and although similar stories exist all over Europe, this version was created by David Pritchard who moved to the village of Beddgelert ('Gelert's grave') in 1793 and wanted to devise a tale to explain the name of his new home (Baring-Gould, 1996). But whatever the origins of the tale, the reason that I enjoy telling it is the emotional resonance it has for me as a childhood memory; this may seem an insupportable reason for choosing a story for classroom use but, as Grainger

(1997) asserts, it is vital that the teller has a real sympathy for the stories that s/he tells:

> The importance of finding short tales which have an instinctive and immediate appeal should not be underestimated. The most successful stories are those which have real meaning and significance for the teller, since unless the tale is in tune with the teller it will not work well. A teacher's enthusiasm for a story is infectious. It allows the story to be 'sung' creatively and fosters commitment from the audience, enticing them to listen, wonder, feel and respond. Teachers working to a tight timetable may need to search for tales for a particular purposes: to enrich cross-curricular work, to examine moral values and practices, and to highlight commonalities and differences across time and between cultures. Traditional tales open doors into the arts, the sciences and the humanities, but such doors must not be forced open at the expense of losing the teacher's interest and critical commitment to the tale. Finding tales that are waiting to be told, that the storyteller really wants to share, for whatever conscious or unconscious reason, remains important. The hunt is not a quick or easy one, but it is always worth the journey. (Grainger, 1997, p. 147)

Grainger's phrase: 'tales that are waiting to be told', is extremely felicitous—it is certainly the feeling I have when I come across a tale that I would like to tell. For me, 'The Dog Gellert' is waiting to be told.

There is a wealth of material to which the storyteller has access, and with the advent of the World Wide Web the choice is tales is bewildering (giving some indication of the problem presented in selecting stories that are appropriate to the needs of a specific group of pupils). The first step, then, is for the teacher to find a story which has a personal resonance from the moment that it is encountered, through adaptation, and to the point where it is unfolded with the students.

Selection criteria

In addition to personal resonance, I would suggest that stories suitable for classroom use should meet the following criteria:

- a coherent narrative;
- linguistic comprehensibility;
- appropriateness to the developmental level of the students;
- cultural relevance;
- a curriculum link;
- a socially constructive message.

Coherent narrative.   Once we have awareness of how coherent narrative is understood (in my methodology through the use of the adapted Actantial schema), we can identify stories that are both suitable for classroom use and easy to learn. If the story is strongly sequential (for instance, the tale of the 'Labours of Theseus' as he travels from Troezen to Athens), then not only should the functions of the global story be present, but also those of each episode should be implicit within the sequence:

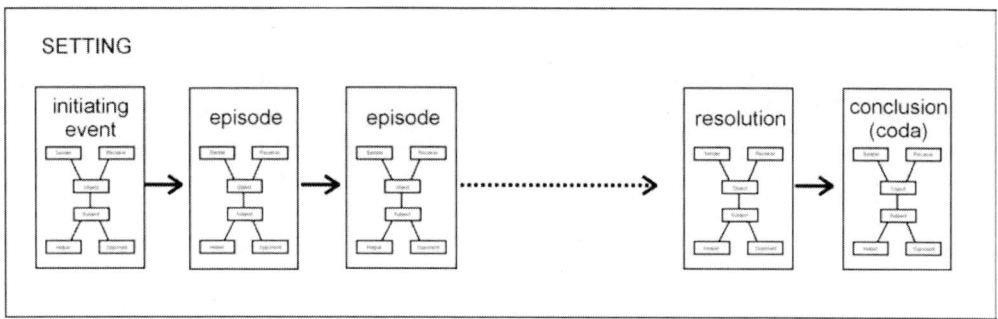

This may seem a burdensome task, but once the method is embedded in praxis, it becomes automatic and self-regulatory.

Linguistic comprehensibility. The telling will need to be comprehensible to the children. This does not mean, however, that the language of the source text needs to be at the appropriate level as the language of oral delivery is dependent on the story-teller, rather than the original printed version. It should also be remembered that as the text is performed it is supported by paralinguistic devices, such as gesture, tone of voice, physical tension and spatial manipulation.

Appropriateness to the developmental level of the students. There is a great differential between the developmental levels of students between Foundation year and Year 6. The story should be appropriate to the emotional and social development of the students. I once made the mistake of telling the story of 'The Three Billy Goats Gruff' from the perspective of the Troll to some children in the Foundation year; it was clear in hindsight that this retelling demanded conceptual jumps outside the children's 'zone of proximal development', and within which the Troll inhabited a role as figurative shorthand for an evil and predatory creature, rather than a character with his own consciousness.

Cultural relevance. It is essential to be aware of the culture within which you are working and its assumptions. The social construction of the child's world must be capable of including the characters, settings and behaviours of a story (even if those behaviours represent a breach of cultural expectations (see Bruner, 1990, 1996).

In the Brothers Grimm story of 'The Fisherman and His Wife', the shrewish wife wishes, in turn, for a house, a castle and a palace. Realising that she can't live in a palace as the wife of a fisherman, she wishes first to be the king, then emperor and then pope. In my telling the papacy is edited from the story on the grounds that few children outside of Catholic families or schools would understand the role of the Pope, or why his status is elevated above that of king and emperor. While it could be argued that this story presents an opportunity to inform students about the historic place of the papacy in European culture, the reference to the pope comes towards the end of the story immediately prior to the wife wishing to be God; to interrupt the narrative in order to make an historical point would destroy the narrative flow and the sense of progressive tension. On the other hand, if one was studying the life of King Henry VIII and his disagreements with the Vatican, this tale could help contextualize the status of the Bishop of Rome.

A story may be also be a means of valuing the different ethnic cultures present in the classroom setting and building a bridge by which pupils can negotiate their way between the dominant, host and minority cultures (Wyse & Jones, 2001, p. 255):

> Story telling can be … [a] particularly successful method of encouraging the multilingual child to negotiate between more than one language. There is evidence that story telling has been a particularly important strategy with bilingual learners in the early years … All cultures have their own histories, myths, legends and stories which are passed on through generations of children. These stories cross cultural boundaries; some are recognisably similar with subtle shades of difference, others will be particular within a specific cultural context. In either case the story itself becomes a powerful shared experience and the telling, the retelling, the writing and reading of the range of possible stories opens a rich vein of language study for the teacher to exploit.

My own experience of working as a storyteller in multicultural schools where there are ethnic tensions has informed my practice. The response of students from Turkish families in some inner-city schools in Belgium to a folktale from Turkey has proved to me the affirming effect of simple storytelling. That the non-Turkish students could also engage with an amusing tale that anyone would be hard-pressed to dislike is also a consideration.

A curriculum link.   The story may be a means of supporting curriculum studies or introducing new themes. For instance, if in science you were looking at the solar system, you could tell a story such as the Native American myth 'How grandmother spider stole the sun' (Bruchac, 1991) to explore the ways in which different peoples have tried to explain what they see in the night sky. The told story (as a creative and shared act) may, by stimulating the imagination, become a spur to critical thinking; restricting storytelling to programmes of study directed purely towards the development of literacy and oracy, therefore, is to ignore a tool for engagement across the curriculum. Egan writes: 'The imagination thus should be … seen as one of our major tools in the pursuit of objective knowledge, and indeed as establishing the very conditions of objectivity' (Egan, 1992, p. 59)

A socially constructive message.   While I don't want to enter a debate on the rights and wrongs of story as social manipulation within the education system, it has to be acknowledged that classroom storytelling remains within the school context and cannot escape being part of the structured environment of learning for the child. In addition to being a primary agent for constructing future society, every teacher faces social issues within the classroom itself, from bullying, to bereavement to the effects of family breakdown, among their students. Although we should beware seeing storytelling as a panacea for the ills of society, the told tale can be a powerful tool in speaking for the marginalized and bolstering the cause of social justice within the school community.

Absence and completion: engagement and story

The longer I practise as a storyteller, the more convinced I become that the key to good storytelling—the key to good teaching—is the principle of *absence and completion*. The word 'absence' can be used in many contexts, not all of them positive: absence of listeners, absence of attention, absence of understanding, absence of humour, but all of these would be despite the teacher and the storyteller. When I speak of 'absence', I am specifically referring to moments where an element of the narrative is missing and has to be provided by the listeners. This absence is controlled by the storyteller; it is intentional and contrived and aimed at stimulating the imagination of the students and directing the imagination along a particular path (or paths) without constricting it.

In this sense, absence may be manifest in a missing word or phrase that the students have to provide (closed response):

> Storyteller: But Siput the snail kept on walking
>
> he kept on walking,
>
> he kept on ...
>
> Students: ... walking!

It may be in supplying information needed to complete the story (open response: if the storyteller is prepared to develop the idea provided by the children):

> Storyteller: The first animal to knock on the witch's door was
>
> the ... the ... You know, I've forgotten; what animal do you think it was?

It may be visual absence, where a person, place or object is 'seen' in what is empty space by the storyteller, but has to be completed by the imagination of the students:

> Storyteller: [*cupping hands and focussing eyes on the space
> between them*] ... and the Lord God looked down at the body of the dead
> swallow and said to the angels, 'You have chosen well ...'

Or, the absence could have additional significance, where an everyday object gains a new meaning through the way it is used in the storytelling:

> Storyteller: The fisherman rowed his little boat out into the blue sea ... [*the storyteller
> takes a long piece of blue cloth and creates ripples in it to signify water*]

With such moments of visual absence, the imagination is engaged in bridging the gap between reality and textual reference (between blue fabric and the sea). It also anchors the whole group to a specific object or space, creating a shared moment of recognition and transformation.

In my efforts to develop storytelling skills, I have made use of a series of scaffolding exercises where students begin by telling an anecdote in which they emphasize elements of the story with over-large gestures; from here they work through several activities until, finally, they make use of subtle visual absence to support their own retelling of an English folktale ('The Pied Piper [of Franchville]': see Jacobs, 1993, p. 225). A key aspect of these activities is peer observation: the observer not only commenting on the ability of their storytelling partner to communicate the narrative, but also reflecting on the skills that they need to develop themselves in order to tell their stories more effectively.

One of the main differences between the read story and the tale that is told is the breadth of opportunities the latter presents for creating moments of absence that engage the listeners and make them participators rather than passive hearers. Sadly, it is the case that many performance activities (whether storytelling, acting, dancing or singing) would be identical whether or not an audience was in fact present. This is not to recommend an 'It's behind you!' approach to every mode of performance, but it is possible to create events where the audience affects the piece. I would echo the director Peter Brook, who rejects the activity of 'watching' a play because of its suggestion of passivity, preferring the French word 'assistance' which has connotations of contribution to the event (Brook, 1972, p. 156):

> In the French language amongst the different terms for those who watch, for public, for spectator, one word stands out, is different in quality from the rest. *Assistance*—I watch a play: *j'assiste à une pièce*. To assist—the word is simple: it is the key.

By creating moments of absence and completion, the storyteller assures the students that their listening is valued, and, at the same time, the children know that the story cannot continue without them. When pupils are asked to contribute to a story and their contribution is incorporated into the narrative, they see that what they bring to the story is integral to the telling and part of the continuous whole.

Conclusion

As we regale friends with the latest disaster in our relationship with the school's photocopier we will use all the elements of storytelling that have been identified in this paper: we will select the story, identifying the elements of narrative and adapting it to our audience; and we will even engage in absence and completion miming the prodding of the green 'start' button and asking, 'Go on, guess what happened next!' Although I may be depriving myself of work, I hope that I have provided ample reasons for every teacher to see themselves as a nascent storyteller. Whether teaching the physical properties of material science, or telling the tale of 'Little Red Riding Hood', the same rules apply:

- A clear, coherent narrative that is unmediated by a written text.
- The use of material that is appropriate to the developmental level of the children and the cultural context in which they exist.
- The controlled and varied use of absence and completion.

Although the structured approach that I have suggested may appear to fly in the face of the very creativity that is implicit in the word 'storytelling', it is my assertion that by maintaining a consistent and structured methodology the teacher-storyteller is able to develop their own metacognitive skills in relation to narrative teaching. This framework for storytelling is, therefore, one in which the teacher takes on the role of principal storyteller in the classroom; it is from this position that can be set a pattern of self-regulation in narrative learning for the students without sacrificing the opportunities for creativity and imaginative play that are inherent in good storytelling.

Notes

1. In a technical sense, this is clearly untrue as the storytelling of the teacher is the medium through which the tale is expressed, but the phrase *unmediated text* succeeds in emphasizing the contrast between the story which is concretized in a set, printed format standing between the teller and their tale and the hearers.
2. Although this interpretation of the *receiver* function is not strictly in line with Greimasian semiotics (in which 'receiver' denotes 'the actant to whom a desire or obligation is given by a sender': Martin & Ringham, 2006), I consider that it does permit a valid and beneficial analysis.
3. Of course, smell and taste are also potent stimuli for memory even if the opportunities to use them strategically in the classroom are limited.

Bibliography

Baring-Gould, S. (1996) *Myths of the middle ages* (ed. J. Matthews) (London, Cassell).

Bettelheim, B. (1991) *The uses of enchantment* (Harmondsworth, Penguin); work originally published 1976.

Booker, C. (2004) *The seven basic plots: why we tell stories* (London, Continuum).

Brook, P. (1972) *The empty space* (Harmondsworth, Penguin).

Bruchac, J. (1991) *Native American stories* (Denver, CO, Fulcrum).

Bruner, J. (1990) *Acts of meaning* (London, Harvard University Press, 1990).

Bruner, J. (1996) *Making stories: law, literature, life* (London, Harvard University Press).

Butcher, S. E. (2006) Narrative as a teaching strategy, *Journal of Correctional Education*, 57(3), 195–208.

Davies, P., Shanks, B. & Davies, K. (2004) Improving narrative skills in young children with delayed language development, *Educational Review*, 56(3), 271–286.

Egan, K. (1989) *Teaching as story telling* (Chicago, University of Chicago Press).

Egan, K. (1992) *Imagination in teaching and learning* (London, Routledge).

Fisher, R. (2004) What is creativity? in: R. Fisher & M. Williams (Eds) *Unlocking creativity* (London, David Fulton).

Grainger, T. (1997) *Traditional storytelling in the primary classroom* (Leamington Spa, Scholastic).

Grainger, T., Goouch, K. & Lambirth, A. (2004) *Creative activities for plot, character and setting ages 5–7* (Leamington Spa, Scholastic).

Greimas, A. J. & Cortes, J. (1982) *Semiotics and language, an analytical dictionary* (trans. Larry Crist *et al.*) (Bloomington, IN, Indiana University Press).

Jacobs, J. (1993) *English fairy tales* (London, Everyman's Library) (Original work published 1890).

Kayashima, M. & Inaba, A. (2003) Towards helping learners master self-regulation skills. Paper presented at *2003 International AIE Conference*. Available online at: http://www.education.umd.edu/EDHD/faculty2/Azevedo/AIED/metacogWorkshopPDFs/kayash.pdf (accessed 28 December 2006).

Lyle, S. (2000) Narrative understanding: developing a theoretical context for understanding how children make meaning in classroom settings, *Journal of Curriculum Studies*, 32(1), 45–63.

Martin, B. & Ringham, F. (2006) *Key terms in semiotics* (London, Continuum).

Polman, J. (2005) True stories, storied truth: stitching narrative and logico-scientific discourse together in an age of 'spin'. Paper presented at the *2005 ISCAR Congress*. Available online at: http://www.umsl.edu/~edujpolm/papers/iscar05-truestories.pdf (accessed 28 December 2006).

Ricoeur, P. (1984) *Time and narrative,* Vol. 1 (Trans. K. McLaughlin & D. Pellauer) (Chicago, University of Chicago Press).

Rosenberg, H. S. (1987) *Creative drama and imagination: transforming ideas into action* (New York, Holt, Rinehart & Winston).

Schreiber, F. J. (2005) Metacognition and self-regulation in literacy, in: S. E. Israel, C. Collins Block, K. L. Bauserman & K. Kinnucan-Welsch (Eds) *Metacognition in Literacy Learning* (Mahwah, NJ, Lawrence Erlbaum Associates).

Smith, P. K., Cowie, H. & Blades, M. (2003) *Understanding children's development* (4th edn) (Oxford, Blackwell).

Toolan, M. (2001) *Narrative, a critical linguistic introduction* (2nd edn) (London, Routledge).

Weimer-Hastings, P. & Glasswell, K. (2003) StoryStation: agent-based scaffolding of metacognitive processes for writing. Paper presented at the *2003 AIED Conference*. Available online at: http://www.cs.usyd.edu.au/~aied/vol9/vol9_roger_Hastings&%20Glasswell.pdf (accessed 28 December 2006).

Wier, C. (1998) Using embodied questions to jump-start metacognition in middle school remedial readers, *Journal of Adolescent and Adult Literacy,* 41(6), 458–467.

Williams, M. (2006) Letting talents shine: developing oracy with gifted and talented pupils, in: D. Jones & P. Hodson (Eds) *Unlocking speaking and listening* (London, David Fulton).

Wood, D. (1998) *How children think and learn* (2nd edn) (Oxford, Blackwell).

Wyse, D. & Jones, R. (2001) *Teaching English, language and literacy* (London, Routledge Falmer).

Zipes, J. (2004) *Speaking out: storytelling and creative drama for children* (London, Routledge).

Supporting the mother tongue: pedagogical approaches

Theodora Papatheodorou

Background information

For centuries, Greece has been a country that exports migrants. There are now as many Greeks living across the world as live in Greece (Katsikas, 1993). Such a Diaspora has led to the formation of well-established and still locally important Greek communities. Generally, Greek communities are well organized and provide many activities and services, especially for the education of the younger members.

As with other ethnic minority groups, hosted in a majority culture, Greek families and their children face the issue of language learning. That is, the need to learn the language and understand the culture of the country that hosts them and, at the same time, to maintain their own language and culture. Usually the statutory educational system of the host country takes responsibility for the first issue, whereas the second remains the responsibility of the family and/or the community. Indeed, Greek communities have established community schools, which operate largely in the early evenings, during weekdays, and on Saturdays, both morning and afternoon. Financially, they are supported by the Greek community of each town/city.

In the UK, Greek communities comprise both Greeks and Greek-Cypriots. Most of the Greek community schools operate under the auspices of the Archdioceses of Great Britain and Thyateira, but there are also a number of schools that operate independently. Both types of schools are recognized by the Ministry of Education and Religious Affairs in Greece and the Ministry of Education in Cyprus. Greek community schools are mainly staffed by qualified teachers, seconded by the Greek or Cypriot governments, but some part-time staff with equivalent qualifications are also employed. Staff development and the quality of education offered are overseen by the educational advisers appointed by the Greek and Cypriot governments.

Some observations and concerns

Although Greek community schools are well established, there are increasing concerns that gradually fewer children attend the schools and attendance patterns are irregular. Over the years and during the long history of the Greek community schools, multiple and complex factors seem to have contributed to this situation. My own personal experience and observations from a threefold role (that of a teacher, parent and committee member of three community schools in the UK for almost 17 years) indicate that contributing factors include:

- parental conflicting attitudes and uncertainties about the value and importance of learning the mother tongue;
- lack of and/or inappropriate learning resources of teaching the mother tongue to young children;
- mismatch between children's educational experiences in UK state schools and the Greek community schools;
- varying perceptions by children and parents about the status and usefulness of the mother tongue.

For some parents the learning of the Greek language by their children is important for practical reasons, especially if they intend to return to Greece or Cyprus in the near or far future. For others learning Greek, and understanding Greek culture and traditions, means that 'Greekness' becomes part of, or even the whole of, the child's identity. For these parents language and identity are closely related and interwoven and they insist that their children are taught and learn the mother tongue. (see Bialystok, 2001)

However, for another group of parents, the Greek language is less of a priority; the learning of English and assimilation in the host culture prevail. In addition, for some members of the community, especially, those who come from mixed parentage, Greekness is not the only nor the defining characteristic of their lives, culture and identity. For them, their children's attendance at Greek community schools becomes a symbolic gesture of belonging and acknowledgement of their cultural heritage. Often second- and third-generation Greeks who have not learned the mother tongue feel that they have missed out. They missed out in communicating and developing relationships with their relatives, as they did not have a common language and understanding of the culture that shapes, and is shaped by, the language (Brunner, 1990; Cummins, 2006). These members of the community come to insist that their children learn the Greek language, even if not proficient themselves.

However, even among those parents who appreciate the importance of learning the mother tongue, there is a lack of awareness of how to support their children with their own residual language skills. Parents, as second- and third-generation immigrants, are often reluctant to speak Greek with their children either because they claim not to know the language well or because they undervalue the particular idiom they speak (such as Greek-Cypriot). Such uncertainty and ambiguity are further reinforced when their children start statutory education and they are taught in English. Fear that the children may not be able to cope with the language of instruction in statutory education means that the home language is sidelined. To make the situation worse, there are still cases where teachers advise parents either not to speak Greek with their children or not to send their children to the Greek community school. Yet research evidence has shown that bilingualism promotes flexibility of thinking and information processing and furthermore, the mother tongue and the language of instruction in school become interdependent and they nurture each other (Baker, 2000; Cummins, 2000).

The impact of parental conflict and confusion on the learning of the mother tongue is further clouded by the dated, mainly didactic, methods of teaching and learning in the Greek community schools. In addition, there are a few up-to-date and appropriate learning resources that emulate the children's experiences (Katsikas, 1993). For example, reading schemes developed and piloted in Germany have been made available to Greek community schools in the UK and other countries. However, the experiences of young children living in Germany and the experiences of children living in the UK have little resemblance. Similarly, the use of books that have been developed and piloted in Greece to be used by native speakers is equally problematic. The experiences of children living in the UK are likely to be more different than similar to the experiences of children living in Greece. In this context, the teaching of the Greek language becomes de-contextualized, with children failing to understand and comprehend the language. This problem is exacerbated by the use of phonetic only approaches to teaching and learning Greek. There is now strong evidence that, though phonetic approaches may help children acquire the mechanics of the structure, syntax and spelling of a language, they may contribute very little to understanding and comprehension (Wyse, 2006).

In addition, Greek teachers themselves often lack an understanding of the culture of the migrant communities that may share many similarities with the indigenous Greek communities, but they are different in many aspects. The teachers often take a deficit approach that emphasizes what members of the Greek communities lack rather than what they have and fail to utilize their current experiences as a resource for further development and action. Teachers' expectations often are that the attitudes, behaviour and practices of members of the Greek communities should be similar to, or mirror, the attitudes, behaviour and practices of the indigenous Greeks living in Greece or Cyprus.

Finally, learning the mother tongue is often rejected by the children themselves. Learning Greek is seen by the children as a means of exclusion from their peer group. The perceived status of minority languages, like Greek, seems to further reinforce such exclusion. In addition, formal and didactic approaches to teaching the mother tongue often conflict with the children's experiences, in early years settings, where learning is largely play-based. As a result, the children's experience of learning the mother tongue becomes less engaging and attractive.

The aim of the study

In this context, a project was developed to address some of the issues raised above. More specifically, the project aimed to modify the pedagogical approach in teaching the mother tongue in order to:

- involve and actively engage children with the learning of the Greek language for functional use;
- involve parents in the learning process and support them in so doing;
- increase children's regular attendance in Greek community schools.

Methodology

A 15-week program, entitled 'Learning Together', was developed and piloted in a class of 11 children in a Greek community school in eastern England. The class comprised of seven boys and four girls, 4–8 years old, of Greek and Greek-Cypriot origin. They were second- and third-generation immigrants, and some were of mixed parentage. The program was discussed and developed in collaboration with the teacher who had been seconded by the Greek government, and arrived in the UK for the first time at the beginning of the school year in which the program was implemented.

For the implementation and evaluation of the 'Learning Together' program an ethnographic case-study methodology was used (David & Sutton, 2004). The researcher and the teacher maintained an insider–outsider perspective in terms of the cultural context of the community, where the project was developed. However, in terms of educational praxis, the researcher and teacher—both qualified teachers—maintained an insider perspective.

Two sets of data were collected for the purpose of the study. Baseline data were collected, before the implementation of the program to establish the actual situation in terms of parental practices and children's experiences with regard to the learning of the mother tongue. Such data included:

- situational data received through informal discussions of the teacher with parents;
- factual and attitudinal data received from parents by using an open-ended questionnaire;
- young children's views elicited by the teacher through individual informal, class-based discussions.

After the implementation of the program, data were collected to examine qualitatively the processes of the 'Leaning Together' program and the extent to which it addressed the aims of the project. Data collected included:

- parents' informal feedback throughout the implementation of the program and via a questionnaire administered after the implementation of the program;
- teacher's informal class-based discussions during and at the end of the program;
- teacher's report on the pupil's attendance;
- teacher's reflection on the implementation of the program;
- work produced by the children.

The collected data were analysed by content analysis to identify the emerging themes and issues from each set of data. Consequently, the emerging themes and issues from each data set were examined to map the emerging picture before and after the implementation of the program in order to identify and discuss conceptual and practical implications (David & Sutton, 2004).

The 'Learning Together' program

The 'Learning Together' program was developed by drawing upon the principles of socio-cultural theories of learning and developmentally appropriate practice in early childhood. According to socio-cultural theories, language and thinking are interdependent and interwoven; they influence and are influenced by each other; they are rooted within the culture of a particular group of people and, in turn, contribute to the change and evolution of that culture (Vygotsky, 1986; Bruner, 1990; Van der Veer & Valsiner, 1991; Kozulin *et al.*, 2003). These ideas are particularly important in understanding the importance of the socio-cultural context of the lived experiences of children in the Greek community. Their experiences are not the same as those of their parents and/or their peers in the host country or the country of their origin. Instead, they are uniquely positioned in a particular socio-cultural context that has been defined by the evolving processes and needs of the Greek communities, and through the interactional processes with the majority culture.

The 'zone of proximal development' and scaffolding, which are key concepts of the socio-cultural theories, are also relevant to teaching the mother tongue. Considering these concepts, socio-cultural theories ascertain that learning is happening in the context of, and should start from, the children's existing experiences which, being mediated by knowledgeable others, should assist them to reach their full potential (Vygotsky, cited in Van der Veer & Valsiner, 1991). In early childhood these concepts have been better exemplified in developmentally appropriate practice, which starts from children's experiences and needs, and adopts experiential, hands-on and playful activities to facilitate and extend their learning (Bredekamp & Copple, 1997).

Appropriating these ideas to the 'Learning Together' program meant that its pedagogical approach invested in and utilized the children's lived experience in their unique socio-cultural context. Experiences derived from, and linked with, the Greek and British communities in the form of stories, historical events, memories, family and community traditions were used to link their emotional impact with the intended outcome of learning the mother tongue. It became important that children's prior knowledge and evolving cognitive frameworks were used to build new language learning (Haritos, 2003; Stechuk & Burns, 2005).

The reading of picture-books introduced in the 'Learning Together' program, were followed by a range of multi-modal and experiential learning activities (e.g. kinaesthetic, role-play, drama, singing, dancing) to produce strong associations and emotional links between the children's lived experience and the intended learning outcomes (Frater, 2000; Stechuk & Burns, 2005). It involved parents as facilitators in the learning process and mediators of their children's incongruent experiences that may arise from their engagement in different cultural contexts and educational settings (e.g. experiences from statutory education settings and the Greek community school).

Emphasis was placed, first, on pleasurable and purposeful engagement with text and books, and second, the functional use of the language. Books and vocabulary introduced referred to familiar stories, events, objects and concepts that were relevant and meaningful to children. The prime aim of the program was for the children to use language to express their needs and wants; communicate basic information and interact with others; express their feeling and emotions and regulate their behaviour (Halliday, 1975; Ofsted, 2004).

More specifically, the pedagogical approach in the 'Learning Together' program aimed to:

- place an emphasis on the cultural and contextual aspects of language learning;
- focus on young children's active engagement in the learning process and utilize their existing experiences;
- encourage and facilitate the functional use of the language;
- strengthen the link between the school and the family;
- support parents in facilitating their children's learning.

The project had two strands that were implemented along side. One strand focused on 'Talking picture-books' and the other 'Making our own books'.

Talking picture-books

One of the main difficulties encountered in teaching the Greek language to young children is a lack of appropriate resources. Picture-books, even those written with Greek native speakers in mind, rely heavily on text. For the purpose of this project, through extensive consultation and inspection of many books, 12 picture-books were selected to be used. The books focused on simple, everyday life events and familiar stories; they had an exciting and memorable story line, with clear and unambiguous language; they had rhythm and intonation, high iconicity related to the text and high levels of within-book intertextuality. The books provided a thematic focus that was used as the basis for the development of multi-modal activities (Gregory, 1996; Facella *et al.*, 2005).

Each week, one book was introduced by the teacher. The introduction of the book was done by setting the story in its context and then reading it. This activity was followed by talking about the story, aiming to clarify key points, and asking questions, making predictions and summarizing the story. Finally, the teacher again reread the story (see Gregory, 1996). The story was role-played by incorporating music, dance or kinaesthetic activities. Music included classical pieces, traditional and contemporary Greek music, as well as children's chosen popular music. The same applied to dance, which included both Greek traditional and contemporary dances. The basic idea was to introduce the Greek culture and blend it with cultural aspects of the children's current experiences from the Greek community and the host majority culture. Its aim was for young children to gain a holistic view of the world in which they live, rather than seeing distinct cultures within and between which they move and shift and drift.

For example, starting with the beetle's experiences during the four seasons of the year (described in one of Aesop's fables), the teacher was able to introduce weather-related vocabulary and questions. The classroom was staged for role play, with each corner of the room decorated to represent one of the four seasons. Pictures were made available and text provided for children to make associations between pictures, spoken and written words and sentences (Figure 1). Vivaldi's *Four Seasons* was used as background music for the children to enact the story. Greek music and different styles of dance were also introduced for the children to express the beetle's emotional state, according to weather changes.

Each picture book was tape recorded by the teacher, producing a copy for each child attending the class. Every week the children borrowed the picture-book and the tape recorder to listen to the story-book at home with their parents. Parents were also given brief information concerning what the children had already done school; guidance on how they could share readings with their child; and how to help with further activities supporting vocabulary learning and the functional use of the language by making reference to cultural aspects and elements. The guidance was structured, but, at the same time, flexible and open enough to incorporate children's individual experiences and encourage personal responses that revealed hidden linguistic and cultural experiences and elements (Dombey, 2003).

Making our own books

Starting either from themes derived from the picture-books, read each week, or from their own experiences, the children were asked to draw a picture (e.g. 'Me

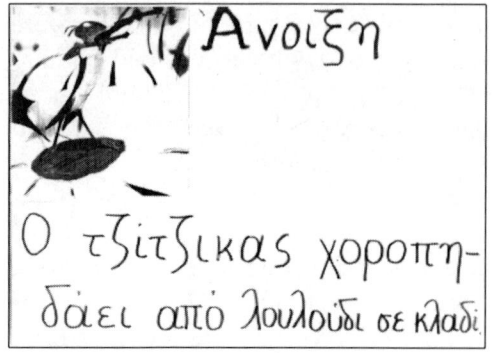

Picture 1: Spring (Ἄνοιξη)

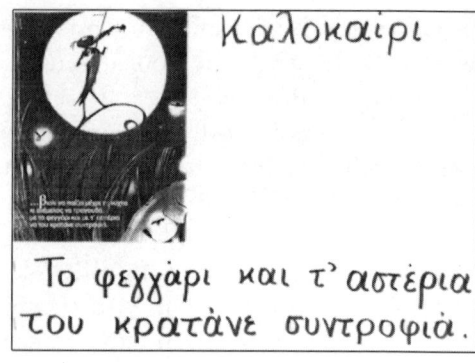

Picture 2: Summer (Καλοκαίρι)

Picture 3: Autumn (Φθινόπωρο)

Picture 4: Winter (Χειμώνας)

Figure 1.   Four pictures (English and Greek text)

and my mum', 'The place where I live', etc.). They then worked in small groups to talk about the pictures and wrote one or two sentences to convey some information about the pictures. The children were encouraged to use 'code mixing' to use elements from both languages (Greek and English) within the same pieces of conversation or writing (Genesee *et al.*, cited in Stechuk & Burns, 2005). Children with different levels of fluency in both languages worked together to support each other in writing the sentence for their pictures. For example, Figures 2 and 3, referring to the topic 'Me and my mum', include both English and Greek text.

This strand of the program, focused mainly on expression and the functional use of the language. It aimed to value equally the Cypriot dialect and the Modern Greek language and allowed code mixing to encourage communication. Most importantly, the activity aimed to build children's confidence in engaging with language rather than the learning of syntax, grammar and spelling. For example, in Figure 3, the sentence in Greek is not correct in terms of its syntax, grammar and spelling.

Figure 2.   Me and my mum in the park (Εγώ και η μαμά μου μέσα στο πάρκο)

Figure 3.   In the garden with my mum (Μέσ στο κιπο με την (εγώ) μαμά μου)

Findings and discussion

The pre-implementation data

The pre-implementation baseline data revealed certain themes and patterns related to the importance of the mother tongue and its place in children's lives and experiences, as suggested below.

Exposure to Greek culture.   Parental responses to the questionnaire revealed that families and children were surrounded by extended family, including grandparents, aunts, uncles and cousins who often lived in the same community. There was regular exchange of visits and participation in family events such as weddings, christening, birthday and name day (Saint's day) celebrations. The Greek Church and the events, organized by the Greek community to commemorate religious festivals, and national and historical events, remain important focal points of the social life. In addition, all families and their children were in regular contact with relatives and friends in Greece or Cyprus. Such contact is mainly maintained by telephone or regular summer visits. All had access to satellite TV channels in Greece and/or Cyprus that provided another way of familiarizing children with the mother tongue. Evidently, children were acquainted with the Greek or Cypriot culture and had rich experiences within the Greek communities, in parallel with their experiences within British society and statutory educational settings.

Exposure to the mother tongue.   All parents who responded to the questionnaire stated that they had a good command of the Greek language; they spoke the language well, read and wrote it well or, at least, to some degree. At home, they spoke to their children in both Greek and English, with roughly equal percentages; for instance, one parent said, 'we speak 50–50 Greek and English'. Code switching, however, was most common between parents; for example, a parent reported, 'I speak in English and my husband speaks in Greek'.

Use of the Greek language ranged from the introduction of simple vocabulary to its more functional use; for example, one parent noted, 'We mainly ask Tony [pseudonym] to do things', whereas another pointed out that: 'We use it at a certain time of the day with the children or when we are teaching the children everyday words.'

Cross-generational communication and functional use of the mother tongue.   Cross-generational communication remains the main reason for children to be exposed to the mother tongue. For example, a few parents responded as follows: 'I sometimes speak to the children in Greek, especially when I am at my mum's house'; 'My wife speaks to the children in Greek, especially at her mother's house'; and 'When my father is with us, we speak in Greek all the time'.

The mother tongue as more than a second language. A few parents mentioned that learning the Greek language was important as the children learned a second language that may be beneficial to their education and future employment. However, some parents also highlighted that learning the mother tongue was *more* than learning a second language, implicitly making the link between language, cultural heritage and identity. As one parent put it: 'We teach the children [the Greek language] and make them realize it's not just a second language.'

The mother tongue and its declining use. The informal discussions of the children with the teacher supported further parental claims that they spoke Greek at home. They pointed out that their parents spoke in Greek, especially when they wanted to explain things to them. As socio-cultural theory contends, thinking is better expressed in the language that is associated with cognitive and conceptual frameworks that develop in, and derive from, a particular cultural context.

All children said that they spoke both Greek and English at home, but English seemed to be the dominant language as 'it's convenient to speak in English'. Children's views about their spoken, reading and writing skills revealed a pattern that showed the mother tongue to be declining. The children stated that they spoke Greek a little, but were not yet able to read or write it. Limited reading and writing skills may be understood in terms of children's age and limited time spent in being systematically taught the mother tongue. However, despite parental claims that they spoke Greek at home, limited verbal skills may indicate that second- and third-generation Greeks may gradually become less competent in using the mother tongue. This may be due to the fact that the mother tongue has functional use only in the home context and within the Greek community.

These data seem to indicate that, even among those parents who are clearly committed to maintain the mother tongue, there appears to be inconsistency between desired and actual practices. The narrow and context-specific function and utility of the mother tongue is inevitably shadowed by the dominant language of the majority culture.

The post-implementation data

Key elements of the 'Learning Together' program. The 'Learning Together' program was positively received by all parents, who commented as follows:

> [It] has made learning more fun and interesting!
> It enabled the children to learn different areas of the Greek language in a fun way.
> It has made learning more interesting and enabled understanding of the text with interaction.
> They [the children] communicate with one another at different ages.
> Children learn more when they read together; it promotes discussion, increases vocabulary.
> Helps promote the Greek language at home, speaking with your child.

> The results of the programme speak for themselves! The current format and structure of the programme seems to be working extremely well.

These views were also consistent and reflected in the following comments made by the children:

> I can play.
> It's fun and interesting.
> I learn new words ... I speak Greek.
> I learn about Greece and Cyprus.
> I am with my friends ... other children.
> I speak Greek at home with my parents and brothers and sisters.

All parents supported their children at home with given homework and most of the parents followed the teacher guidance and assisted their children daily. A few parents, however, were of the view that daily homework was too much for their children; they argued that either the children were too young or too tired to do additional homework. Indeed, these comments reflected parental differences on the wider issue of homework in general.

The comments were further supported by feedback offered informally during the implementation of the programme. For example, some parents said that the 'Learning Together' program brought the Greek language into their home, and others pointed out that they themselves felt more confident to speak the language, even if they were not fluent speakers. This, in turn, improved their own language skills and brought to the forefront residual language skills and passive vocabulary. One parent was particularly impressed when she overheard her son using Greek vocabulary in playing with his toys.

Code mixing.   In the 'Making our own books' strand of the program, the children were encouraged to use the Greek language to express, articulate and communicate the messages depicted in their pictures. Consequently, they wrote down their message in both English and Greek. Correct spelling and syntax were of less importance at this stage. For example, in Figure 3, the children wrote in Greek, 'Μέσ στο κιπο με την (εγώ) μαμά μου', which depicts the message of the picture, but in terms of syntax and spelling this sentence should read 'Μέσα στο κήπο με την μαμά μου'.

Considering that the children had different levels of fluency in Greek, they were also encouraged to use code mixing to articulate their message. Code mixing was not only between Greek and English, but between Modern Greek and the Cypriot idiom too. In his reflections, the teacher commented that the children gradually grew in confidence in expressing themselves in Greek and code mixing between the two languages gradually decreased.

Introduction of an inter-lingual lexicon.   Vocabulary that does not sit comfortably with the concepts deriving from one or the other culture is usually appropriated to produce a unique new word that reflects the meaning of such concepts. For example, in Greek there is no equivalent word for translating 'fish and chip shop'. This is because 'fish and chip shop' is a culture-specific concept and tool. The nearest translation in Greek may be 'psaradiko' (ψαράδικο), which means the shop where fresh fish is sold. But the two concepts are more different than similar. As a result, the concept of 'fish and chip shop' has been appropriated into the Greek language with the introduction of the word 'fishadiko' (φισσάδικο). Such interlingual lexical development, often referred to by the children and members of the community as 'Greeklish', has two components that derive from two languages and cultures; the word *fish*, from English, and the endings *-adiko*, from the Greek word 'psaradiko' (ψαράδικο). The word 'fishadiko' then becomes a new word in the vocabulary of Greek migrants to reflect the meaning of a culturally bound concept. The children endlessly used the dominant cognitive frameworks and understandings to make meaning and communicate meaning with others.

Introduction of such an inter-lingual lexicon may be seen as a distortion of either or both languages, but paying attention to the meaning given, it can be seen as conceptual and linguistic enrichment. The mother tongue is learned within the ever-evolving cultural context of the Greek communities in the Diaspora, a culture that is at the receiving end of influences from the indigenous Greek and Greek-Cypriot cultures and the majority culture of the host country.

Therefore language and its meaning are not independent of cultural context; instead, they influence and are influenced by each other. Consequently, de-contextualization and de-culturization of learning resources and teaching strategies are set only to fail. The learning and teaching of the mother tongue should start with and utilize the children's lived experiences and extend them to make sense of the cultural context where they live.

Children's attendance at the Greek school. Children's engagement in, and enjoyment of, the learning took place in the 'Learning Together' program had an impact on their attendance at the Greek school. They all attended the weekly sessions regularly and until the end of the academic year. The initial 15-week pilot study was extended until the end of the academic year and continued the following academic year changing the teaching and learning culture of the Greek community school at least for this age group.

Issues arising from the 'Learning Together' program. Despite the overwhelming positive support received by parents, and the increased regular attendance of the children in the Greek community, the 'Learning Together' program was not without its difficulties. The first difficulty had to do with the quality of the tape recording: recording made with professional equipment would have produced better results that could be enhanced by appropriate background music, etc. In addition, the two-hour sessions once a week were considered inadequate to implement both strands of the program within the same week. Despite the teacher's recommendation for the children to attend the classes twice a week, parents felt that this was too much for the children.

Conclusion and recommendations

The findings of this study indicate that mother tongue *matters*. It matters for cross-generational communication, and for awareness and understanding of cultural heritage and identity. Yet, there is much ambiguity among parents concerning the place of the mother tongue within the majority culture of the host country. In addition, as the functional use of the mother tongue is limited to the family and Greek community only, its use tends to be gradually declining. Despite the best intentions of parents in maintaining use of the mother tongue, the language of the host country gradually takes over.

Playful, interesting and interactive learning activities are seen as the best means of encouraging children to engage with learning the mother tongue. Resources that start from and build on children's experience, and, at the same time, extend such experience, are the best means to support the mother tongue. Parents, however, remain the main source of support in facilitating the learning of the mother tongue, by using their residual language skills and understanding of both the heritage culture and the culture of the host country.

Finally, code mixing and an inter-lingual lexicon may not be desirable processes for linguists who would wish to see languages maintain their syntactical and grammatical purity, but they may be seen as appropriate means to communicate the cognitive and conceptual frameworks of different cultures. Borrowing from socio-cultural theorists, code mixing and inter-lingual lexicon become the cultural tools that evolve through the history of migrant communities developing their own culture as an amalgamation of their past and present experiences. However, such conclusions deserve a note of caution; this is a small study and its findings can be generalized or be seen as applicable only to situations which share similar contextual characteristics and elements.

Acknowledgement

The researcher would like to thank the teacher, who implemented the 'Learning Together' program, and acknowledges the funding received from the local authority to make this project possible. To maintain the anonymity of the Greek community school, the teacher and the local authority cannot be named here.

References

Baker, C. (2000) *A parent and teacher guide to bilingualism* (2nd edn) (Clevedon, Multilingual Matters).
Bialystok, E. (2001) *Bilingualism in development: language, literacy and cognition* (Cambridge, Cambridge University Press).
Bredekamp, S. & Copple, C. (Eds) (1997) *Developmentally appropriate practice in early childhood programs* (rev. edn) (Washington, DC, NAEYC).
Bruner, J. (1990) *Acts of meaning* (Cambridge, MA, Harvard University Press).
Cummins, J. (2000) *Language, power, and pedagogy: bilingual children in the crossfire* (Clevedon, Multilingual Matters).

Cummins, J. (2006) *Bilingual children's mother tongue: why is it important for education?* Available on line at: http://www.iteachilearn.com/cummins/mother.htm (accessed 7 August 2006).

David, M. & Sutton, D. C. (2004) *Social research: the basics* (London, Sage).

Dombey, H. (2003) Moving forward together, in: E. Bearne, H. Dombey & T. Grainger (Eds) *Classroom interactions in literacy* (Maidenhead, McGraw-Hill/Open University Press).

Facella, M. A., Rampino, K. M. & Shea, A. K. (2005) Effective teaching strategies for English language learning, *Bilingual Research Journal*, 29(1), 209–221. Available online at: http://brj.asu.edu/content/vol29_no1/art12.pdf (accessed 7 August 2006).

Frater, G. (2000) Observed in practice: English in the National Literacy Strategy: some reflections, *Reading*, 34(3), 107–112.

Gregory, E. (1996) *Making sense of a new world: learning to read in a second language* (London, Paul Chapman).

Halliday, M. A. (1975) *Learning how to mean: explorations in the development of language* (London, Edward Arnold).

Haritos, C. (2003) Listening, remembering and speaking in two languages: how did you do that? *Bilingual Research Journal*, 27(1), 73–99. Available online at: http://brj.asu.edu/content/vol27_no1/documents/art4.pdf (accessed 7 August 2006).

Katsikas, S. (1993) *Studies for the Greek Diaspora* [in Greek]. Available online at: http://www.ggae.gr/ggae/studies/intro/default.el.asp (accessed August 2006).

Kozulin, A., Gindis, B., Ageyev, V. S. & Miller, S. M. (Eds) (2003) *Vygotsky's educational theory in cultural context* (Cambridge, Cambridge University Press).

Office for Standards in Education (Ofsted) (2004) *Reading for purpose and pleasure* (London, Ofsted).

Stechuk, R. A. & Burns, M. S. (2005) *Making a difference: a framework for supporting first and second language development in preschool children of migrant farm workers* (Washington, DC, AED Centre for Early Care and Education). Available online at: http://www.ece.aed.org/publications/locator.htm (accessed 7 August 2006).

Van der Veer, R. & Valsiner, J. (1991) *Understanding Vygotsky: a quest for synthesis* (Oxford, Blackwell).

Vygotsky, L. S. (1986) *Thought and language* (3rd edn) (Cambridge, MA, MIT Press).

Wyse, D. (2006) Rose tinted spectacles: synthetic phonics, research evidence and the teaching of reading. Keynote speech presented at the *TACTYC Annual Conference: Literacy Plus 'Reading between the Lines'*, Birmingham, 4 November.

A longitudinal investigation of mothers' mind-related talk to their 12- to 24-month-old infants

S. Degotardi and J. Torr

Introduction

Contemporary approaches to early literacy emphasize the importance of children's metacognitive understanding in the processes of literacy acquisition (Watson, 2001; Olson, 2002; Astington & Pelletier, 2005; Israel *et al.*, 2005). Metacognition, defined by Flavell (1979) as 'knowledge about cognition and cognitive phenomena' (p. 906), incorporates children's understanding of diverse mental states and processes such as thinking, knowing, believing, remembering and understanding. Such awareness, it is argued, enables children to reflect upon and discuss their own and others' mental processes, allowing children to monitor and regulate their own literacy learning strategies (Griffith & Ruan, 2005) and to use language in literacy-oriented, abstract and decontextualized ways (Dickinson & Tabors, 1991; Olson & Torrance, 1991; Snow, 1993).

In developmental psychology, children's metacognitive understanding is regarded as an integral part of their 'theory of mind'. This term highlights the fact that psychological states are opaque, so children need to develop the ability to draw upon their inferences of emotions, desires, knowledge and thoughts to gain an appreciation of the other person's perspective (Wellman, 1990; Perner, 1991). A wide body of research indicates that this development begins early, with concepts relating to emotions, desires and intentions emerging during infancy (Bartsch & Wellman, 1994; Carpenter et al., 1998). During the preschool years, children acquire belief-related concepts, and begin to understand the subjectivity of their own and others' mental states (Wellman, 1990). This rich period of development means that children are relatively competent 'mind-readers' by the time that they enter school (Flavell & Miller, 1998).

Recent theory-of-mind research emphasizes the importance of children's understanding of, and talk about, the mind for their emerging literacy development. Metacognitive understanding during children's first years of school is related to their reading ability (Pelletier, 2004) and their comprehension of narrative content, themes and character motivation (Astington & Pelletier, 2005). Children's use of metacognitive talk has been found to predict their comprehension of written narrative at age 8 years (Griffin et al., 2004), and their change in reading ability between the age of 4 and 5 (Astington & Pelletier, 2005). Such findings bolster claims that the ability to think and talk about the mind constitutes a vital tool for narrative understanding and the intentional and selective employment of cognitive processes, such as attention and memory, that are implicated in the processes of literacy learning (Astington & Pelletier; 2005; Griffith & Ruan, 2005).

The role of adult talk in children's metacognitive understanding

The apparent significance of an understanding of the mind for emergent literacy has prompted a call for metacognitive instruction in the classroom through explicit teaching (Olson & Astington, 1993; Israel et al., 2005). Formal schooling is, however, only one context to support children's metacognitive development. As research has linked family talk to later literacy development (Snow, 1993; Beals & de Temple, 1993; Beales, 1997; Purcell-Gates, 2001), so has children's theory-of-mind development been found to be strongly predicted by the types of talk that children are exposed to within the family context. In this paper, we have focused on mothers' use of mind-related talk to their infants on the basis that it is an important contextual feature that supports and facilitates metacognitive understanding. Three broad categories of maternal talk have been argued to provide young children with important messages about the content and nature of the mind: mental-state talk, encouragement-of-autonomy talk and modulation-of-certainty talk (the use of modal verbs and adjuncts to modulate certainty). These therefore constitute the categories of interest in the present study.

The most extensively studied type of maternal talk is mental-state talk, or talk which explicitly refers to emotions, desires, and cognitions. Relationships between mothers' use of mental-state language and children's subsequent understanding of these terms are well established (e.g. Dunn *et al.*, 1991; Moore *et al.*, 1994; Adrian *et al.*, 2005), suggesting that such talk plays a causal role in children's theory-of-mind development (Ruffman *et al.*, 2002). Another type of talk with implications for children's understanding of the mind is talk that encourages autonomy. Research has found that mothers who de-emphasize autonomy through their use of controlling talk (Dunn & Brown, 1994) or through behavioural directives (e.g. 'Eat your meat', 'Get the ball') have children who show lower theory-of-mind understanding, relative to the children of mothers who encourage autonomy (Vinden, 2000). Encouragement-of-autonomy talk therefore appears to provide children with subtle messages about psychological individuality and intentional behaviour (Markus & Kitayama, 1998; Meins *et al.*, 2001). A further relevant talk category is mothers' use of modal verbs or adjuncts, such as 'probably', 'possibly', 'might' and 'maybe', to modulate certainty. Such talk foregrounds the existence of subjective opinions (Moore & Furrow, 1991; Torr, 1998), and has been associated, both contemporaneously and longitudinally, with children's understanding of the mind (Moore *et al.*, 1990; Brown *et al.*, 1996).

Much of the above-mentioned research on mothers' mind-related talk to their children has focused on children in the two to five year old age range; yet, by the age of two, children are already beginning to use mind-related talk to refer to their own autonomy and mental states (Bretherton & Beeghly-Smith, 1982; Shatz *et al.*, 1983; Budwig, 1989; Bartsch & Wellman, 1995) and to modulate certainty of their knowledge (O'Neill & Atance, 2000). This suggests that, by the age of three, an understanding of the mind is already under way. The idea that metacognitive understanding starts in infancy is corroborated by three recent studies that report longitudinal relationships between infants' exposure to mental-state talk and their subsequent understanding of the mind (Meins *et al.*, 2003; Symons *et al.*, 2005, 2006; Taumoepeau & Ruffman, 2006). Such findings emphasize the importance of early mind-related talk for children's development, and highlight the need for increased information about this feature of infants' social context.

Aims of this study

In this paper, we investigate mothers' use of mind-related talk to their 12- to 24-month-old infants with the aim of contributing towards a deeper appreciation of the discourse context that may orient infants towards an understanding of the mind. We focus our investigation around the question of variability in mothers' use of such talk as little is currently known about the extent, and relative stability, of individual variation during the infancy period. There is, however, evidence to suggest that variability in mothers' mind-related talk use is related to their infants' age. Beeghly *et al.* (1986) found that mothers significantly increased their overall use of mental-state talk to their 13- to 28-month-old infants, with a closer analysis finding that cognitive-oriented talk increased but talk about perception and desire actually decreased during this time. More recently, Taumoepeau and Ruffman (2006) report similar findings in their analysis of desire and belief-related talk to infants at 15 and 24 months, but found no significant change in mothers' use of modulation-of-certainty talk. In this paper, we aim to determine whether these findings are supported by the present data, and extend previous research by including encouragement-of-autonomy talk in order to address a lack of longitudinal studies of mothers' use of this type of mind-related talk.

Finally, we investigate the relationship between mothers' educational attainment and their use of such talk with their infants. There are long-established links between maternal education, language and literacy (Purcell-Gates, 1996; Senechal & LeFevre, 2001; Storch & Whitehurst, 2001), and evidence exists to suggest that socioeconomic status (of which educational attainment is a contributing factor) is associated with the extent to which mothers explicitly verbalise the fact that their children have a separate and individual perspective on the phenomena they experience (Hasan & Cloran, 1990; Hasan, 1991). Yet little information currently exists about specific associations between mothers' educational attainment and their use of mind-related talk to their infants. The use of a longitudinal design, in the present study, enables us to determine whether such associations exist, and whether educational attainment interacts with infant age to bring about differential patterns of change in maternal use of mind-related language over time.

Method

Participants were 22 mother–infant dyads recruited from a longitudinal study being conducted at that time by the Centre for Child Development, Macquarie University, Sydney, Australia. Mothers were recruited from government-run antenatal clinics and private obstetric practices, and were contacted by telephone to be invited to participate in the present study. A copy of the video taped play footage was offered to the mothers on completion of the study.

All mothers spoke English as their first language, nominated themselves as the primary caregiver of their infant and, at commencement, cared for their infant at home for at least five days per week. At commencement, all mothers lived in or around the metropolitan area of Sydney. Mothers ranged in age from 23 to 39 years of age ($M = 30$ years, $SD = 4.90$), and had completed between 10 and 16 years of formal education ($M = 13.32$ years, $SD = 1.86$). There were 12 boys and 10 girls, of whom 11 were first-born, six were second-born and five were third-born.

Procedure

Each dyad was visited in the family home when the infants were 12, 18 and 24 months old (mean number of days from target age = 7, $SD = 3.79$). Visits took place at a time when the mother felt her infant was likely to be 'awake, happy and in a good mood'.

On arrival at each mother's home, the first author outlined the visit procedure to ensure that the mother understood and was comfortable with the requirements.

Mother–infant interaction was video taped using the procedure employed in many mother–infant interaction studies (e.g. Bakeman & Adamson, 1984; Carpenter *et al.*, 1998; Markus *et al.*, 2000). Mothers and infants were presented with a standard set of eight toys, selected to encourage flexible, open-ended use and promote shared mother-infant interaction. Mothers were asked to play with their infant as 'you would normally do if you had 10 minutes to spare', and were given free choice of the toys in the box. Video taping commenced when the mother and infant had established play with the first selected toy, and ceased approximately 10 minutes later. Interruptions occurred if the infant wandered off camera or the mother's attention was drawn away from the infant (such as by a phone call) for a period of 20 or more seconds. As these interruptions were judged to be outside the control of the mother, taping ceased until the mother rejoined her infant, and recording then continued until 10 minutes of footage had been obtained.

Coding of mothers' talk

All of the mothers' talk in the 10 minutes of codable video footage was transcribed and divided into utterances, defined primarily by natural speech intonation contours, and the presence of pauses in the flow of speech (Snow *et al.*, 1996). Rapidly repeated words, such as 'shake shake shake', were defined as a single utterance when there was no definite pause between each word. If a mother changed topic during the flow of speech with no indication through intonation or pause, the utterance was bounded by topic. Occasional unintelligible utterances were excluded from analysis. Overall, the 64 transcripts contained a total of 10,756 utterances; 3,628 utterances in the 12-month, 3,467 in the 18-month and 3,661 in the 24-month transcripts.

Each utterance was coded according to the presence of one or more of the following talk types:

- *Encouragement-of-autonomy talk* included directives or requests that encouraged independent infant action and joint infant-mother agency (Vinden, 2000; Meins *et al.*, 2001). In order to be included in this category, the utterance had to allow the infant choice and control over the directed behaviour, so the footage of the mothers' physical behaviour was observed in order to ensure that this was the case. For example, if a mother said, 'Let's open the box' and then immediately opened the box without allowing her infant time to comply, this would not qualify as encouragement-of-autonomy talk, but instead would be coded as non-psychological.
- *Mental-state talk* included explicit references to mental states and processes. This category was split into two sub-categories: *non-belief mental-state talk* included references to perception, likes, emotions and desires; and *belief mental-state talk* included references to beliefs, such as knowing and thinking, and to symbolic activities such as tricking, teasing and pretending.

- *Modulation-of-certainty talk* included utterances containing modal verbs or adjuncts, such as 'might', 'could' or 'maybe'. Note that the term 'think', such as in 'I think there's a bear in the box', could be coded as a modulation-of-certainty as well as belief mental-state talk, as it meets the criteria for inclusion in both categories. However, multiple coding of the same single term would artificially inflate the occurrence of psychological statements, so, following Ruffman *et al.* (2002), all references to 'think' were coded as belief mental-state talk rather than modulation-of-certainty talk.
- *Non-psychological talk* included all other utterances, and comments about and descriptions of objects and events, social overtures, orienting utterances and questions. As these utterances were outside of the focus of this study, they were not included in the present analysis.

Scoring and reliability

Each utterance was coded, but utterances could be coded in multiple ways if they contained more than one separate mind-related talk type (Ruffman *et al.*, 2002). For example, the statement "I think that you can do it yourself", would be coded as belief mental-state talk ('I think that ...'), and as encouragement-of-autonomy ('... you can do it yourself'). The frequency of each talk category occurring in 10 minutes of footage was used to measure the variability in mothers' talk, on the assumption that variability in exposure to talk types does matter because infants are developmentally sensitive to the amount of stimulation they receive (Bornstein *et al.*, 1992).

One coder coded all utterances and a second coder independently coded 20% of the full data set. Inter-rater reliability was calculated for each separate talk category based on agreement of the presence or absence of each talk category within the utterance. This had the advantage of revealing the level of reliability for each individual category rather than just one overall agreement rating which could potentially mask the occurrence of a low level of agreement for a particular category (Ruffman *et al.*, 2002). Examples, and the Cohen kappa statistics for each talk category are presented in Table 1.

Mothers' education

Mothers' educational attainment was coded according to whether or not they had participated in a tertiary academic program. Mothers were classified as *lower educated* ($n = 8$) if they had attained between 9 and 12 years of high school education or *higher educated* ($n = 14$) if they had attained 12 years of school education, and had completed or partially completed university tertiary educational qualifications.

Results

Results are presented as follows. We first provide descriptive statistics to illustrate individual differences for each talk variable at each infant age and then assess the

Table 1. Examples and interrater reliabilities for each category of mothers' talk

Mothers' talk category	Examples	Cohen's κ
Encouragement of autonomy	Can you put that on there?; You try to open it; Let's try to fix that.	.86
Non-belief mental-state	Can you see it?; You like that one, don't you; That was scary; Which one do you want?	.88
Belief mental-state	You know what's in there; Can you remember this from last time?; Do you think he's in there? Are you tricking mummy?; Pretend Teddy's asleep.	.90
Modulation of certainty	He might jump up soon; This should work; It's probably inside there.	.91
Non-psychological	It's a ball; We're clapping; Peekaboo!; Hey!; Look at this; What's that?	.91

stability of individual differences over time. Next, we explore changes in mothers' tendency to use each talk type over the 12-month time period. Finally, we assess the effect of educational attainment on mothers' use of each talk type. In all analyses, two-tailed tests of significance were used, and exact probability levels are reported.

Table 2 presents the descriptive statistics for the mothers' talk variables. The most frequent mind-related talk type at each infant age was maternal encouragement-of-autonomy talk, constituting approximately 20% of the mothers' talk at each infant age. Non-belief mental state talk constituted approximately 10% of all utterances across the infants' second year, whereas the mean frequencies of belief mental-state talk and modulation-of-certainty talk were relatively low. The range at each infant age demonstrated pronounced individual differences in mothers' propensity to use each talk type. Kendall's Coefficient of Concordance revealed that mothers' tendency to use each type of mind-related talk was stable over the three time points: encouragement of autonomy, $W(21) = 0.60$, $p = 0.014$; non-belief mental state talk, $W(21) =$

Table 2. Means, standard deviation (in parentheses), and range of the frequency of mothers' use of each talk type to their 12, 18 and 24-month-old infants.

Mind-related talk type	Infant age					
	12 months		18 months		24 months	
	M	Range	M	Range	M	Range
Encouragement of autonomy	19.09 (13.87)	4–53	19.05 (9.02)	2–38	23.27 (13.77)	4–47
Non-belief mental state	11.27 (7.45)	2–26	10.41 (8.02)	1–31	9.50 (6.95)	0–33
Belief mental-state	2.50 (2.97)	0–10	2.77 (2.71)	1–11	4.77 (4.63)	0–17
Modulation of certainty	1.45 (1.97)	0–7	0.95 (0.99)	0–3	2.09 (2.99)	0–9

Table 3.   Means and standard deviations (in parentheses) of higher and lower-educated mothers' use of each talk type

| Mind-related talk type | Maternal education | | | |
	Higher (*n*=14)		Lower (*n*=8)	
12m Encouragement of autonomy	22.71	(15.22)	12.75	(8.61)
18m Encouragement of autonomy	19.93	(9.43)	17.50	(8.64)
24m Encouragement of autonomy	23.14	(14.63)	23.50	(13.10)
12m Non-belief mental state	14.79	(6.97)	5.13	(2.90)
18m Non-belief mental state	13.78	(8.17)	4.50	(2.45)
24m Non-belief mental state	11.64	(7.68)	5.75	(3.20)
12m Belief mental state	3.50	(3.32)	0.75	(0.71)
18m Belief mental state	3.93	(2.67)	0.75	(1.16)
24m Belief mental state	7.07	(4.32)	0.75	(0.71)
12m Modulation of certainty	2.14	(2.18)	0.25	(0.46)
18m Modulation of certainty	1.36	(1.01)	0.25	(0.46)
24m Modulation of certainty	3.14	(3.32)	0.25	(0.46)

0.77, $p = 0.001$; belief mental-state talk, $W(21) = 0.68$, $p = 0.003$; modulation-of-certainty talk, $W(21) = 0.62$, $p = 0.009$. The propensity to use mind-related talk therefore constituted a relatively stable trait in these mothers.

Next we used a series of repeated measures ANOVAs to assess the effect of infant age on each separate talk type. Belief mental-state talk did significantly increase over time, $F(2,42) = 4.60$, $p = 0.016$, with the main increase occurring between the infant ages of 18 and 24 months, $F(1,21) = 5.50$, $p = 0.03$. There was no significant effect of infant age on mothers' use of encouragement-of-autonomy talk, non-belief mental-state talk, or modulation-of-certainty talk.

Finally, a series of repeated measures ANOVAs with mothers' education as the between subject factor were conducted to assess the effect of maternal education on the four separate mind-related talk types. The means and standard deviations of higher- and lower-educated mothers are presented in Table 3.

The analyses revealed no effect of mothers' education on their use of encouragement-of-autonomy talk. The effect of mothers' education on non-belief mental-state talk was significant, $F(1,20) = 11.77$, $p = 0.003$, $\eta^2 = 0.37$; and pairwise comparisons showed that higher-educated mothers used significantly more non-belief talk than lower-educated mothers at 12 and 18 months: $F(1,20) = 13.75$, $p = 0.001$, $\eta^2 = 0.41$, $F(1,20) = 9.64$, $p = 0.006$, $\eta^2 = 0.33$; and, to a lesser extent, at 24 months, $F(1,20) = 4.22$, $p = 0.053$, $\eta^2 = 0.17$. The effect of mothers' education on their use of belief-related mental state talk was considerable, $F(1,20) = 22.64$, $p < 0.001$, $\eta^2 = 0.53$. A near significant infant age × maternal education interaction, $F(2,40) = 2.85$, $p = 0.069$ reflected increasingly pronounced differences between higher-educated and lower-educated mothers over time: 12 months, $F(1,20) = 5.24$, $p = 0.033$, $\eta^2 = 0.20$; 18 months, $F(1,20) = 10.04$, $p = 0.005$, $\eta^2 = 0.33$; and 24 months, $F(1,20) = 16.51$,

$p = 0.001$, $\eta^2 = 0.45$. Higher-educated mothers increased their use of belief talk, while lower-educated mothers' use remained low and constant. Finally, there was a significant effect of maternal education on modulation-of-certainty talk, $F(1,20) = 10.96$, $p = 0.003$, $\eta^2 = 0.35$, again, with higher-educated mothers significantly more likely than lower-educated mothers to use this type of talk at each infant age: 12 months $F(1,20) = 5.77$, $p = 0.026$, $\eta^2 = 0.22$; 18 months $F(1,20) = 8.48$, $p = 0.009$, $\eta^2 = 0.30$; and 24 months $F(1,20) = 5.86$, $p = 0.025$, $\eta^2 = 0.28$.

Discussion

This study explored mothers' use of mind-related talk to their infants, in their second year of life, during play. Such talk constitutes an important developmental context within which young children's theory of mind and early literacy understandings develop (Ruffman *et al.*, 2006; Symonds *et al.*, 2006). Our study extends previous analyses of mothers' mental-state talk to their infants (Beeghly *et al.*, 1986; Taumoepeau & Ruffman, 2006) to include encouragement-of-autonomy talk and modulation-of-certainty talk, as these types of talk have also been found to relate to children's subsequent understanding of the mind (Brown *et al.*, 1996; Vinden, 2000). This inclusion contributes towards a more comprehensive understanding of the nature of mind-related talk that supports and guides children's gradual acquisition of metacognitive awareness.

Our first aim was to describe the variation that occurred in mothers' use of mind-related talk to their infants over a 12-month period. We found that the mothers varied considerably in their use of mind-related talk, and that this individual variation was stable over time. Increasingly, evidence supports the notion that children's exposure to mind-related talk from infancy to pre-school age plays a causal role in their theory-of-mind development (Meins *et al.*, 2003; Ruffman *et al.*, 2002; Symonds *et al.*, 2006; Taumoepeau & Ruffman, 2006). Our findings demonstrate that young children's differential experiences with such talk is enduring, so any developmental effects of such talk are likely to begin in infancy and become consolidated and more pronounced over time.

We found that mothers most frequently used encouragement-of-autonomy talk and non-belief mental-state talk, compared with their use of belief mental-state talk and modulation-of-certainty talk, which was relatively infrequent. Consistent with Beeghly *et al.* (1986) and Taumoepeau and Ruffman (2006), our findings suggest what mothers focus on in their talk are the salient, observable aspects of their children's behaviour and development. During their second year, infants become increasingly intentional and autonomous, and their desires and emotions are particularly noticeable as they attempt to exert this independence, so it is likely that mothers are responding to these visible behaviours in their choice of mind-related talk.

Our next aim was to examine changes in mothers' use of mind-related talk over time. Like previous studies (Beeghly *et al.*, 1986; Taumoepeau & Ruffman, 2006), we found that mothers increased their use of belief mental-state talk as their infants became older, suggesting that they were responding to their infants' developing capabilities in some way. It was notable that the significant period of change occurred between the infant ages of 18 and 24 months. The period of late infancy sees the emergence of symbolic play (e.g., Harris, 1994) and systematic problem-solving abilities (e.g. Chen & Siegler, 2000), so it may be that the mothers were responding to these developments by increasing the frequency in which they talk about knowledge and thinking. Further, Taumoepeau and Ruffman (2006) suggest that mothers may be influenced by rapid increases in vocabulary and grammatical development which enable older infants to share and exchange information with others. Our findings highlight the need for future studies to investigate relations between mothers' belief mental-state talk and infant development in order to determine which skills or behaviours provide mothers with insights into their infants' knowledge and thinking.

Our final aim was to examine relationships between mothers' educational attainment and their use of mind-related talk. Our findings are consistent with previous research with older children (Brown *et al.*, 1996; Ruffman *et al.*, 2006), in that higher-educated mothers did tend to use more mind-related talk than lower-educated mothers. Our inclusion of additional categories of mind-related talk showed, however, that while substantial differences existed in their use of both mental-state categories and modulation-of-certainty talk, there was no significant difference for encouragement-of-autonomy talk. It is possible that our findings reflect other observations that maternal education has been associated with the ability to reason in more abstract terms (Snow, 1993, 1999). While encouragement-of-autonomy talk is firmly grounded in the tangible aspects of immediate, intentional behaviour, mental-state talk and modulations-of-certainty require the speaker to make inferences about underlying mental states or perspectives.

Our finding that maternal education was associated with non-belief mental-state talk is inconsistent with Jenkins *et al.*'s (2003) study of mothers' talk to older children, which found that maternal educational attainment was associated with mothers' use of belief mental-state talk, but not other types of mental-state talk. While the relatively small sample size of the present study indicates that our results need to be interpreted with caution, it is possible that our findings can be explained by our focus on the talk context of infants, and thus may reflect the overall salience of non-belief concepts for mothers at this particular time in their child's life.

It is noteworthy that in our sample, higher-educated mothers decreased their use of non-belief mental-state talk over time, so that the difference between the higher and lower educated became less pronounced over time. These same mothers increased their use of belief mental-state talk, in contrast to the lower-educated mothers, whose use of both categories of mental-state talk remained static and consistently low. These findings, while exploratory, may indicate that higher-educated mothers' use of mental-state talk is more dynamic than their lower-educated counterparts, and that the apparent responsiveness to infant development captured by our and others' analyses (Beeghly *et al.*, 1986; Tamoepeau & Ruffman, 2006) may predominantly be a characteristic of higher-educated mothers.

Limitations of the study

Although many of the present findings are consistent with those of previous research, the small sample size means that our results should be regarded as exploratory. In particular, our suggestion that the dynamics of mind-related talk may differ as a function of maternal education warrants replication with a larger sample. Further, our talk sample was drawn from a relatively short, 10-minute free play session. While not unusual in studies of mothers' talk to infants, we recognize that such a small talk sample provides only a 'snapshot' of talk that infants are exposed to on a daily basis. Research with older children has demonstrated how mental-state talk occurs in many different contexts, including book reading (Symons *et al.*, 2005), picture talks (Ruffman *et al.*, 2002) and family and friend conversations (Dunn, 1996; Hughes & Dunn, 1998). Given the significance of early face-to-face and routine-time family interactions for infants' language and cognitive development (Bruner, 1983; Nelson, 1996), future research would benefit from analysing longer talk samples from a wider range of potentially facilitative talk contexts.

Implications of the study for early education

Our findings have important implications for early childhood education, pedagogy and practice. Early-childhood teachers need a thorough understanding of language structure and function and the role it plays in children's learning, so that they can become consciously aware of the language experiences they provide. Educators cannot assume that all children who enter their classrooms will have had similar exposure to mind-related talk. In particular, children whose mothers left school at an early age are unlikely to have experienced the types of mental-state and modulation-of-certainty talk that have been associated with theory-of-mind and literacy-oriented discourse. This stresses the importance of providing early childhood teachers who themselves have tertiary qualifications and who are aware of the importance of such talk, as this may enhance their capacity to provide infants and toddlers with an additional learning context to contribute to their development of metacognitive understanding. Once aware of the differential discourse backgrounds of the children in their care, educators can potentially provide targeted language and literacy experiences for these children, building on and complementing their home experiences in sensitive and positive ways.

References

Adrian, J. E., Clemente, R. A. & Villanueva, L. (2005) Parent–child picture-book reading, mothers' mental state language and children's theory of mind, *Journal of Child Language*, 32, 673–686.

Astington, J. & Pelletier, J. (2005) Theory of mind, language and learning in the early years: developmental origins of school readiness, in: B. D. Homer & C. S. Tamis-LeMonda (Eds) *The development of social cognition and communication* (Mahwah, NJ, Lawrence Erlbaum), 205–230.

Bakeman, R. & Adamson, L. B. (1984) Coordinating attention to people and objects in mother–infant and peer–infant interaction, *Child Development*, 55(4), 1278–1289.

Bartsch, K. & Wellman, H.M. (1995) *Children talk about the mind* (New York: Oxford University Press).

Beals, D. (1997) Sources of support for learning words in conversation: evidence from mealtimes, *Journal of Child Language*, 24, 673–694.

Beals, D. E. & de Temple, J. M. (1993) Home contributions to early language and literacy development, in: D. J. Leu & C. K. Kinzer (Eds) *Examining central issues in literacy research, theory and practice: Forty-second yearbook of the National Reading Conference* (Chicago, National Reading Conference, Inc.), 207–215.

Beeghly, M., Bretherton, I. & Mervis, C. B. (1986) Mothers' internal state language to toddlers, *British Journal of Developmental Psychology*, 4, 274–261.

Bornstein, M. H., Tal, J., Rahn, C., Galperin, C. Z., Pecheux, M., Lamour, M., Toda, S., Azuma, H., Ogio, M. & Tamis-LeMonda, C. S. (1992) Functional analysis of the contents of maternal speech to infants of 5 and 13 months in four cultures: Argentina, France, Japan and the United States, *Developmental Psychology*, 28, 593–603.

Bretherton, I. & Beeghly–Smith, M. (1982) Talking about internal states: The acquisition of an explicit theory of mind, *Developmental Psychology*, 18(6), 906–921.

Brown, J. R., Donelan-McCall, N. & Dunn, J. (1996) Why talk about mental states? The significance of children's conversations with friends, siblings, and mothers, *Child Development*, 67(3), 836–849.

Bruner, J. (1983). *Child's talk* (Oxford, Oxford University Press).

Budwig, N. (1989) The linguistic marking of agentivity and control in child language, *Journal of Child Language*, 16(2), 263–284.

Carpenter, M., Nagell, K. & Tomasello, M. (1998) Social cognition, joint attention, and communicative competence from 9 to 15 months of age, *Monographs of the Society for Research in Child Development*, Serial no. 255, 63(4).

Chen, Z. & Siegler, R.S. (2000) Across the great divide: Bridging the gap between understanding of toddlers' and older children's thinking, *Monographs of the Society for Research in Child Development*, 65(2, Serial No. 261).

Dickinson, D. & Tabors, P. O. (Eds) (1991) *Beginning literacy with language* (Baltimore, MD, Brooks).

Dunn, J. (1996) Family conversations and the development of social understanding, in: B. Bernstein & J. Brannen (Eds) *Children, research and policy: essays for Barbara Tizard* (Philadelphia, PA, Taylor & Francis), 81–95.

Dunn, J. & Brown, J. (1994) Affect expression in the family, children's understanding of emotions, and their interactions with others, *Merrill Palmer Quarterly*, 40(1), 120–137.

Dunn, J., Brown, J. R., Slomkowski, C., Tesla, C. & Youngblade, L. (1991) Young children's understanding of other people's feelings and beliefs: Individual differences and their antecedents, *Child Development*, 62(6), 1352–1366.

Flavell, J. H. (1979) Metacognition and cognitive monitoring: A new area of cognitive–developmental inquiry, *American Psychologist*, 34, 906–911.

Flavell, J. H. & Miller, P. H. (1998) Social cognition, in: W. Damon (Ed.) *Handbook of child psychology*, Vol. 2 (5th edn) (New York, Wiley), 851–898.

Griffin, T.M., Hemphill, L., Camp, L. & Palmer Wolf, D. (2004) Oral discourse in the preschool years and later literacy skills, *First Language*, 24, 123–147.

Griffith, P. & Ruan, J. (2005) What is metacognition and what should be its role in literacy instruction? In S. Israel, C. Block, K. L. Bauserman, & K. Kinnucan–Welsch, (Eds.), *Metacognition in literacy learning* (Mahwah, NJ: Erlbaum), 3–18.

Harris, P. (1994) Understanding pretense, in: C. Lewis & P. Mitchell (Eds), *Children's early understanding of mind: origins and development* (Hove: Erlbaum), 287–293.

Hasan, R. (1991) Questions as a mode of learning in everyday talk, in: T. Le & M. McCausland (Eds) *Language education: interaction and development* (Launceston, University of Tasmania Press), 70–119.

Hasan, R. & Cloran, C. (1990) A sociolinguistic study of everyday talk between mothers and children, in: M. A. K. Halliday, J. Gibbons & H. Nicholas (Eds) *Learning, keeping and using language* (Amsterdam, John Benjamins), 104–131.

Hughes, C. & Dunn, J. (1998). Understanding mind and emotion: longitudinal associations with mental-state talk between young friends, *Developmental Psychology*, 34(5), 1026–1037.

Israel, S., Block, C., Bauserman, K. L. & Kinnucan–Welsch, K. (2005) *Metacognition in literacy learning* (Mahwah, NJ: Erlbaum).

Jenkins, J., Turrell, S., Kogushi, Y., Lollis, S. & Ross, H. (2003) A longitudinal investigation of the dynamics of mental state talk in families, *Child Development*, 74(3), 905–920.

Markus, H. R. & Kitayama, S. (1998) The cultural psychology of personality, *Journal of Cross-Cultural Psychology*, 29(1), 63–87.

Markus, J., Mundy, P., Morales, M., Delgado, C. E. F. & Yale, M. (2000) Individual differences in infant skills as predictors of child–caregiver joint attention and language, *Social Development*, 9(3), 302–315.

Meins, E., Fernyhough, C., Fradley, E. & Tuckey, M. (2001) Rethinking maternal sensitivity: mothers' comments on infants' mental processes predict security of attachment at 12 months, *Journal of Child Psychology and Psychiatry and Allied Disciplines*, 42(5), 637–648.

Meins, E., Fernyhough, C., Wainwright, R., Clark-Carter, D., Das Gupta, M., Fradley, E. & Tuckey, M. (2003) Pathways to understanding mind: construct validity and predictive validity of maternal mind-mindedness, *Child Development*, 74(4), 1194–1211.

Moore, C. & Furrow, D. (1991) The development of the language of belief: the expression of certainty, in: D. Frye & C. Moore (Eds) *Children's theories of mind* (Hillsdale, NJ, Erlbaum), 173–193.

Moore, C., Pure, K. & Furrow, D. (1990) Children's understanding of the modal expression of speaker certainty and uncertainty and its relation to the development of a representational theory of mind, *Child Development*, 61(3), 722–730.

Moore, C., Furrow, D., Chaisson, L. & Partiquin, M. (1994) Developmental relationships between production and comprehension of mental terms, *First Language*, 14(40:1), 1–17.

Nelson, K. (1996) *Language in cognitive development: the emergence of the mediated mind* (Cambridge, Cambridge University Press).

Olson, D. (2002) What writing does to the mind, in: E. Amsel & J. P. Byrnes (Eds) *Language, literacy and cognitive development: the development and consequences of symbolic communication* (Mahwah, NJ, Lawrence Erlbaum), 153–166

Olson, D. & Torrance, S. (Eds) (1991) *Literacy and orality* (Cambridge, Cambridge University Press).

Olson, D. R. & Astington, J. (1993) Thinking about thinking: Learning how to take statements and hold beliefs, *Educational Psychologist*, 28(1), 7–23.

O'Neill, D. K. & Atance, C. M. (2000) 'Maybe my daddy give me a big piano': The development of children's use of modals to express uncertainty, *First Language*, 20(58:1), 29–52.

Pelletier, J. (2004) Relationships among theory of mind, metacognitive language, reading skills and story comprehension in L1 and L2 learners, in: A. Antonietti, O. Liverta-Sempio & A. Marchetti (Eds) *Theory of mind and language in developmental contexts* (New York, Springer), 77–89.

Perner, J. (1991) *Understanding the representational mind* (Cambridge, MA: MIT Press).

Purcell-Gates, V. (1996) Stories, coupons, and the TV guide: relationships between home literacy experiences and emergent literacy knowledge, *Reading Research Quarterly*, 31(2), 406–428.

Purcell-Gates, V. (2001) Emergent literacy is emergent knowledge of written, not oral, language, in: P. R. Britto & J. Brooks-Gunn (Eds) *The role of family literacy environments in promoting young children's emergent literacy skills* (San Fransisco, CA, Jossey-Bass), 7–22.

Ruffman, T., Slade, L. & Crowe, E. (2002) The relation between children's and mothers' mental state language and theory-of-mind understanding, *Child Development*, 73(3), 734–751.

Ruffman, T., Slade, L., Devitt, K. & Crowe, E. (2006) What mothers say and what they do: The relation between parenting, theory of mind, language and conflict/cooperation, *British Journal of Developmental Psychology*, 24(1), 105–124.

Senechal, M. & LeFevre, J. (2001) Storybook reading and parent teaching: links to language and literacy development, in: P. R. Britto & J. Brooks-Gunn (Eds) *The role of family literacy environments in promoting young children's emergent literacy skills* (San Fransisco, CA, Jossey-Bass), 39–52.

Shatz, M., Wellman, H. M. & Silber, S. (1983) The acquisition of mental verbs: A systematic investigation of the first references to mental state, *Cognition*, 14(3), 301–321.

Snow, C. (1993) Families as social contexts for literacy development, in: C. Daiute (Ed.) *The development of literacy through social interaction: new directions for child development 6* (San Fransisco, CA, Jossey-Bass), 11–24.

Snow, C. (1999) Facilitating language development promotes literacy learning, in: L. Eldering & P. P. M. Leseman (Eds) *Effective early education: cross-cultural perspectives* (New York, Falmer), 141–161.

Snow, C., Pan, A., Imbens-Bailey, A. & Herman, J. (1996) Learning to say what one means: a longitudinal study of children's speech act use, *Social Development*, 5(1), 56–84.

Storch, S. A. & Whitehurst, G. (2001) The role of the family and home in the literacy development of children from low-income backgrounds, in: P. R. Britto & J. Brooks-Gunn (Eds) *The role of family literacy environments in promoting young children's emergent literacy skills* (San Fransisco, CA, Jossey-Bass), 53–72.

Symonds, D. K., Fossum, K. M. & Collins, T. B. K. (2006) A longitudinal study of belief and desire state discourse during mother–child play and later false belief understanding, *Social Development*, 15(4), 676–691.

Symonds, D. K., Peterson, C. C., Slaughter, V., Roche, J. & Doyle, E. (2005) Theory of mind and mental state discourse during book reading and story-telling tasks, *British Journal of Developmental Psychology*, 23(1), 81–102.

Taumoepeau, M. & Ruffman, T. (2006) Mother and infant talk about mental state relates to desire language and emotion understanding, *Child Development*, 77(2), 465–481.

Torr, J. (1998) The development of modality in the pre-school years: language as a vehicle for understanding possibilities and obligations in everyday life, *Functions of Language*, 5(2), 157–178.

Vinden, P. (2000) Who's gonna do that?: how requests teach children about mind, self and agency. Paper presented at the *Jean Piaget Society Annual Meeting*, Montreal, Canada, 1–3 June.

Watson, R. (2001) Literacy and oral language: implications for early literacy acquisition, in: S. B. Neuman & D. K. Dickinson (Eds) *Handbook of early literacy research* (New York, Guilford Press), 43–53.

Wellman, H. M. (1990) *The child's theory of mind* (Cambridge, MA: MIT Press).

Constructing language: evidence from a French–English bilingual child

Gee Macrory

Introduction

An understanding of language development is fundamental to all those involved in the care and education of young children. As I have argued elsewhere (Macrory, 2001), an understanding of typical development as well as the range of individual variation is important, but this needs to be underpinned by an appreciation of *how* language is acquired, so that appropriate contexts can be provided to foster this successfully. This is all the more so in the case of children growing up bilingually or multilingually. Moreover, an understanding of the theoretical perspectives underpinning and informing training courses and books is vital for professionals working in early years settings. Only in this way can they bring to their role an informed understanding of the development of children in their care and a critical view of any advice offered.

Competing views of language development

Central to an appreciation of bilingual acquisition is an understanding of the wider field of child language. A long-standing tension in this field is that between theory and data-driven approaches. A well-known and landmark debate between Skinner *et al.* (1957) and Chomsky (1959) turned the field away from the empiricist and descriptivist traditions of psychology towards a more mentalist/nativist perspective, and at the same time, accorded a key role to grammar. The centrality of grammar in explanations of language acquisition arises from Chomsky's now famous tenets relating to the generative nature of grammar, the apparent speed with which children acquire the language to which they are exposed and the apparently degenerate nature of the input.

This has resulted in explanations that centred on the notions of a Language Acquisition Device and a Universal Grammar, and more recently Principles and Parameters Theory, which allowed the acquisition device to make the necessary adjustments that the grammars of different languages required. Such modifications to the nativist explanation arose first, in the 1970s, in the form of accounts arguing for a semantic basis to children's early grammars (e.g. Bowerman, 1973), and later from research in input and interaction (see Snow & Ferguson, 1977; Gallaway & Richards, 1994; Snow, 1999), as well as the broader areas of discourse and pragmatics. More recently, however, the field of Cognitive Linguistics has made a significant contribution to non-nativist accounts of language acquisition. From this perspective, linguistic constructions are essentially cognitive schemas that are of the same type that exist in other domains of cognition, and derive from recurrent events with respect to which the people of a culture have recurrent communicative roles (Tomasello, 1998).

The implications for acquisition are that what is needed is a sophisticated ability on the part of the child to understand the event structures of the particular cultural context in which they are developing, and crucially, the intentions of others as demonstrated through their actions and their language (Tomasello, 1992). As Snow stresses, the social precocity of the young infant is impressive, and this in turn implies a pragmatic precocity in understanding the interpersonal and intentional nature of communication (1999, p. 261). Tomasello (2000, 2001, 2003) suggests not only that children have multiple ways of understanding adults' intentions, including the knowledge that adults use words to announce their intended actions, but that they also have a powerful capacity for imitative learning.

Within this context, Tomasello argues that children's first multi-word constructions are based on specific lexical items from which they discern patterns, and progress to the formation of abstract categories and schemas based on patterns of usage in adult language. Crucially, he claims that these schemas and categories are not innate, but are generalizations children make on the basis of their own categorization skills working on the language they hear. If early multi-word constructions are, however, lexically specific, this suggests the possibility that language development is a more piecemeal and less incremental process than hitherto thought.

The item-based nature of early acquisition is not, of course, an entirely novel proposition. Previous research has revealed the use of routines in language acquisition in both first and second language acquisition (Nelson, 1973; Clark, 1977, 1982; Wong Fillmore, 1979; Peters, 1983; Lieven *et al.*, 1992; Myles *et al.*, 1998). However, earlier notions that located such use within an individual differences perspective have developed over the past decade or so to suggest that they may play a broader role in development than was previously thought. For example, in their data Pine and Lieven (1993) chart the emergence of the kind of positional patterns described by Braine (1976, 1988) out of initially unanalysed phrases; Lieven *et al.* (1995) suggest also that this may well continue beyond the earliest stage of multi-word utterances. Thus young children's 'novel' utterances may rely heavily on those they have previously used. Finally, in more recent years, frequency in the input has been identified as a likely factor in acquisition (Rowland & Pine, 2003).

In summary, there is a tension between traditional nativist accounts that would predict a more across-the-board appearance of linguistic structures and the approach outlined above which implies a slower and more gradual build-up towards adult competence, and one which accords a role to frequency in the input as well as to the child's own usage.

However, monolingual contexts are not the only source of data. Studies of bilingual children offer a unique opportunity to consider development of not one but two languages. Clearly, as Bosch and Sebastián-Gallés (2001) note, the study of bilingual development is needed from a social and educational perspective. But as other researchers also point out, it may also contribute to our more general understanding of language acquisition (de Houwer, 1995; Meisel, 1995). Paradis and Genesee (1996, p. 22) suggest that 'bilingual children provide a sensitive test of proposed universals and language-specific differences in acquisition'. Although it was once thought that the two languages of young bilingual children were a single undifferentiated system, an argument used to explain the mixed utterances often observed in bilingual children, it has been generally accepted in recent years that young children can differentiate their languages from early in development at a phonological, lexical and grammatical level. Furthermore, the issue of similarity with monolingual acquisition is seen as crucial. de Houwer (1995) suggests that proof that a bilingual child's development follows the same path as that of a monolingual child of similar age would provide strengthened evidence that the bilingual child is developing two separate morpho-syntactic systems. For example, the French/German children studied by Meisel (1989, 2001) produced different word-order sequences in both languages as soon as they began to produce multi-word utterances. There is now an increasing body of evidence that the 'piece-meal' development observed in monolingual children is also evident in bilingual children (Serratrice, 2001; Van der Linden & Hulk, 2005). If this is the case, there are important theoretical and practical implications to consider.

The aim of the present study

The aim of the study described in this paper was to examine data from a French/English bilingual child, analysing the emergence and development of structures in two languages in order to consider what light this might throw on the theoretical debate outlined above (Macrory, 2001, 2004). In particular, the aim was to investigate: (1) whether the acquisition of French and English in one child resembled their acquisition in monolingual children; (2) whether there was any evidence that either or both of the two languages appeared to emerge as new-upon-old, that is with new utterances relying on previously learned language; (3) whether there was evidence that structures, once acquired, were used to differing degrees; and (4) whether there was any evidence of a relationship between the child's language and the input from her parents. Given that it was not possible to examine the whole of the grammatical system of a language, it was important to focus on a particular aspect of it. This study took as its focus the development of questions in French and English, and I report below on the emergence and development of yes/no questions for the verbs 'want' (French: *veux*) and 'can' (French: *peux*) in both languages.

Methodology

This is a case study of a bilingual child living in England with a French mother and an English father, thus fitting into Romaine's 'type 1' category (1995, pp. 183–5), '*one person–one language*', whereby the parents have different native languages and with each having some degree of competence in the other's language, and where the language of one of the parents is the dominant language of the community, and the strategy adopted is that the parents each speak their own language to the child from birth. An issue, of course, is that although the 'one parent–one language' is a strategy that childcare experts tend to feel they can recommend (de Jong, 1986, p. 36), this may be a little simplistic. At the very least, one parent must change languages to speak to the other parent. This underlines the importance of describing clearly for any study what the particular situation is, so that results can be considered in context. Adèle was a first-born child whose parents had opted for this approach and followed it as diligently as they could. Adèle was cared for in her home by her mother who spoke only French to her, and who had opted for full-time parenting in order to maximize Adèle's opportunity to grow up speaking French; the sole exception was in the company of her mother-in-law who spoke no French. Although some French friends and their children visited from time to time, and Adèle had access to French books and video tapes, the majority of her input was from her mother. Adèle's father spoke only English to her and the parents conversed in English, although Adèle's mother still addressed her in French in her father's presence, as he understood French but did not speak it fluently.

The data were collected at monthly intervals from the age of 2;3.0 to 3;5.22, and audio/video recorded in samples of one hour. An hour of French with her mother was followed later the same day by an hour of English with her father. The data were transcribed in full using CHILDES (MacWhinney, 1991) and all questions extracted from the data. For ease of handling the data, the 15 data collection points were divided into seven stages, spanning comparable time periods. Before considering the findings, however, it is important to set out the key differences between the question systems of French and English.

Question systems of French and English

Yes/no questions in English

Inversion. First, a key feature of yes/no questions in English is that of inversion. If the lexical verb in the statement is part of *to be*, or occasionally *to have*, then subject and lexical verb can be inverted in a question, such as:

> *She is nice—is she nice?*
> *She had a cat—had she a cat?*

With any other lexical verb, the auxiliary verb *do* has to be imported; it is thus the auxiliary and the subject which are inverted: '*She likes cats—does she like cats?*' It is therefore the auxiliary verb that carries the markers for tense and number. Statements with other auxiliaries are treated in the same way : '*He can fly—can he fly?*' Inversion in yes/no questions is accompanied by rising intonation.

Intonation. English does allow intonation-only questions, where canonical order (normally SVO) is retained and a rising intonation signals the function of question; e.g. '*You'll have a coffee?*' These are described as *declarative questions* by Quirk *et al.* (1972).

Yes/no questions in French

There are essentially three ways of forming yes/no questions in French (see Price, 2003), as follows.

Intonation. Canonical order (normally SVO) is retained and a rising intonation rather than a falling one signals the function of question.

Question marker *est-ce que* (with elision before a vowel, resulting in, for example, '*est-ce qu'il...?*' rather than '*est-ce que Pierre....?*') precedes statement. This is accompanied by a rising intonation.

Inversion. (a) subject pronoun and verb: straightforward inversion of verb and subject pronoun, with the addition of / t / between verb and pronoun where pronoun begins with a vowel, hence, for example, '*Vous mangez*' becomes '*Mangez-vous?*', but '*Elle mange*' becomes '*Mange-t-elle?*'

> (b) where the NP consists of a name, or noun preceded by modifiers, the NP remains intact and the relevant subject pronoun is inserted into the question, and the verb and pronoun are inverted as in (a) above, so that, for example, '*Le garçon mange un biscuit*' becomes '*Le garçon, mange-t-il un biscuit?*'.
>
> (c) tenses formed with auxiliary verbs, such as the perfect, pluperfect, immediate future and the conditional perfect, require the inversion of the auxiliary verb and the subject pronoun: '*Il a mangé un biscuit*' therefore becomes '*A-t-il mangé un biscuit?*'

The key issue to note in respect of questions is that inversion is typically used in English rather than intonation. In contrast, in French, intonation is the most common, followed by the use of the question marker *est-ce que*, and with inversion, the least used in everyday spoken French, belonging to the most formal register (Batchelor & Offord, 1982).

Findings

Separate systems

The overall findings appear to confirm earlier research that suggests the two languages are developed separately from an early age. It is the case that each language broadly follows the pattern of acquisition that is typical of a monolingual learner of that language. Most noticeably, Adèle showed a preference for inverted questions in English and for questions formed by intonation only in French, as can be seen in Table 1.

There are other indications that the pattern of acquisition broadly follows that which is expected in monolingual children. In English, in the very early stages, some questions are produced with intonation only (the 41% in Table 1 disguises the fact that many of these questions appear in the early stages), before auxiliary verbs and inverted questions appear, reflecting previous research (Bellugi, 1965). When they do, *can* as the first auxiliary verb to appear echoes previous findings (Fletcher, 1985), as does the relative lack of tag questions (Richards, 1990). In the French data, the order of acquisition observed in Adèle broadly reflects what is known about monolingual acquisition of French. For example, both Clark (1985) and Redard (1976) (in one of the few studies to consider the acquisition of questions in French) note that questions formed with intonation only are produced first, and are much more evident than questions produced with the question marker *est-ce que* or questions formed by inversion. This is what the data from the current study also tell us.

In summary, the view that the language development of young bilingual children parallels that of monolingual speakers of the languages is well supported by the data here. This is important to note prior to examining, in more detail, the emergence of particular structures and their subsequent development. While, on the one hand, Adèle's languages resembled their monolingual development, on the other hand, it is necessary to compare her acquisition of one language with the acquisition of the other. In order to do this, a more detailed analysis of particular structures was

Table 1.   Percentage of Adèle's questions formed by inversion or intonation-only in French and English

	French	English
Intonation-only	99.7%	41%
Inversion	0.3%	59%

undertaken in both French and English. We report below on the emergence and development of *want* and *can* in French and English.

Sequence of emergence: the case of 'want'

Although Adèle presented a case of what is considered to be simultaneous bilingual development, as noted above, the context of individual cases needs always to be taken into account. Here, at the beginning of the study, Adèle spoke more French than English, due, no doubt, to her almost exclusively French-speaking daytime environment. Perhaps unsurprisingly, then, French was sometimes used in place of English when she was talking to her father, but the opposite seldom occurred. Again, unsurprisingly, some structures appeared in her French before their equivalents did in English. Nevertheless, the *sequence* in which they appeared showed an interesting similarity. The questions fulfilled the same functions in both languages, used typically to request permission, to ask the parent to do something or to offer the parent something, or an opportunity to do something. In both languages, among the questions to appear early were questions with want and can: '*Can I ...?*', '*can you...?*' and '*do you want ...?*', and their French equivalents.

In both languages, items were first offered to the parent simply with a rising intonation on the noun phrase—e.g. *NP?* In English, Adèle's first questions with 'want' were of the sort '*You want NP?*' at the age of 2;9, followed a month later by '*Do you want NP?*'. Only five months later (3;3.0) was this frame *do you want* used with a verb phrase *Do you want + V (verb)?*, or sometimes *You want + V?*. Only after this was used did she produce questions with other verbs beginning with *do you want—do you want to V?*

What did we observe in French? First of all, after producing nouns with rising intonation, Adèle's first questions with a verb consisted of *tu veux + NP?* This was at the age of 2;2.0 but not used with a VP until some seven months later: *tu veux + V?* (2;9). At the age of 3;2 she produced her first question fronted with the marker *est-ce que*, when she used this with *tu veux + NP?*, resulting in: *est-ce que tu veux ... NP?*

What does this pattern of linguistic development tell us (Table 2)? First, we should recall that the 'do' support required of English questions is a key element in the question system. Adèle could have used it in other sorts of questions (e.g. do you like?), or with other persons of the verb (e.g. does he want? does he like?), but in fact her early usage was very constrained, offering support to Tomasello's contention that

Table 2.   The development of '*want*' and '*veux*'

French	English
NP?	NP?
Tu veux NP?	You want NP?
Tu veux VP?	Do you want NP?
Est-ce que tu veux NP?	Do you want VP?

children's early multi-word constructions are based on specific lexical items from which they discern patterns of usage; Adèle appeared to build systematically on language acquired earlier, trying out 'do' on a familiar verb (want). Secondly, from a bilingual perspective, she appears to be constrained in a very similar way in French, limiting her use of '*veux*' to second person and also like 'do' trying out '*est-ce que*' in familiar and well-used territory (i.e. her frequent use of *tu veux?*). In both languages she appears to be adopting a strategy of new-upon-old, reflecting the kind of behaviour drawn to our attention by researchers such as Elbers (1995), who suggested that much of young children's syntactic development derives from analysis of their own linguistic production. Lieven *et al.* (2003) found that a high percentage of novel utterances in the output of the child they studied were closely related to utterances produced previously.

Differential usage: the case of 'can'

A related issue to emerge in the findings was the differential usage of certain verbs. Thus, some were much more heavily used than others. As noted above, Fletcher (1985) found that '*can*' is the first modal auxiliary verb to be produced. While the findings of this study confirm this, the interesting finding was the differential usage of verb '*can*' and its French counterpart '*peux*'.

In English, '*can*' emerged used in the question *can I + VP?*, followed a month later by questions with *can you + VP?* There were, in total, 64 questions with '*can I?*' and 75 with '*can you?*'. This contrasts markedly with the three questions with '*can we?*', and the complete absence of questions with he/she/they. Thus, in a similar fashion to the acquisition of '*want*', a clear preference for first- and second-person singular pronouns is evident. While this may be, in part, explained by the dialogic nature of her interaction with her parents, there were nevertheless ample opportunities for reference to other people and things. Turning to consideration of her French usage of '*peux*', a similar pattern emerges. The first question with '*peux*' to appear is, *je peux + VP?*, of which there are 33 in the data, followed by *tu peux + VP?*, of which there are only nine. On the one hand, this contrasts with the use of '*can*', noted above. However, some interesting issues are raised by this. Adèle is clearly not using cross-language equivalents. Rather, a closer look at the data shows that she shows a preference for asking her mother to do something by saying '*tu veux + VP?*' and '*can you +VP?*' to her father (Table 3).

Why might this be? One explanation relates to the acquisition of '*veux*'. This is so frequently used by Adèle herself (see Table 2) that it is an easy step from using it with

Table 3.   Adèle's use of '*peux*' and '*can*'

Je peux + VP? [33]	Can I + VP? [64]
Tu peux + VP? [9]	Can you + VP? [75]
Tu veux + VP? [23]	(Do) you want to + VP? [12]

an object to using it with a verb phrase as a request. On the other hand, in English, '*can*' is an easier structure to produce than *(do) you want to*. This is not to suggest that '*can*' has been analysed and used as an independent component. The differential usage noted above suggests the possibility that both *can I ...?* and *can you ...?* may be being used as convenient routines. However, children's own usage is by no means the whole story. As noted above, frequency in the input has been identified as a possible factor in acquisition. Accordingly, an analysis of the parents' questions was carried out.

Parents' questions

The questions used by Adèle's parents were analysed at three points: beginning, middle and end of data collection. Using CHILDES, all questions were extracted from the data and analysed for frequency. In the case of the mother, in French, it was evident that she frequently asked questions of the *tu veux* + *V?* type (37 examples), but there were no examples of *tu peux* + *V?* in the data at all. Similarly, in the father's data, he asked 12 questions of the *(do) you want to* +*V?* type but 23 of the *can you* + *VP?* variety. What does this suggest?

It may be that the explanation for Adèle's differential usage lies, at least in part, with the input she receives. Tomasello and Brooks accord a key role to the input, arguing (1999, p. 179) that 'children's progress toward adult-like constructions is mostly driven by the adult language they hear', and that 'the language children hear is a key element in providing numerous exemplars of similar utterances from which they can extract commonalities of form and function' (1999, p. 181).

In the case of the mother, in particular, the data from the current study are strongly suggestive of a relationship between what the child hears and what she produces. On the other hand, there is a weaker case to be made for the father, although we can see that he uses one sort nearly twice as often as the other. Were we to extrapolate up from this not only to all the data, but to what the child hears on a daily basis, this is a substantial difference. If there are slightly stronger parallels between child and mother and child and father, this is consistent with research that shows that maternal and paternal input may differ. Barton and Tomasello (1994, p. 119) state that findings from studies of paternal and maternal speech to young children have repeatedly shown that secondary caregiver fathers' verbal interactions with their children are different from their mothers'. They regard as of central interest Berko Gleason's (1975) suggestion that fathers provide a 'bridge' to the outside world. According to this hypothesis, fathers in Western societies are more likely to be at work outside the home, and mothers more likely to be the parent with daily and continuous interaction with children, allowing a greater level of interactional fine-tuning.

In this particular case, however, the mother had recognized the potential pitfalls of a bilingual upbringing where one language is much more frequent in the input than the other, and had chosen to remain at home largely for this reason. Adèle thus had her English input from a greater diversity of sources than her French, which was primarily provided by her mother. Thus an alternative explanation to the bridging hypothesis is that the child's English is diluted by other speakers, and as the major influence is the mother, she may be more likely to model the input frequencies of the mother rather than the father. Thus there may be differences between the relationships the child has with her two parents. These are not, however, sufficiently large as to call into question the general point at issue here. Despite some variation, there does appear to be a modelling in the input of the syntax that the child acquires in each language.

Conclusion and implications

To summarize, the research reported above suggests that, in the case of this particular child at least, and within the domain of questions, there is persuasive evidence that both languages emerged in a somewhat piecemeal way, suggested by the way in which the verb *want* and its French counterpart *veux* appeared in the child's speech, and were used to carry the first uses of key elements of the question system in both languages (*do* and *est-ce que*). This lends support to the view that children use their own output as input (Elbers, 1995). Furthermore, the differential usage of the auxiliary verbs reported here mean that Adèle is reinforcing some structures more than others in her speech, adding potentially to the piecemeal nature of acquisition.

Yet the analysis of the parents' data suggests that this cannot be the whole story. The distribution of frequency of the parents' questions is such that it is difficult to avoid the conclusion that Adèle is using the language she most frequently hears. While this at one level is unsurprising, from a theoretical perspective it lends weight to a constructivist view of how language is acquired rather than a nativist viewpoint, in that the child is not simply generating language from scratch. That this should be the case with not just one, but two, languages simultaneously further reinforces this perspective. The fact that each language appears to pattern off itself and to be related to the input in that language may, of course, be the very mechanism that serves to keep the two languages separate. Equally, to return to the issue raised at the beginning of this paper, it suggests that theory should indeed be derived from the data that young children offer us.

From a practical perspective, that is from the perspective of those who work with young children, it suggests a language learning process that may need continued support long past the early stages. In the case of bilingual (or, for that matter, multilingual), this is even more pressing. It is often the case that one language receives much less input than the other. I have written elsewhere about the implications that this may have on a practical basis for early years practitioners (Macrory, 2006). From the data presented above, I would wish to argue that we need a detailed understanding of how to monitor and assess linguistic development in order best to support it, an issue that merits the urgent attention of policy-makers when planning to meet the needs of young bilingual children in early years settings, and when planning guidance for those professionals to whom this task is entrusted.

References

Barton, M. E. & Tomasello, M. (1994) The rest of the family: the role of fathers and siblings in early language development, in: C. Gallaway & B. J. Richards (Eds) *Input and interaction in language acquisition* (Cambridge, Cambridge University Press).

Batchelor, R. E. & Offord, M. H. (1982) *A guide to contemporary French usage* (Cambridge, Cambridge University Press).

Bellugi, U. (1965) The development of interrogative structures in children's speech, in: K. F. Riegel (Ed.) *The development of language functions: 8* (Michigan, University of Michigan, Center for Human Growth and Development).

Berko Gleason, J. (1975) *Fathers and other strangers—men's speech to young children: Georgetown University Roundtable on Language and Linguistics* (Washington, DC, Georgetown University Press).

Bosch, L. & Sebastián-Gallés, N. (2001) Early language differentiation in bilingual infants, in: J. Cenoz & F. Genesee (Eds) *Trends in bilingual acquisition research* (Amsterdam, John Benjamins).

Bowerman, M. (1973) Structural relationships in children's utterances: syntactic or semantic? in: T. Moore (Ed.) *Cognitive development and the acquisition of language* (New York, Academic Press).

Braine, M. D. S. (1976) Children's first word combinations, *Monographs of the Society for Research in Child Development*, 41 (Serial No. 164).

Braine, M. D. S. (1988) Modelling the acquisition of linguistic structure, in: Y. Levy, I. M. Schlesinger & M. D. S. Braine (Eds) *Categories and processes in language acquisition* (Hillsdale, NJ, Lawrence Erlbaum).

Chomsky, N. (1959) Review of *Verbal behavior*, by B. F. Skinner, *Language*, 35, 26–58.

Clark, E. V. (1985) The acquisition of romance, with special reference to French, in: D. I. Slobin (Ed.) *The cross-linguistic study of language acquisition*, Vol. 1 (Hillsdale, NJ, Lawrence Erlbaum).

Clark, R. (1977) What's the use of imitation? *Journal of Child Language*, 4, 341–358.

Clark, R. (1982) Theory and method in child language research: are we assuming too much? in: S. A. Kuczaj (Ed.) *Language development, Vol. 1: Syntax and semantics* (Hillsdale, NJ, Lawrence Erlbaum).

Elbers, L. (1995) Production as a source of input for analysis: evidence from the developmental course of a word-blend, *Journal of Child Language*, 22, 47–71.

Fletcher, P. (1985) *A child's learning of English* (Oxford, Blackwell).

Gallaway, C. & Richards, B. J. (Eds) (1994) *Input and interaction in language acquisition* (Cambridge, Cambridge University Press).

de Houwer, A. (1995) Bilingual language acquisition, in: P. Fletcher & B. MacWhinney (Eds) *The handbook of child language* (Oxford, Oxford University Press).

de Jong, E. (1986) *The bilingual experience: a book for parents* (Cambridge, Cambridge University Press).

Lieven, E. V. M., Pine, J. M. & Baldwin, G. (1995) Lexically based learning and early grammatical development, *Journal of Child Language*, 24, 187–219.

Lieven, E. V. M., Pine, J. M. & Dresner Barnes, H. (1992) Individual differences in early vocabulary development: redefining the referential-expressive distinction, *Journal of Child Language*, 19, 287–310.

Lieven, E. V. M., Behrens, H., Speares, J. & Tomasello, M. (2003) Early syntactic creativity: a usage-based approach, *Journal of Child Language*, 30, 333–370.

Macrory, G. (2001) Language development: what do early years practitioners need to know? *Early Years*, 21(1), 33–40.

Macrory, G. (2004) *The acquisition of questions by a French–English bilingual child.* Unpublished PhD thesis, University of Manchester.

Macrory, G. (2006) Bilingual language development: what do early years practitioners need to know? *Early Years*, 26(2), 159–170.

MacWhinney, B. (1991) *The CHILDES Project: tools for analyzing talk* (Hillsdale, NJ, Lawrence Erlbaum).

Meisel, J. (1989) Early differentiation of languages in bilingual children, in: K. Hyltenstam & L. Obler (Eds) *Bilingualism across the lifespan: aspects of acquisition, maturity and loss* (Cambridge, Cambridge University Press).

Meisel, J. (1995) Parameters in acquisition, in: P. Fletcher & B. MacWhinney (Eds) *The handbook of child language* (Oxford, Blackwell).

Meisel, J. (2001) The simultaneous acquisition of two languages: early differentiation and subsequent development of grammars, in: J. Cenoz & F. Genesee (Eds) *Trends in bilingual acquisition research* (Amsterdam, John Benjamins).

Myles, F., Hooper, J. & Mitchell, R. (1998) Rote or rule? Exploring the role of formulaic language in classroom foreign language learning, *Language Learning*, 48(3), 323–363.

Nelson, K. (1973) Structure and strategy in learning to talk, *Monographs of the Society for Research in Child Development*, 38(1–2) (Serial No. 149).

Paradis, J. & Genesee, F. (1996) Syntactic acquisition in bilingual children: autonomous or interdependent? *Studies in Second Language Acquisition*, 18(1), 1–25.

Peters, A. (1983) *The units of language acquisition* (Cambridge, Cambridge University Press).

Pine, J. M. & Lieven, E. V. M. (1993) Re-analysing rote-learned phrases: individual differences in the transition to multi-word speech, *Journal of Child Language*, 20, 551–571.

Price, G. (2003) *A comprehensive French grammar* (5th edn) (Oxford, Blackwell).

Quirk, R., Greenbaum, S., Leech, G. & Svartvik, J. (1972) *A grammar of contemporary English* (London, Longman).

Redard, F. (1976) Étude des formes interrogatives en français chez les enfants de trois ans, *Études de Linguistique Appliquée*, 21, 98–110.

Richards, B. J. (1990) *Language development and individual differences: a study of auxiliary verb learning* (Cambridge, Cambridge University Press).

Romaine, S. (1995) *Bilingualism* (2nd edn) (Oxford, Blackwell).

Rowland, C. F. & Pine, J. M. (2003) The development of inversion in wh-questions: a reply to Van Valin, *Journal of Child Language*, 30, 197–212.

Serratrice, L. (2001) The emergence of verbal morphology and the lead-lag pattern issue in bilingual acquisition, in: J. Cenoz & F. Genesee (Eds) *Trends in bilingual acquisition research* (Amsterdam, John Benjamins).

Skinner, B. F. (1957) *Verbal behavior* (New York, Appleton-Century-Crofts).

Snow, C. E. (1999) Social perspectives on the emergence of language, in: B. MacWhinney (Ed.) *The emergence of language* (Hillsdale, NJ, Lawrence Erlbaum).

Snow, C. E. & Ferguson, C. A. (Eds) (1977) *Talking to children: language input and acquisition* (Cambridge, Cambridge University Press).

Tomasello, M. (1992) *First verbs: a case study of grammatical development* (Cambridge, Cambridge University Press).

Tomasello, M. (Ed.) (1998) *The new psychology of language: cognitive and functional approaches to language structure* (Hillsdale, NJ, Lawrence Erlbaum).

Tomasello, M. (2000) Do young children have adult syntactic competence? *Cognition*, 74, 209–253.

Tomasello, M. (2001) Perceiving intentions and learning words in the second year of life, in: M. Bowerman & S. C. Levinson (Eds) *Language acquisition and conceptual development* (Cambridge, Cambridge University Press).

Tomasello, M. (2003) *Constructing a language: a usage-based theory of child language acquisition* (Cambridge, MA, Harvard University Press).

Tomasello, M. & Brooks, P. (1999) Early syntactic development: a construction grammar approach, in: M. Barrett (Ed.) *The development of language* (Hove, Psychology Press).

Van der Linden, E. & Hulk, A. (2005) Special issue: Emergent grammars in bilingual children, *International Journal of Bilingualism*, 9(2), 133–136.

Wong Fillmore, L. (1979) Individual differences in second language acquisition, in: C. J. Fillmore, D. Kempler & W. S. Y. Yang (Eds) *Individual differences in language ability and language behavior* (New York, Academic Press).

Digital story telling in a science classroom: reflective self-learning (RSL) in action

Yordanka Valkanova and Mike Watts

Introduction

In this article we focus on the role of digital video in promoting oral language development through reflective self-learning (RSL) in seven-year-old children. In particular we explore children's narratives, story telling, during the making of sound 'voice-over' tracks for their own video films. We provide evidence for Evan's evocation in the first article of this issue that the development of oral language requires innovative pedagogical practices to stimulate dialogic learning, particularly those practices that fuel metacognitive, in this case reflective, approaches to oracy. We describe a very contemporary research-based perspective on language acquisition and language learning in a specific context: early enculturalisation within school science.

The material we present is part of a larger project that seeks to explore the relationship between reflection on learning and the impact of such reflection on acquisition of knowledge (Valkanova *et al.*, 2004b). Here we describe the nature of children's self-reflection as this bears upon their language development. Our work involves examining children's own visual story-making as poly-vocal self-evaluation, in which children, individually and in groups, attempt to construct a narrative addressing others as a specific audience. In particular, ours is an empirical exploration of the assumption that making video diaries about one's own everyday classroom experiences can serve as a means of developing oracy and enhancing RSL.

Why use video to enhance expressive self-reflection in children?

Self-reflection is recognised as a central component in the process of building self-consciousness and self-conscious language (Piaget & Inhelder, 1967; Moon, 1999; Vygotsky, 1999; Hmelo & Lin, 2000; Bandura, 2001). Research in developmental psychology indicates that in late childhood (7- to 12-year-old children) children have the ability to learn from experience through self-reflection (Andersen & Williams, 1985; Adams-Webber, 2000; Zelazo, 2000; Zelazo & Lourenco, 2003). In a number of studies reflection is seen as an important mediating influence in children's abilities to move out of knowledge-telling into knowledge (Guberman & Greenfield, 1991; Buehl, 1996; Holmstrom & Rosenqvist, 2004). For our particular purposes, such studies also indicate that self-reflection enables children to develop understanding of scientific ideas (Ginsburg & Golbeck, 2004).

Recent developments within emerging technologies offer the promise of using new ways to encourage self-reflection on learning experiences. For instance, several studies have reported on aspects of video recording and video editing that lead to improved self-understanding and behavioural changes in young children (Lonnecker *et al.*, 1994; Atienza *et al.*, 1998; Endres *et al.*, 1999; Kimball *et al.*, 2004). Young children can make video documentaries about their school experiences, explore scientific, historical and social issues, create animations and explore their own creativity. By doing so, they develop new skills that both shape traditional forms of oracy as well as underpin a new type of literacy, making it possible even for seven-year olds to narrate a visual text on the basis of combining moving images, still images, sounds and texts in order to give expression to their ideas (Sefton-Green & Parker, 2000; Valkanova *et al.*, 2004a, b). It is the traditional forms we discuss in this article.

The usual caveats apply, however, because the studies we cite show that this new medium has great potential for children's learning (Petrosino & Cunningham, 2003; Kukulska-Hulme *et al.*, 2004; Thurston, 2004), children's use of video is still only emergent. It is also clearly difficult, technically, to capture children's spontaneous reflection and hence the need to build a particular kind of (video) learning environment through which to prompt 'recordable' self-reflection. But while developments in digital video offer new opportunities, 'digital language skills' are not yet part of the mainstream (Becta, 2005) and the use of digital video requires much greater in-depth exploration to become established.

Some background theory

Theories concerned with self-reflection are polarised. The first viewpoint consists of predominant cognitively directed enquiries on introspection, while the second consists of socially contextualised *inter-subjective* enquiries. The cognitive perspective tends to be criticised for the limitations it places on studying the individual as a whole, in emphasising only the cognitive and failing to prioritise social dimensions of the reflective self. Inter-subjective rhetoric, on the other hand, does not explain how self-reflection relates to an individual's learning and how, in our case, this action influences the cognitive growth in the process of learning science. These issues have developmental dimensions that cannot be ignored, and their recognition is crucial for the investigation of self-reflective language in children at seven to eight years of age.

Devoid of a clear methodological backbone, both sets of theories largely fail to cope with two main issues important to the processes of self-reflection in the science classroom. The first concerns its contextualisation within types of instruction and characteristics of curriculum; the second relates to the dynamics of an individual's motivation for reflection and how this relates to linguistic growth. The 'external' attributes of learning have never found an easy accommodation either within introspective theory or inter-subjectivity. The occurrence of self-reflection has been treated as an outcome that must be explained through cognitive variables, such as the uncertainty over one's own thinking and the effect of the cognitive level of teachers' questions (Harlin, 2000; Moorefield, 2005). But the consideration of instruction and the content of learning in developing reflection in learning falls outside of theories of introspection. On the other hand, inter-subjective elaborations dismiss the curriculum contextualisation as simply a support for self-reflection. In our view, both perspectives fall short of accounting for the objectification of self-reflection within lived language activity.

In our view, a well-articulated, holistic understanding of self-reflection is better provided by drawing on cultural–historical activity theory (CHAT) (Davydov, 1988; Abramova, 2006). While CHAT is rooted in inter-subjectivity, it works to develop the externalisation of self-reflection from the realm of the inner world. Externalisation is considered in relation to internalisation. Both are thought of as two sides to human activity that cannot exist in isolation. Reflection is seen as an action that relates to the context of activity. Indeed, self-reflection is frequently regarded as a component of the process of internalisation (Davydov, 1988; Kaptelinin, 1996). It provides a basis for studying individuals in relation to the particular activity in which they are involved (Leontiev, 1981, 1983; Engeström, 2000; Daniels, 2004a, b).

We are interested in the specific emphasis CHAT places on self-reflection in the process of making articulated sense of an individual's own experience (Stahl, 2003; O'Reilly *et al.*, 2005). CHAT regards the self as embedded in the social realm and acknowledges the role of dialogue with others in the process of self-reflection (Stetsenko & Arievitch, 2004). Moreover, the emergence of action is seen as accompanied by a shared meaning of the action as consciously reflected by the actor (Engeström, 1999). Therefore, it is safe to assume that mediation should support both, sharing meanings gained by self-reflection during learning science as well as sharing knowledge about how to reflect on one's own experiences, extant in children's language during different acts of participation in learning as an activity. Our research task has been to articulate those descriptions and to explore their implications for learning.

About procedures

Researchers who study self-reflection in children stress its hidden nature (Copple, 2003), which presents practical challenges and compound difficulties in recognising reflection in the bustle of a normal busy classroom (Driver *et al.*, 1994). In this study we examine children's spoken stories produced as 'voice-over' to fragments of their own video clips. The goal has been to identify how these children's creative accounts, their narratives and learning from, about and through stories, shape and develop their learning. Our professional intention is to illustrate how such processes can enhance children's development of language, in particular the language of science.

The methodological problem is oxymoronic: how to contrive naturalistic research moments. To achieve this we created an experimental context through which children explain their thoughts about their own learning experiences. We devolved power to the children to decide what and how they reported their own learning and how to present their 'learning identities'. We analysed their self-recorded voice-over narratives as forms of self-reporting produced in (almost) naturalistic classroom conditions. This tranche of our research has been conducted in a London primary school well equipped with appropriate PCs and software for digital video editing (QuickTime Pro for operating system Windows). Thirty pupils aged seven and eight years participated in the study, 15 girls and 15 boys.

The pupil population was a mixture of children from multinational backgrounds, native and bilingual, comprised mainly children born and raised in London. While different occupational backgrounds were represented, the majority of families were working class. The class consisted of both native English speakers and those for whom English was a second language, none with any reported history of speech and hearing difficulties. Since all the bilingual children were born in London, they had acquired a good level of fluency in English. Only one child from the Year 3 class, a female, was born overseas. She spoke English fluently. The study took place over a 12-week period—long enough for children to learn the new skills of video editing and produce their finished film, but short enough to avoid possible maturational effects. For an overview of the key foci of this research, see Figure 1.

The central focus of the work was a video recording, by us, of one classroom science lesson where children undertook National Curriculum Key Stage 2 experiments with light and shadows. The ensuing recorded 40-minute video film was then given to the children as 'work print' files for editing into their own short 3-minute films. The children were told that the purpose of their editing was to produce a short film to show to family and friends what they had learned in science. As an element of film making, children were asked to produce verbal explanations of the events in their films. The data were analysed by discourse and narrative analysis. During the course of their film making we recorded their discussions (both monologues and dialogues).

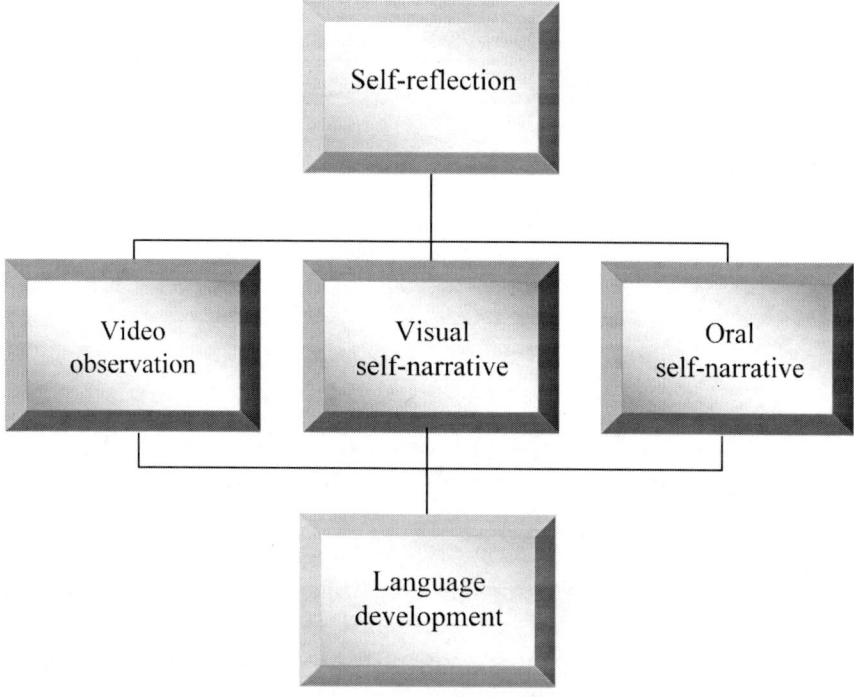

Figure 1. A schematic of the key foci of the research

All associated information and communication technology (ICT) class lessons were also observed and both video- and audio-recorded. Five such ICT sessions were held:

(1) Session 1: Introduction of QuickTime Pro Player—moving markers, copying portions, pasting portions, saving the files (an example of a QuickTime Pro Player title screen is shown in Figure 2).
(2) Session 2: Video revision of work print clips. Revising 14 short QuickTime Pro video clips and choosing 4 of them for their own video film story.
(3) Session 3: Adding text (titles, captions, subtitles). Creating a title with Paint and pasting it into the film. Assembling clips in order and rearranging them.
(4) Session 4: Creating the oral 'voice-over' and, in some instances, subtitles to the film. The recordings needed to be synchronised (where seen as important) with the events on the screen.
(5) Session 5: Presentation to parents in the computer room.

The total length of each session within the study was 40 minutes.

The National Curriculum's Unit 3F on 'Light and Shadows' focuses on relationships between light, various objects (such as lollipop sticks and children) and the formation of their respective shadows. Children observe the apparent movement of the Sun and other sources of light (torches), and the associated changes in shadows. They undertake experimental and investigative work that entails making and recording

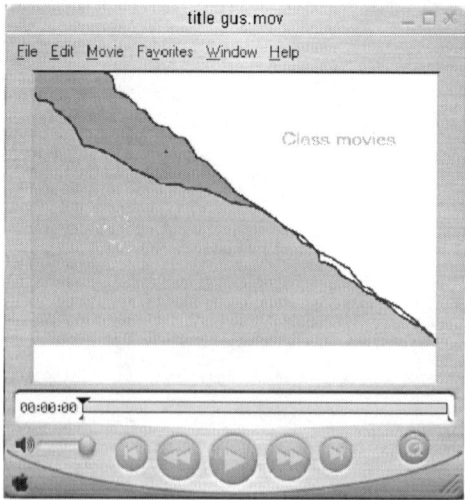

Figure 2.   Example of a title page on screen

measurements and observations, drawing conclusions, suggesting explanations for their observations and statements (see Figure 3). Work in this unit also offers children opportunities to describe and explain shadows using scientific knowledge and to recognise the hazards and risks in looking at the Sun. These seven-year-old children are introduced to words and phrases relating to light and shadow formation: terms such as *light, shadow, light travels, direction, block, transparent, opaque*. They meet expressions of reason using 'because', expressions of comparison, for example, *shortest, highest*, and expressions that allow them to make generalisations.

As noted, as part of creating their three-minute video documentary, they were taught to import video clips and images, trim parts of the film, assemble and split

Figure 3.   Example of the science activity

clips, add text (titles, subtitles) and record sound tracks for the video clips. We chose to use QuickTime 5 Pro because the interface of the programme is simple. It is cheap, easy to use and works as a word processor with which the children were already familiar. Once their own films were complete, we organised presentations of their finished video projects in the ICT room, to be seen by parents, teachers and friends. Copies were recorded on CDs or analogue video cassettes for children to take home.

The children were motivated to reflect on their learning in different contexts by viewing and reviewing the video and then creating visual and spoken self-narrative about this learning. Those narratives were recorded by the children themselves in the computer room. They were given audio recorders and left on their own to narrate the voice-over for their own films, without any direction in the recording process from the researchers.

Video-recorded data were transcribed and analysed through discourse and narrative analysis, based on the analysis of oral versions of personal experience, as introduced by Labov and Waletzky (Labov, 1997). We focussed on five themes: 'learning', 'knowledge', 'science', 'collaboration' and 'project ideas'. All statements—reflective and non-reflective—were analysed (Valkanova *et al.*, 2004b). This discourse analysis was used to clarify the ways in which children structure and maintain self-reflective language.

We also used a version of the Knowledge Monitoring Assessment (KMA) tool (Tobias & Everson, 2002), which is a paper-and-pencil test to assess changes in science curriculum vocabulary. The KMA was designed to assess knowledge by evaluating differences between learners' knowledge in a particular domain and their actual knowledge revealed by their performance in a follow-up test which examines actual knowledge of those words. The method has been demonstrated to have high reliability in contrast with other assessments of metacognition (Osborne, 1998; Osborne, 2001). Watson and Allen (2002) describe KMA is as an 'elegant' method for measuring metacognitive awareness.

Teachers and teacher assistants administered the 38-item exercise to children individually, the children being asked to mark each word that they thought they could recognise. This written task was then followed by a discussion, undertaken by the teacher or a teacher assistant, which sought to identify whether children knew the meaning of the words they had indicated as 'known'. This procedure was undertaken as a pre-/post-test process before and after the Unit 3F on light and shadows. Of the 38 words, 9 were drawn from the curriculum vocabulary of the science unit (e.g. reflection, direction, illumination) and mixed with 17 easy words from everyday language (e.g. day, candle, Earth) with a further 12 words that related to the topic of the curriculum unit but with which the children were supposedly unfamiliar (e.g. dispersion, sensor, photon). The whole process was then administered to a second, parallel class, as a form of limited experimental control.

Some outcomes: children's discussions with 'others'

Some children order their descriptions of events in free-flow narratives in parallel to the original events. These children recapitulate their experiences through the sequence of events they have created in their films, and the narrative is then interspersed with evaluative comment. For example, Tracy (all names psuedonymised) describes her sequence as she follows it from the screen, how she used a 'lollipop stick' and then measured the length of its shadow:

> Ok, this is me doing science ... I just got ... I like science ... uhm ... And there we are measuring a lollipop stick and we are recording the measurements on *that* and... (Tracy)

During the recapitulation and evaluation of their experiences, children describe their classmates or teachers, the descriptions are expressive and often emphasise their attitude to others. Harry addresses his intended audience:

> And I'm gonna talk to you about science ... and we are working on light and shadows ... This is my teacher. I suppose she is helping us with the science. And we are doing a lot now, and we are looking at whatever a shadow is ... and that's my teacher as well, she's my favorite teacher. (Harry)

Caroline has a mixed agenda:

> I'm talking about light and shadows. This is me and my class doing light and shadows. Sebastian's my boyfriend. Sebastian's doing work in shadows too. Sebastian... (Caroline)

Here, science talk is interspersed with personal statements. Watching their own films stimulates animated thought and observations on themselves and others. Their observations allow some broad categorisation of their reflective behaviour so that children who, for example, are most reflective are able to represent ideas thoughtfully, evaluate their ideas, appreciate the state of their own knowledge, maintain social contact and interaction, and evaluate emotions. In the next extended quote, we emphasise some of Sylvia's talk to highlight her reflective moments:

> And here we are doing light and shadows and then we are measuring it and then we are recording it on the top of this. And then, and then, we work that to get this ... [She points to the screen] *What's going on? Uhmm, to go and ... actually I'm not sure about this ...* Then we go around here to my shadow, and then we are working together as part of a group, as me, Cassy and Rumy. Our own work is with Sarah [the teacher assistant] trying to measure each stick. And now we are using ... we are using a torch, some paper and the stick and we are using a ruler ... *and maybe I could use all those and record it all down with the others ...* And then we are going to show people and show to the next group how to do it. (Sylvia)

Sylvia's narrative begins with a positive description of how she participated in the task along with others, though her talk shows a sense of unease, losing confidence during the course of the narrative in her ability to recall exactly how to measure the shadows. In fact, the recording of the whole classroom session shows she was not actually able to do the task in hand. Sylvia asked the teacher assistant, Sarah, repeatedly to help her and her calls to Sarah dominated some of the work around her table. This invoked a negative reaction in others in the group and provoked one of the children to tell her to 'stop moaning'. Her uncertainty in this matter, to which she gives voice, is a reflection of the uncertainty she expressed during the lesson about her ability to perform the learning task.

But two things are interesting here. First, while Sylvia exorcises the negativity of the others in the group, she chooses not to omit the 'difficult' issues from her narrative.

This example shows that she is quite forthright while reflecting on her learning experience. But, second, here in the process of describing her actions, she begins to make sense of what happened and she starts to see how she might have performed the task to measure the shadow, and says:

> And now we using ... we using a torch, some paper and a stick and we using a ruler and maybe I could use all those and record it all down with the others.

While individual children's stories carry such moments of self-reflective comment, groups of children, exclusively boys, were much more interactive in their stories, with children bouncing ideas and sharing imaginative story lines (e.g. Figure 4). Working together, especially within all-boy groupings, gave rise to inventive projection, original characterisation and persona as the 'others' who both featured in the films and who were the audience:

> *Barry*:   Welcome to the 'Pick Nose Monster'. Of course you have to be over 15 or 50 to see this movie.
>
> *Stephen*: ...Or to be like those boys ... [themselves on the film]
>
> *Barry*:   Oh-h that is tasty. I like some bits of this colour here [points at the spots of colour in the backdrop]. I might do some myself. You're working hey! Mummy is a bit stressed!
>
> *Jonathon*: And not in here [colouring]. You're getting a new stress. You're wearing that ... they're like stars! But where is the monster?

The substance of their films was exactly the same as for all other children in the class, a narrative about the session on light and shadows; though, here, the boys have chosen to tell *a* story rather than simply tell *the* story. This was a strategy several groups used, allowing the medium of video film and visual construction to free their talk. In such situations the medium was used as a vehicle for inventive thinking and communication. These exchanges pushed each child along a shared imaginative route, so that the product of their creation could be the eventual narrator of their science story.

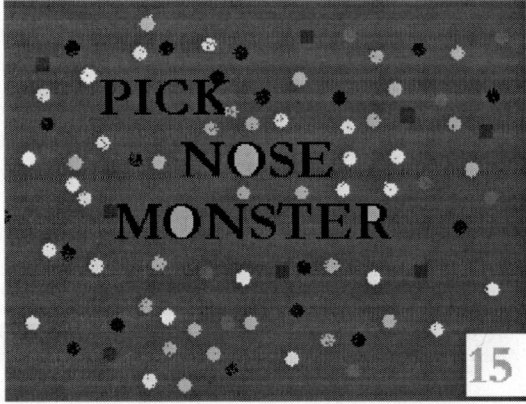

Figure 4.   Title page 'Pick Nose Monster'

The creation of the monster became the focus of their work, who tells the story of their science work, an invented narrator who moves between the light and the shadows, but certainly not the sequence of the recorded classroom events. The comment, 'Mummy is a bit stressed!', comes unconnected to anything else within the recording and seems to be heard by Jonathon as 'dress'. The point here is that the free flow of their talk intersperses task-actions with imaginative inventions and thoughts, comments and responses that surface, the internal becoming external, as they are working.

In the following dialogue, two boys are also in the middle of designing the frontspiece for their video and have taken an original, if macabre, route (see Figure 5). They are using the computer to create images then erasing these as they try different effects, and then eventually return to task.

John: Look, there's both of them
Philip: It's in this book!
John: He should kill her. A man is always strangling…
Philip: Strangle and die once!
John: La-la-la-la!
Philip: There you go!
John: This is all right!
Philip: What are you doing?
John: He trashed her…
Philip: Oh, Ok … Now we need a new title
John: No, we'll do the movie first…
Philip: Yeah but what about when it leads to that bit?

These instances indicate how children play with stories to make sense of ideas and knowledge, using metaphoric interpretations to facilitate the assimilation of knowledge. This observation is consistent with views expressed by Pramling and Pramling Samuelson earlier in this issue. Similar approaches to making meaning in science is

Figure 5.   Title page 'Strangle and die'

observed by Hasse (2002), who undertook anthropological research on Danish university students' science knowledge acquisition. She suggests that male students tend to engage in playful exploration of concepts through invented activities, similar to jumping up and down in an elevator to test gravitational forces, while these playful activities were at times disruptive to female students. Maccoby (1990) further suggests that these modes of exploration lead to new understandings, and they create particular kinds of connections between the male children engaged in play. However, this assumption, although consistent with our results, requires further research.

Story telling is a key element of constructing the film and is a means of understanding children's talk. Through these short productions, children produce self-reflective statements, represent ideas thoughtfully, evaluate their ideas, appreciate the state of their own knowledge, maintain social contact and interaction, regulate their own actions and evaluate emotions. This is motivated by the dynamics of the events and by their desire to represent themselves to others. Their talk develops through social interaction and through the joint construction of meaning.

Further outcomes: the discourse of science

Moving to the KMA paper-and-pencil exercises, our expectation was that reflections on one's own learning by creating documentaries about class activities would positively affect language performance. This was confirmed. The KMA results show statistically significant gains in children's monitoring of curriculum vocabulary (Figure 6). Gains in other learning outcomes were supported by the Teacher Science Assessment.

In this chart the 'treatment group' of 30 children outperformed their parallel school-mates; so that while both had been taught the Unit 3F, the 'video' class recognised and understood a greater and wider range of terms and expressions related to

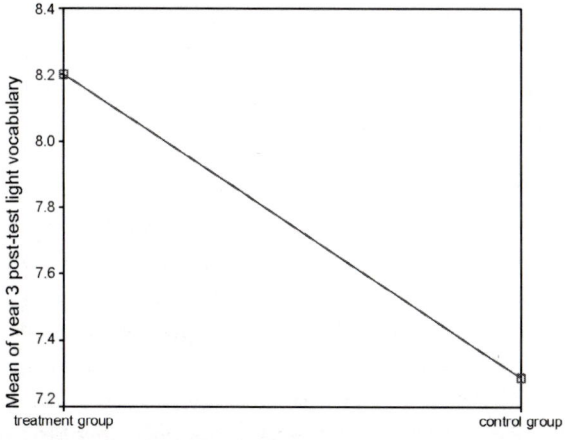

Figure 6. Pivot table based on the post-test measure of cognitive monitoring of science vocabulary words

light and shadows. They were, as the chart below indicates, also able to recognise more of the words associated with the topic that were deemed to be difficult.

Summary comments

So, has our focus on developing oral language through digital video RSL been worthwhile? Our aim has been to motivate young children to reflect on their language and learning by creating films and sound tracks about their work in science. Children produced reflective statements provoked by a desire to explain to others the events they had chosen to present on screen.

First, at the mundane research level, but not at a mundane pedagogical level, we are heartened by the facility with which children learn and develop visual skills and digital literacies. The teachers worked hard within the constraints and demands of busy schooling to provide appropriate learning environments and materials (e.g. computer, visual, audio, print reading, information, multimedia) to enable these children to create their own visual and oral messages. Children appropriate such skills fearlessly and add these to their toolkits of inventive, creative strategies. Assimilation of such resources is not just a cognitive act, but also a communicative one, a social act, enabling children to express themselves verbally and visually in artistic, ingenious and productive ways.

So, although we chose a quasi-experimental design to allow some parallel-group comparisons to be made, our work has been conducted in a very normal London school, amidst all of the usual trials and tribulations of learning and teaching in such contexts. In this classroom, we recognise how talk is intrinsic to both oral and visual literacies and to our ability to form relationships with others and generated evidence for enhancing communicative competence and narrative thinking and talking. Children have been enabled to make sense of the world in ways that are meaningful to them. One strategy they use in such situations is to use imaginative story telling as vehicles of thinking and communication.

Second, we were reassured that creating a film about one's own experience of learning enhances self-reflective learning in seven- to eight-year-old children. The whole research exercise made a measurable difference to the 'video-makers' knowledge and understanding of technical terms and expressions within primary school science. Within this class (and we presume other classes too) there appears to be a spread among the children between those who can present their reflections more readily and others. Some children take to creating films more easily than others and, in doing so, use this facility to present and share their reflections about their learning. Some children use a narrative that follows the events of their film within which they produce more recognisable reflective statements, while other children adopt a more complex, projective and imaginative approach. Using CHAT allowed us to categorise data with regard to the way learning is presented in children's language and discourse, explore the external plane of oral development and the internal reflective plane.

Finally, the discussion of the exploration of the experimental system provides general pointers for further applications of digital video technology in the design of integrative science classroom environments and shows how purpose-driven developments may increase the applications of self-reflection and the construction of science knowledge in primary school children. These results suggest ways in which the self can be recast to accommodate the variation in subjective self-narrative. They also suggest ways in which the oral and visual self-narratives of personal experience may contribute to classroom domain learning.

References

Abramova, N. A. (2006) Reflectivny podhod k probleme vzaimoponimaniy [Reflection as an approach to understanding others], in: N. A. Abramovoy, K. S. Ginsberga & D. A. Novikova (Eds) *Chelavecheskiy faktor v upravlenii* [Human factors in management] (Moscow, Komkniga), 55–87.

Adams-Webber, J. (2000) A further test of a model of self-reflection with children ages 10 and 11, *Journal of Constructivist Psychology*, 13, 289–301.

Andersen, S. M. & Williams, M. (1985) Cognitive/affective reactions in the improvement of self-esteem: when thoughts and feelings make a difference, *Journal of Personality and Social Psychology*, 49(4), 1086–1097.

Atienza, F., Balaguer, I. & Garcia-Merita, M. (1998) Video modeling and imaging training on performance of tennis service of 9- to 12-year-old children, *Perceptual & Motor Skills*, 87(2), 519–529.

Atienza FL, Balaguer I & ML., G.-M. (1998) Video modeling and imaging training on performance of tennis service of 9- to 12-year-old children, *Perceptual & Motor Skills*, 87(2), 519–529.

Bandura, A. (2001) Social cognitive theory: an agentic perspective, *Annual Review of Psychology*, 52, 1–26.

Becta (2005) *Robert James' paper and discussion*. Available online at: forum.ngfl.gov.uk/WebX?13@41.WLJOaXnewYN.0@.efa283f (accessed 27 August 2005).

Buehl, D. (1996) Improving students' learning strategies through self-reflection, *Teaching and Change*, 3(3), 227–243.

Copple, C. (2003) Fostering young children's representation, planning, and reflection: a focus in three current early childhood models, *Journal of Applied Developmental Psychology*, 24(6), 763–771.

Daniels, H. (2004a) Activity theory, discourse and Bernstein, *Educational Review*, 56(2), 121–132.

Daniels, H. (2004b) Cultural historical activity theory and professional learning, *International Journal of Disability Development and Education*, 51(2), 185–200.

Davydov, V. V. (1988) The mental development of younger schoolchildren in the process of learning activity, *Soviet Education*, 30(9), 48–83.

Driver, R., Asoko, H., Leach, J., Scott, P. & Mortimer, E. (1994) Constructing scientific knowledge in the classroom, *Educational Researcher*, 23(7), 5.

Endres, J., Poggenpohl, C. & Erben, C. (1999) Repetitions, warnings and video: cognitive and motivational components in preschool children's suggestibility, *Legal and Criminological Psychology*, 4(1), 129–146.

Engeström, Y. (1999) Activity theory and individual and social transformation, in: Y. Engeström, R. Miettinen & R. Punamaki (Eds) *Perspectives on activity theory* (New York, Cambridge University Press), 19–38.

Engeström, Y. (2000) Activity theory as a framework for analyzing and redesigning work, *Ergonomics*, 43(7), 960–974.

Ginsburg, H. P. & Golbeck, S. L. (2004) Thoughts on the future of research on mathematics and science learning and education, *Early Childhood Research Quarterly*, 19(1), 190–200.

Guberman, S. R. & Greenfield, P. M. (1991) Learning and transfer in everyday cognition, *Cognitive Development*, 6(3), 233–260.

Harlin, R. P. (2000) Developing reflection and teaching through peer coaching (vol. 1, n1, Fall 2000) (Association for Childhood Education International: Olney, MD), 10.

Hasse, C. (2002) Gender diversity in play with physics: the problem of premises for participation in activities, *Mind Culture and Activity*, 9(4), 250–269.

Hmelo, C. E. & Lin, X. (2000) Becoming self-directed learners: strategy development in problem-based learning, in: D. H. Evensen & C. E. Hmelo (Eds) *Problem-based learning: a research perspective on learning interactions* (Mahwah, NJ, Lawrence Erlbaum), 227–250.

Holmstrom, I. & Rosenqvist, U. (2004) Interventions to support reflection and learning: a qualitative study, *Learning in Health and Social Care*, 3(4), 203–212.

Kaptelinin, V. (1996) Activity theory: implications for human-computer interaction research, in: B. A. Nardi (Ed.) *Context and consciousness: activity theory and human–computer interaction* (Massachusetts, MIT Press), 102–116.

Kimball, J. W., Kinney, E. M., Taylor, B. A. & Stromer, R. (2004) Video enhanced activity schedules for children with autism: a promising package for teaching social skills, *Education & Treatment of Children*, 27(3), 280–298.

Kukulska-Hulme, A., Foster-Jones, J., Jelfs, A., Mallett, E. & Holland, D. (2004) Investigating digital video applications in distance learning, *Journal of Educational Media*, 29(2), 125–137.

Labov, W. (1997) Some further steps in narrative analysis, *Journal of Narrative and Life History*, 7(1–4), 395–415.

Leontiev, A. N. (1981) *Problemy razvitiy psihiki* [Problems of the developmental mind] (Moscow, Izdatel'stva Moskovskogo Universiteta).

Leontiev, A. N. (1983) *Izbrannie psihologicheskie trudy* [Selected psychological works] (vol. 2) (Moscow, Pedagogika).

Lonnecker, C., Brady, M. P., McPherson, R. & Hawkins, J. (1994) Video self-modeling and cooperative classroom behavior in children with learning and behavior problems: training and generalization effects, *Behavioral Disorders*, 20(1), 24–34.

Maccoby, E. E. (1990) Gender and relationships: a developmental account, *American Psychologist*, 45(4), 513–520.

Moon, J. (1999) *Reflection in learning and professional development: theory and practice* (London, Kogan Page).

Moorefield, L. (2005) Reflective discipline: providing students a tool for self-reflection can decrease classroom disruptions and help identify the problems behind them, *Teaching Pre K-8*, 36(1), 70–71.

O'Reilly, M. F., O'Halloran, M., Sigafoos, J., *et al.* (2005) Evaluation of video feedback and self-management to decrease schoolyard aggression and increase pro-social behaviour in two students with behavioural disorders, *Educational Psychology*, 25(2–3), 199–206.

Osborne, J. (2001) *Assessing metacognition in the classroom: the assessment of cognition monitoring effectiveness.* The Department of Educational Psychology, University of Oklahoma (unpublished manuscript).

Osborne, J. W. (1998) *Measuring metacognition: validation of the assessment of cognition monitoring effectiveness* (Buffalo, NY, State University of New York).

Petrosino, A. & Cunningham, A. (2003) Situating authentic tasks with digital video: scaffolding the development of critical thinking and reflection in preservice teacher preparation, *Technology and Teacher Education Annual*, 2, 1524–1530.

Piaget, J. & Inhelder, B. (1967) *The child's concept of space* (New York, Norton).

Sefton-Green, J. & Parker, D. (2000) *Edit-play: how children use edutainment to tell stories* (London, British Film Institute).

Stahl, G. (2003) Meaning and interpretation in collaboration, in: B. Wasson, S. Ludvigsen & U. Hoppe (Eds) *Designing for change in networked learning environments: proceedings of the international conference on computer support for collaborative learning (CSCL'03)* (Norway, Kluwer), 523–532.

Stetsenko, A. & Arievitch, I. M. (2004) The self in cultural–historical activity theory, *Theory and Psychology*, 14, 475–503.

Thurston, A. (2004) Promoting multicultural education in the primary classroom: broadband videoconferencing facilities and digital video, *Computers & Education*, 43, 165–177.

Tobias, S. & Everson, H. T. (2002) *Knowing what you know and what you don't: further research on metacognitive knowledge monitoring* (New York, College Entrance Examination Board).

Valkanova, Y., Jackson, A. & Watts, M. (2004a) Digital video in a primary science classroom: a tool for self-reflection and learning, paper presented at the *International Conference on Education and Information Systems Technologies and Applications EISTA '04*, Orlando, FL, 21–25 July.

Valkanova, Y., Watts, M. & Jackson, A. (2004b) Enhancing self-reflection in children: the use of digital video in the primary science classroom, *International Journal of eLiteracy*, 1, available online at: http://www.jelit.org/9/01/Jelit_Paper_11.pdf.

Vygotsky, L. (1999) *Thought and language* (Cambridge, MA, MIT Press).

Watson, J. B. & Allen, B. S. (2002) The effect of metacognitive prompts on student navigation, comprehension, and metacognitive awareness in a multimedia science tutorial, *Annual Meeting of The American Educational Research Association (AERA)* (New Orleans, EyeCues).

Zelazo, P. D. (2000) Self-reflection and the development of consciously controlled processing, in: P. M. K. Riggs (Ed.) *Children's reasoning and the mind* (London, Psychology Press), 169–189.

Zelazo, P. D. & Lourenco, S. F. (2003) Imitation and the dialectic of representation, *Developmental Review*, 23(1), 55–78.

INDEX